THE OFFICIAL
PREPPY
HANDBOOK

EDITED BY
LISA BIRNBACH

CONCEPT
JONATHAN ROBERTS

WRITERS
LISA BIRNBACH
JONATHAN ROBERTS
CAROL McD. WALLACE
MASON WILEY

PHOTOGRAPHY
ROBIN HOLLAND

ILLUSTRATION
OLIVER WILLIAMS

WORKMAN PUBLISHING
NEW YORK

Cover and book design: Paul Hanson

Library of Congress Cataloging in Publication Data

Birnbach, Lisa.
The official preppy handbook.

1.   Preparatory schools—United States—Hand-
books, manuals, etc.   2.   Preparatory school
students—United States—Handbooks, manuals, etc.
I   Title.
LC58.7.B57   373.2'22'0973   80-51892
ISBN 0-89480-140-6 (pbk.)

Workman Publishing Company, Inc.
1 West 39 Street
New York, New York 10018

Manufactured in the United States of America.
First Printing September 1980
10 9 8 7 6 5

ACKNOWLEDGEMENTS

Many, many Preps assisted me in the preparation of this book. You might say that *The Official Preppy Handbook* is living, tangible proof that the Old Boy Network works. Ask one Southerner for help, and he coops another friend, and before long you wonder how the Confederacy ever lost.

Grateful as I am to everyone, there is simply not enough space to enumerate every contribution as I would like. There are several, though, who must be thanked especially. Gail MacColl, Jonathan Roberts, Carol McD. Wallace, Mason Wiley, Paul Hanson, Robin Holland, and Oliver Williams worked tirelessly on this project, their enthusiasm as unflagging as their energy. I would also like to thank Richard Smith, Sally Kovalchick, and Peter Workman for their support, encouragement, and good humor.

Many thanks are also owed to: Bradford Warren Agry, Wendy Avrett, Jonathan S. Birnbach, Maks L. Birnbach, Naomi S. Birnbach, Norman D. Birnbach, Steven Bloom, Scott Borene, Kathleen McCabe Bovers, David Breskin, Mark Charles, Leslie Citron, Arlene Meyer Cohen, Alison Verity Collins, Jacqueline Collins, Brenda, la Comtesse de Morelos, y Guerrero, Mary Lou Dinardo, Katy Dobbs, Ellis Duncan, John Eding, Edward "Trip" Emerson, III, Kay Evans, Bruce Feirstein, Stephen Fenichell, Scott Fields, David Finkle, John H. Friedman, Janie Hawkens Furse, Donald Gettinger, Erica Gjersvik, Steven Gottleib, Jon J. Gould, Elissa Gretz, Priscilla Haack, Jeffrey Harper, James Sherwood Harrison, Edward Herbert, Richard Hawkins, Rodney Hobbs, Marcia Jacobs, Evelyn Konrad Jereski, Freeborn Garrettson Jewett, III, Susan Kane, Ronnie Kent, Gregory Kiernan, Joan Kingsly, Susan Knopf, Beth Mudd Kotelec, Charles Kreloff, Nancy Krueger, Joe Laun, Norman Lefkovits, Dana Levenson, Amy Lewis, Anne Beals Lewis, Barbara Livenstein, Mary Anne Maloy, Mike Marden, Deborah Matlovsky, Mary McCarthy McDevitt, Ellen Meltzer, Frederick R. Newman, Richard E. Newman, B. Gregory Palitz, Steven Paradis, Stephanie Pierson, Stephen Pollack, Louis Postel, Christopher Power, Jeremy Richard, Sara Risher, Raymond A. Roel, Jennifer Rogers, Randall A. Rothenberg, Susie Schwartz, Erich Segal, Kibbe Smith, Nancy Stone, Frederick Morgan Taylor, William Neville

Tifft, Laurie Anderson Thorp, Thomas Ruffin Vandeventer, Bart Walker, David Weeks, Betsy West, Tad Wise, Thomas Caine Wynbrandt, Craig D. Wynne, Jeff Yablonka.

I would also like to thank the following suppliers for the use of their products: Capezio at Lincoln Center, Elisabeth Stewart Swimwear, Foot-Joy, J.G. Hook, Herman's World of Sporting Goods, Leon Levin Sportswear, Lord & Taylor, and Scully & Scully, Inc. And my special thanks to Burton Ltd. and Burton Ltd. Ladies' Division for their clothes, accessories, support, and friendship.

L.B.

CONTENTS

CHAPTER III

THE BEST YEARS OF YOUR LIFE

The College Years

CHAPTER IV

DRESSING THE PART

The Basic Look

CHAPTER V

THE REAL WORLD

The Young Executive Years

CHAPTER VI

YOU'RE ALL GROWN UP NOW

The Country Club Years

CHAPTER VII

PREP SPOKEN HERE

Initiation

It is the inalienable right of every man, woman, and child to wear khaki. Looking, acting, and ultimately being Prep is not restricted to an elite minority lucky enough to attend prestigious private schools, just because an ancestor or two happened to arrive here on the *Mayflower.* You don't even have to be a registered Republican. In a true democracy everyone can be upper class and live in Connecticut. It's only fair.

The Official Preppy Handbook will help you get there. Within this book lies an abundance of detail that would make even the most knowledgeable Preppy gape—advice on parents, choosing secondary schools and colleges, picking careers, finding a fiancée and planning the wedding, decorating dwelling places from the first dorm room to the suburban living room, what to wear, how to throw a party, what to drive, where to vacation and, finally, what to say and how to pronounce it. All this, and more, in seven chapters as neatly arranged as a sit-down dinner for twelve.

You'll be able to travel from crib to coffin, from desk to date, from the city to the island without one false step, knowing full well that whenever emergencies arise, you'll know what to do, be it gatoring, debuting, or choosing a charity. And you can wear lime green all along the way.

So stop thinking you're a lost cause simply because you've never been to either the Harvard-Yale game or Martha's Vineyard. Even Preppies had to learn at one point not to wear socks with loafers. Remember: Preppies don't have to be rich, Caucasian, frequenters of Bermuda, or ace tennis players. But they do have to read this book (Monarch Notes not yet available). It's the preferred self-help. It's key.

CHAPTER 1

RIGHTS OF THE BIRTHRIGHT

The Years at Home

THE
FAMILY

A Preppy begins grooming for Prep school at the moment of birth. Mummy and Daddy have carefully selected first and middle names (at least one of each) for the newborn that correspond to the names of dormitories at their Prep alma maters. An announcement of birth is sent by messenger to the alumni newsletter to alert the school's admission office of a future applicant. And Prep tots are carted along on Homecoming weekends so that the campus will seem like a second home by the time they are fifteen.

But just as important as guaranteeing their offsprings' entrée into the Right School is the Prep parents' need to impress their children with the desirability—nay, inevitability—of their going Prep. No use sacrificing Bermuda vacation money for tuition for a kid who's going to run off and join a modern dance troupe. Nor does the Prep parents' responsibility stop with simply ensuring their children's acceptance at a school: they've got to make certain that once the progeny are enrolled, they're not going to lock themselves in the computer lab for the whole four years and miss out on house party invitations, "after-hours alcoholic sprees," and the joy of shopping for madras.

Thus, the Prep child's indoc-

THE
ANCESTRAL GALLERY

COUSIN "BLACK" JACK

The family's single dashing ancestor, reportedly once stabbed by a cuckolded husband. Although he squandered the family fortune, he's forgiven due to his legacy of quotable quips, fox-hunting victories, and rakish exploits that are the bulk of present-day reminiscences.

AUNT EVELINE

Beloved but eccentric spinster aunt. Renowned at one time for her now faded beauty. Lived alone in great grandparents' house for years, but didn't do much maintenance (Mummy and Daddy had to spend tons to renovate before moving in). She spent her final years instructing grand-nieces on the intricacies of bee-keeping.

trination to the preferred way of life begins immediately. Mummy and Daddy make certain that he or she will not stray from the family fold because he or she won't know that other folds exist. The Prep child grows up surrounded by relatives who are all going, have gone, or, like him or her, will go to the same schools. Both sets of grandparents, Brother Bobo, Sister Biffy, Uncle Icky, Aunt Teeny, Cousin Amanda and Cousin Bob all rhapsodize about the fun they've always had with fellow Preppies, and what upstart is about to think otherwise? When you spend all your time

They are Prep's foggy past, now hardened in oil for the benefit of their inheritors' house's Not Decorated Look. Their pictures hang in the dining room or over the fireplace in the formal living room or along the staircase to the second floor.

THE GENERAL

Went to four military academies in four years. Was decorated for obscure scrimmage during Civil War—then wore his uniform in lieu of formal dress and bored others with his war stories for the rest of his life. Independent, strong-willed and respected, although family still hasn't recovered from his refusal to invest in the horseless carriage.

GRANDMOTHER

Doting, loving, senile. Daddy doesn't let her drive anymore since the accident. Stays at beach cottage during August; everyone goes to her house for Thanksgiving. Her diary in bound annual volumes documents for future generations exactly what she ate for breakfast, lunch, and dinner over a fifty year period.

I GAVE BIRTH TO A PREPPY

One year after marriage, I gave birth to a baby girl. I was looking forward to a blissful mother-daughter relationship, but my tiny offspring immediately began to assert herself in very distinctive ways. She flatly refused Pampers and demanded 100 percent-cotton diapers clasped with a gold kilt pin. She eschewed pacifiers and rings and preferred to teethe on an add-a-bead necklace.

As a young child, she continued to have her own ideas about proper moppet behavior. She didn't play "house," she played "cottage." Instead of playing "store," she favored "investment banking." While the other little girls lavished attention on their baby dolls, my daughter pretended to find a baby-sitter for hers.

The other children were quite happy with their little red wagons; she would accept nothing but a woody. When she learned that she would be receiving a Barbie doll, she marched straight to Tiffany's to register Barbie's silver pattern.

Yes, the first five years with my daughter have been quite an experience. I am certainly going to miss her, but she is determined to go off to a good boarding kindergarten. She's busy going through the catalogs now, looking for one with a close proximity to a boys' kindergarten and with liberal overnight allowances.

with your family and other Prep families at the beach, on the slopes, at the country club, and at innumerable family reunions; when all your birthday and Christmas presents are either monogrammed or have Izod labels, it's unlikely that you will have the normal childhood aspirations of becoming a fireman or a nurse.

Preppies inherit from Mummy and Daddy, in addition to loopy handwriting and old furniture, the legacy of Proper Breeding. Preppies soon learn that any deviation from the prescribed style of life is bound to bring disaster. Attending a déclassé school, marrying wrong, selecting uncharted neighborhoods, choosing demanding vocations, or simply taking up bowling can unravel the tightly woven social fabric that binds the comfortable Preppy community.

Because Mummy and Daddy instruct their children in all matters of Taste and Tact, Preppies don't really have to worry about going astray. When the time comes, the children will know what to write on a Prep school application essay, who to marry, and how to ensure serenity and security for *their* children by putting their tooth-fairy dollars in a money market fund. Like everything else, Preppiness begins in the home.

NICKNAMES

A nickname is a gift. Whether given deliberately by the family or unintenionally by a peer, it bespeaks a certain In-ness and inaccessibility to outsiders. It's like being tapped for a secret society, minus the degrading rituals. It's tangible proof that you've gained entrance into an exclusive camaraderie.

12 MOST POPULAR NICKNAMES FOR GIRLS

1. Muffy. For any name—first or middle—commencing with the letter "M," such as Margaret, Martha, Madeleine, Murchison, Mead.

2. Missy. Short for Melissa. Often a term of endearment like "honey."

3. Buffy. Popularized in the TV sitcom of 1960's, "Family Affair." A catchall. For Buxtons and Bundys.

4. Bitsy. Applies to the diminutive blonde. Slightly old-fashioned. From Beth, Melinda, Susan, Bryant.

5. Bootsy. Very New England, much Preppier than Betsy. Barbara or Elizabeth.

6. Bunny. Anyone cute and furry. All-purpose and coed (see boys' list below). From Louise, Pierce, Simpson, Lisa, but based more on personality than name.

7. Kiki. For any permutation of Katherine; also Kathleen, Karen, Kirkland.

8. Tiffy. Athletic with strong coltish legs. Good name to scream at field hockey games. Tilford, Truman, Tamara.

9. Topsy. Margaret, Tripler, Esmé, Sarah, Warren. Reminiscent of Beatrix Potter stories (also Flopsy and Mopsy.)

10. Cuffy. Usually a female of generous proportions. From Catherine, Caroline, Claudia, Crosby.

11. Corkie. Also indicates perkiness. Also from "C" names—Corcoran, Crane, Chris, Kelly. Corkie's best friend is Pookie (Polly).

12. Molly. Connotes wholesomeness and sometimes an artistic bent, in which case hair always worn in a scarf. From Mary or Martha.

12 MOST POPULAR NICKNAMES FOR BOYS

1. Skip. When son is named after Daddy. Outdoorsy, suntanned, always on the winning team. From Geoffrey, Stephen, Thatcher.

2. Chip. From Charles. Preppier than Chuck or Charlie. Also indicates chip off the old block. Future golfer.

3. Kip. Free-for-all, used when nothing else is appropriate. Nathaniel, Archer, Hill, Loomis. On the football or swimming teams.

4. Trip. Also Tripp. When son has a "III" after his name. Well-rounded athlete who prefers drama club.

5. Bif. For little boys. From any part of name beginning with "B." Blackwell, Burnham, Bartholomew. Bif *lives* on the tennis courts.

6. Bunny. Surprising but true. High society. Nonathletic, but cool. Comes from any name. Robert, Edmund, George.

7. Bink. Rugged, big shoulders; a skier. Beekman, Brinsley, Richardson.

8. Van. When "van" is part of the last name, as in van Dine, van der Hoff, van Doren. Indicates clubability, heavy après-ski action.

9. Win. Applies to attractive blond men, lends Scandinavian flair. Winthrop, Winter, Witherspoon.

10. Wog. Nickname for young man who classmates like, but think is a dolt. Michael, Howell, Pruitt.

11. Rocky. Replaces macho element that Prep supplanted with chivalry. Real name is irrelevant. Varsity lacrosse star.

12. Jock. From John. More classy than Jack. Connotes horsey set and Whitneys.

T HE YEARS AT
HOME. These chil-
dren are off to a fly-
ing start. They don't
know that there is
anything special
about the way they
are dressed; within a
few years they will be
choosing their clothes
without the slightest
idea that they are
being Consciously
Prep. Note the back-
ground—the family
has finally bought the
Big House.

*little Lacoste,
collar already
turning up*

tennis forearm

*hands in pockets,
just like Dad*

*in the pocket: 50¢
(allowance for emptying
the wastebaskets) and
several pieces of string*

cuffs, even now

little Top-Siders

*little Shetland
sweater,
worn as scarf*

little web belt

*white briefs
(too young for
boxers)*

little khakis

*Old English
sheep dog pup
named
Jack Daniel*

PREP PERSONA
No. 1

short hair until she's 10
and can take care of it herself

Mummy's
herb garden

dress bought at Women's Exchange,
hand smocking done by nuns,
with deep hem (hand-me-down)

in the pocket:
green crayon about
to go through
the wash

no jewelry; tacky on children
no watch; Nanny knows what time it is

Steiff bear named "Teddy"

white cotton socks—always plain,
never scalloped or trimmed with lace

oxfords; support for the growing feet

OF MAHOGANY AND MACRAME
Decorating Haves and Have Nots

There is only one look in Prep decorating: Not Decorated. Nothing is consciously coordinated, but everything works together through a successful marriage of utility and excellence. Furnishings have always been in the family, but are not treated like museum pieces. Everything is used: The Georgian silver is on the table at all meals, the Canton china is chipped regularly by the dishwasher. And not using certain rooms except for special occasions would be like wearing curlers in public.

If it must be pinned down, the look is English-American, with a dash of seaside resort and women's handicraft. It is where the Chippendale secretary meets the needlepoint-covered brick doorstop, and the lobster-trap coffee table meets the prized Kerman rug.

Understatement is essential—perfect proportions and clean lines are preferred over ornate detail. The key words are *classic*, *handsome*, *patina*, and *Mother's*. To achieve the Not Decorated Look, remember:

HAVE	HAVE NOT
Upholstered pieces covered with flowered chintz.	Vinyl protectors.
Many small, worn oriental rugs.	Wall-to-wall.
Prints of dogs, ducks, horses, boats, birds.	Abstract art.
Antiques bought at auction.	Louis-the-Anything furniture.
Museum-documented, eighteenth-century wallpaper patterns.	Flocked wallpaper.
Lots of old table lamps.	Indirect, track, or spot lighting.
Mahogany and brass.	Chrome and glass.
Standard, black dial phones.	Novelty phones. This includes beige.
Pastel sketches of the children.	Pastel sketches by the children.
Portraits of ancestors.	Portraits of U.S. presidents (unless they are ancestors).
Lots of fireplace equipment.	Macrame.
Ship models, nautical memorabilia.	Hummel figurines.
Dust.	Dirt.
Georgian paneling.	Masonite paneling.
Dishes of beach glass.	Dishes of candy.

THE DUCK MOTIF

The duck is the most beloved of all totems. The duck suggests hunting, water, Maine—all the things worth thinking about. The basic duck is the mallard. The most common view of the duck is the silhouette, although the duck in flight runs a close second. Three-dimensional decoys are nearly as popular and may appear as lamp bases, planters, doorstops, candlesticks, and paperweights. Ducks themselves—real ducks—may be of little interest. It is the representation of the duck that counts. And the less an object has to do with ducks, the more it cries out for duck adornment. Ducks are stenciled, printed, painted, engraved, embroidered, embossed, debossed, appliquéd, mounted, and otherwise emblazoned on wood, brass, fabric, leather, silver, glass, crystal—anything.

CARRIERS OF THE MOTIF

WASTEBASKETS
PRINTS
GLASSWARE
BELTS AND BELT BUCKLES
NEEDLEPOINT PILLOWS
KEY TAGS
EMBROIDERED PANTS AND
    SWEATERS
SCRIMSHAW
LUGGAGE, INCLUDING
    HANDBAGS
DIRECTOR'S CHAIRS
TOILET KITS
HOSTESS DRESSES
TRAYS
DOORMATS
MAILBOXES
WEATHERVANES
BEER STEINS AND MUGS
PLATES
ANDIRONS
COAT HOOKS
LIGHT SWITCH PLATES
QUILTS
BOXER SHORTS
BUTTONS
MAGNETS
SOUP TUREENS
BOOKENDS
CAR DECALS
HOOD ORNAMENTS

LEADING SUPPLIERS OF THE MOTIF

Wherever Prep merchandise is sold the duck motif will be found. However, a few mail-order catalog sources stand out: Gokeys, of St. Paul, Minn.; Orvis, of Manchester, Vt.; the Audubon Society's gift catalog (see *Where to Shop–Catalogs*).

One catalog stands beak and tail feathers above the rest: The Sporting Life, P.O. Box 9136, 5302 Eisenhower Ave., Alexandria, Va. 22304. With only a few exceptions, *everything they sell*—a full line of men's and women's sportswear and accessories—bears the duck motif. It's duck heaven.

THE DEN OF INEQUITY
A Model Family Room

There's the living room you look at and then there's the living room you live in. The latter is known as the family room, or the den, or the library, but its purpose is clear—to keep everyone out of the other living room. Because of the casual nature of its raison d'être, this room is the culmination of the Not-Decorated Look, the room where the Duck Motif reaches a well-deserved crescendo of exposure. Daddy smokes his pipe in here, the children do their homework on the floor while watching "Gilligan's Island" re-runs, Mummy has sherry with Cousin Elizabeth while the turkey is roasting. There are moccasins on the floor, glass rings on the table, newspapers under the easy chair—the comfortable, practical, outdoorsy look of Prep at its very best.

1. French windows.
2. Walls painted authentic Williamsburg green.
3. Curtains, not drapes.
4. Dog prints.
5. Horse prints.
6. Antique decoy ducks.
7. Liquor in large-size bottles: gin, scotch; soda siphon.
8. Large, old, color TV with rabbit ears (reception is terrible this far from the city).
9. Wood from apple tree that fell down in last hurricane.
10. Pinecones for kindling (bought at roadside stand with pumpkins and Indian corn last fall).
11. Duck print.
12. Andirons and bellows bought at antique show in Suffield.
13. Fire screen with duck in flight.
14. Painting entitled "The Three-masted Schooner *Henrietta C. Mather* under Full Sail Rounding Cape Ann at Neap Tide Hard on the Wind."
15. Silver cigarette box lined with cedar. Prize for 1965 Labor Day regatta.
16. Red leather chair in which dog is not allowed.
17. *Best of Life* (last book bought).
18. Mummy's owl collection.
19. Sextant used in Bermuda Race of 1953.
20. Model of *Cutty Sark*.
21. Brass candlesticks. Bayberry candles from Williamsburg.
22. Sofa slipcovered in chintz for the summer.
23. Needlepoint pillows. One says "If You've Nothing Nice to Say Come Sit By Me," one is stitched in the bargello pattern, one has a duck embroidered on it.
24. Conch shell from Eleuthera.
25. Tintypes of grandparents from Daddy's side in silver frames.
26. Duck-paneled magazine rack. Magazines include: *Town & Country; Antiques; Smithsonian; Gourmet; Time* (to keep up); *The New Yorker; Architectural Digest; National Geographic; Yachting; Fortune; Blair & Ketchum's Country Journal;* the appropriate alumni bulletins.
27. Ivy in hand-painted cachepot from Orvis.
28. Butler's tray table. Plaque is engraved with initials of Mummy and Daddy's wedding party.
29. Mahogany cabinet. Contains: A set of monogrammed highball glasses. A set of coasters with ducks on them. Plastic swizzle sticks, half-used matchbooks, cocktail napkins of varying designs from various affairs.
30. Books include: complete Ralph Waldo Emerson in matched volumes; complete Winston Churchill; 13th edition of the *Encyclopædia Britannica*; Agatha Christie in first editions; old *Horizons;* five years worth of *American Heritage;* J.J. Audubon's *Birds of America; This Fabulous Century;* Will and Ariel Durant's *The Story of Civilization;* Modern Library editions of Jane Austen and Thomas Wolfe; the appropriate college and secondary school yearbooks.

NEVER ON THURSDAY
Help in the House

The Prep family may pride themselves on their Spartan camping trips with just them, the great outdoors, and every item in the L. L. Bean catalog, but when they get home they want clean sheets and dinner on the table. For this reason, the family depends upon auxiliary support, known as help. Servants may live in, come in only once a week, or just appear for special occasions, but they are all spiritually linked for the services they provide: labor, loyalty, and the ability to tell entertaining stories about crazed brothers-in-law and other human activity that goes on outside the Preppy universe.

Governess/Nanny. Surrogate Mummy who never spanks. Feeds, bathes, and reads aloud in heavy Scottish brogue.

Houseman. Helps with heavy work around the house. Sometimes chauffeurs Daddy to work in an old Packard.

Cook. Knows to step out of the way and to praise the result when Mummy decides to try something from Julia Child. Feigns role of strict dietician but is actually quite generous

---

THE LOOK FOR LIVE-INS

If the help is live-in the appropriate room includes:
1. Hide-a-bed
2. Black-and-white TV
3. Milk-glass hobnailed lamp
4. Sink
5. Two bookshelves
6. Framed prints of floral still lifes
7. Three throw pillows
8. Old copies of *Vogue* and *Town & Country*

---

with between-meal snacks.

Cleaning lady. One, two, or three times a week. Changes linen and is a champion duster. Forgets instructions and accidentally "cleans" your desk, throwing away directions to party in the country scribbled on the back of canceled check.

Gardener. Unnecessary for city dwellers. Mummy entrusts her roses to him, but sons mow the lawn to earn the down payment on an MG.

Laundress. Once-a-week visitor. Washes by hand and machine. Watches soap operas or listens to "easy listening" radio station while ironing.

KEEPERS OF THE FLAME

The Status Quo Institutions

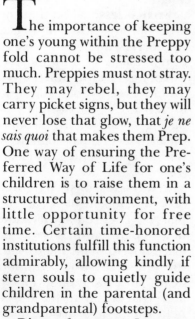

The importance of keeping one's young within the Preppy fold cannot be stressed too much. Preppies must not stray. They may rebel, they may carry picket signs, but they will never lose that glow, that *je ne sais quoi* that makes them Prep. One way of ensuring the Preferred Way of Life for one's children is to raise them in a structured environment, with little opportunity for free time. Certain time-honored institutions fulfill this function admirably, allowing kindly if stern souls to quietly guide children in the parental (and grandparental) footsteps.

Piano lessons. Lessons should be commenced before children reach the tenth birthday. Musical knowledge is charming and enhances the Total Preppy Being. It allows children to understand what is heard at the Boston Pops. It lends them a certain dignity at the Young People's Concerts. Additionally, the child's lessons provide a much-needed excuse for the looming presence of the Steinway baby grand in the living room— apart from its obvious function as a dramatic means of displaying photographs, flowers, and more photographs.

Ballet lessons. For daughters exclusively, beginning when they are very tiny. They will plié obligingly, visions of sugarplums (and a possible role in *The Nutcracker*) dancing in their heads. Ballet will, with any luck, teach her Proper Deportment, insuring a graceful young woman for debut balls and afternoon teas. Care is taken that she doesn't

THE HORSE PHASE

The Horse Phase is a standard condition of a girl-Prep's adolescence. More aesthetic than pimples, less worrisome than cars, but colossally boring while it lasts, it is *the* activity for girls ages ten to fourteen.

The first step is the request for riding lessons, which no loving parent can legitimately refuse. Acquisitions begin with jodhpurs, a black velveteen hard hat, jodhpur boots.

Then the child's enthusiasm becomes exhausting. She converses at breakfast about posting and stirrups, and reads *Misty of Chincoteague* for the fifth time. She upgrades her jodhpurs into breeches and tall boots, and adds a riding jacket to the wardrobe. She draws horses jumping in the margins of her algebra textbook.

Her interest intensifies; she wears tattersall shirts with bow ties, tweed hacking jackets, scarves with snaffle bits on them. She knows just how much it will cost to convert the garage into two box stalls.

Then one day, she discovers Boys. The breeches hang in the closet, the horse-show ribbons get dusty on the wall, and the objects of her affections thereafter walk on two legs instead of four.

become overly zealous—if she decides to pursue dance seriously, she'll never agree to college, and hence will not meet the Right People.

Dancing school. Seventh-grade boys and girls go once a week, so that they can learn Poise and Good Manners together and thus be prepared at a young age for any sort of Prep gathering imaginable. The fox trot, waltz, and cha-cha are standards, but such terpsichorean esoterica as the rhumba, merengue, egg-beater, and frug are also taught.

French lessons. So that the little darlings will sound like Aristocrats, and will be able to communicate with the *au pair*, governess, and maitre d'. Tutor travels to your house, so there's no embarrassment in having to lug *cahiers* around for all to see. Prepares children for European and Caribbean travel.

Tennis lessons. Whether they develop into "A" or "B" players, children must know how to play tennis. They must learn how to shake hands with the linesmen, what "sudden death" and "sweet spot" mean, and what to say to the opponent after a victory. More deals and wedding proposals are offered on the courts than in any board room, after all.

Two hours of lessons with the club pro (the twenty-year-old son of friends) are ritually terminated by a dunk in the pool, before heading home.

Sailing lessons. Preparation for a lifetime of regattas and summers in Newport. From the initial swimming test—fifteen minutes of treading water in complete foul-weather gear—to the first yacht, boats will always play a key role in the Preppy's life. While still on their maiden voyages on a Bluejay, youngsters will learn to call rope "line," the bathroom "the head," and to regard lifejackets cavalierly.

Riding lessons. Private, once a week outings that require special outfits, all imported from England, some elements of which can be adapted to the casual everyday wardrobe. Prepares youth for life among the Landed Gentry, even if they are city-dwellers.

Summer camp. Where children are sent to learn self-reliance, and to give a weary Mummy and Daddy their much-needed vacation. Not every sleep-away camp is Prep; the most sought-after are those where you get grounded for a week for wearing a pastel-colored Lacoste shirt with your white tennis shorts. Chase Tennis Camp, (the New Hampshire campus, *not* Pennsylvania), Buck's Rock Work Camp, and anything in Maine where you have to dispense with your bodily fluids out of doors are key.

PREP ON ALL FOURS

The Proper Pet

Having the right pet is as important as having the right polo shirt—and the true Prep pet is the dog. It is allowed to contradict in its behavior every established rule and value of the Prep household. While the Prep adult and child are impeccably well behaved, the pet is not. All the affection that the Prep family holds back from each other is lavished upon the dog (or dogs)—therefore it is hideously spoiled. It leaps, it froths, it paws—it eats steak.

Any eccentricity of character is indulged, no matter how extreme—dogs that pee on the Sheraton sofa, or attack anyone outside the immediate family, or regularly disperse the contents of neighborhood trash cans will be accommodated for years. Labradors think they're lap dogs, Great Danes eat off the table. Golden retrievers, smiling foolishly, dig huge holes in the rose garden, and basset hounds sunbathe on highways.

The proper dog should also be absolutely filthy on a regular basis (from swimming and then rolling in sand or dirt, or plowing through underbrush after a good rain), guzzle beer from a dish (particularly fashionable if there are teenaged

THE PREFERRED BREEDS

Golden retriever. Wonderfully good-natured. Can always be praised for bringing the neighbor's newspaper to the breakfast table undamaged, due to its soft mouth—evolved, of course, for retrieving.

Labrador retriever. Comes in two colors, yellow and black—either is fine. Its feathery tail is ideally formed for making a clean sweep of the coffee table.

English or Irish setter. English is, perhaps, preferred. A nervous breed and therefore particularly difficult to control. Maintains a high level of saliva production, making it all the more desirable.

Old English sheepdog. Popular because it's so very hairy, and because it's English. High potential for generating large clumps of matted fur—can achieve that sought-after unkempt look with very little effort.

sons in the house), bark at the least consequential movement or noise while cheerfully ignoring any unannounced visitor, shed profusely, nap on the living room sofa, and sleep on a family member's bed.

NAMES

Nothing cute will do; nor will anything ethnic. Don't give an Irish setter an Irish name, and never call a dog Muffin. Several categories of names, however, are encouraged.

Liquor. In every town there are at least three blond dogs named Brandy or Whiskey.

Family names. Prep families have so many names, that, even after giving three or four to each child, they still are left with some to assign; hence dogs called Bayard, Tyler, Hubert.

Biblical or mythical names. To show that you are intellectual. Moses, Joshua, Nimrod, Juno.

ODE TO THE BIG DOG
by Jeffrey Harper

While by the fire, sipping grog
I stroke the warm back of our dog;
She is no simple mutt; for me,
This creature nears the deity.

No names like Champ or Rex or Spot
Our dog is never hot to trot
She ambulates with arrant glee
Befitting noble pedigree.

A wondrous hound with flowing mane
A Lab, a setter, a Great Dane,
This canine I bequeath to thee
Who laps not water but Earl Grey tea.

And raised on victuals of great fame—
No Ken-L-Ration Gravy Train
But weaned on shrimp, Coquilles St. Jacques,
Pheasant-aspic and veal stock.

And girded thus with finest things
In gladful howls our beast does sing
Rejoicing of its canine creed
Adopted child of the nobler breed.

Most Un-Prep

Newfoundland. Massive size and saliva output make this breed almost uncontrollable and nearly impossible to keep indoors—no one outside the serious Prep Family even considers this dog for a pet.

Basset hound. Usually two. So dignified they can barely walk, often seen in the company of older couples.

Pugs. Only qualifies if there are at least five, so that they have every opportunity of getting constantly underfoot and yapping in unison.

Also favored: Brittany spaniels, German shorthaired pointers, standard poodles, corgis, St. Bernards.

REGULATING THE CASH FLOW

Well-to-Dos and Don'ts

The thing about money is that it's nice that you have it.

You're not excited to get it. You don't talk about it. It's like the golden retriever by the chair—when you reach out for it it's there. You find this comforting.

Nice people don't discuss their money. If in private they are voracious readers of *Barron's*, *The Wall Street Journal*, *Forbes*, and *Fortune* and are wily manipulators of their own fortunes, the general impression is still that they treat their money with benign neglect.

Nice people *do* discuss *other* people's money. They speculate on whether that money was earned, inherited, married, borrowed, or stolen. Is it his? Is it hers? Is it really there at all?

The true Preppy traffics his money with the following rules in mind:

1. Your money is handled by a man called a trustee until you reach a certain age, usually in your twenties. It is important that you give your trustee the impression that you are a solid citizen. It is imprudent to discuss drugs, sex, or your skepticism about capitalism with him. When he takes you to lunch let him pay, so he knows you're frugal. He's making his own income from your money anyway. Agree with anything he says.

2. Give to charities that will list your name as a sponsor.

3. Be alternately spendthrift and parsimonious. Spend a lot

of money on a bottle of Scotch and good cigars, but save subway fare by walking to work.

4. Be a little bit careless with money. Forget how much cash you have with you, for instance—it helps give the impression that you don't think too much about money.

5. Never carry cash, anyway. Borrow, or charge.

6. Don't get grabby over lunch checks. If you intend to pay, take your guest to your club, where he has no choice.

7. No matter how rich you are, give your children only modest allowances. Encourage them to earn more money by helping to vacuum the pool, or repair the dock, or roll the tennis court.

8. Charge at any store, whether or not you have an account. Simply give them your name and address in the most disinterested manner possible.

9. Never replace anything until you have exhausted all possibility of repair, restoration, or rehabilitation. No matter what it is, they don't make it as well as they used to.

10. Be quick to pick up small tabs—for drinks, taxis, and such. Your friends should remember only the frequency of your generosity, not the amount, and they will end up picking up the big tabs.

11. Don't say *wealthy*. Say *rich*.

12. Be in debt.

IN DADDY WE TRUST

If Daddy has foresight, he will provide for the future of his young by endowing them with a trust fund. With more growth potential than a Christmas Club savings account, the trust fund has connotations of comfortable paneled dens, silver trays laden with bottles of imported sherry— in a word, Security.

Daddy deposits a certain amount of money into the fund each year, and the total interest accrued is dispersed to the beloved offspring in monthly allotments. The trust fund means that looking for a job can be a leisurely hobby. It means that you can rent a car when you don't feel like taking a three-hour bus ride.

If Daddy doesn't establish a trust fund, it need not mean he doesn't love his child. He may invest in real estate in the child's name; he may buy stocks, certificates of deposit, bonds for the child's portfolio. Or, for that touch of class, he may buy a bottle of extraordinarily fine wine on each of the child's birthdays, to be put in a wine cellar that will be given over to the lucky inheritor on the 21st birthday.

BEFORE TRUTH, THE RIGHT FORK

A Preppy Value System

The Prep value system is a hybrid of the Puritan ethic and noblesse oblige combined in an unspoken code that is, nevertheless, as solid as the rock on Mummy's engagement ring. True Preppies assimilate these commandments through osmosis—Mummy and Daddy never lecture. In fact, these values are so ingrained, Mummy or Daddy would have a hard time trying to codify them if called upon to do so. These values are second nature—like wearing loafers without socks.

ONE
CONSISTENCY

This is the Preppy euphemism for sameness. Generation after generation will dress, dine, walk, talk, decorate, vacation, work, get educated, get married, and name babies all in the same way. Children perpetuate the traditions because they haven't been exposed to any other way of life. This primary value ensures that the Prep style of life will remain intact, that future generations will know which fork to use.

TWO
NONCHALANCE

While Preppies take pride in their social position, they are loathe to flaunt it to the world. Understatement is key. They know they have wealth and power, so why show it off? Mummy may have inherited a king's ransom in sables, but she prefers to wear her four-year-old ski parka.

THREE
CHARM

This quality is mistaken by non-Preppies as mere politeness, as if simply saying "ma'am" and "sir" to elders were all that distinguished a Preppy. On the contrary, charm is the Preppy's suit of armor, the facade of unflappable gentility that doesn't crack under pressure. The hostess who breaks up a drunken fistfight at a party and then turns to her other guests remarking, "just a little excitement," is not just salvaging her soiree. She's preserving the Prep status quo.

F O U R
DRINKING

A Preppy's ambition is directed toward imbibition. Failure
to master the skill of consum-
ing large amounts of alcohol
will result in a lifetime of denied invitations. The cocktail's
ubiquitous presence proves
that pleasure is life's major
concern—it also provides
something to do with the
hands when standing and talking.

F I V E
EFFORTLESSNESS

If life is a country club, then all
functions should be free from
strain. Since Preppies want always to appear capable and
comfortable, everything they
do or wear must look as if it
were done without a second
thought. Forget about the time
spent practicing a bow tie knot
or forehand topspin return;
the important issue is that it
looks like a cinch in public.

S I X
ATHLETICISM

Vacations and leisure activities
usually revolve around locations for sports—ski slopes,
golf courses, beaches—so it's
necessary to at least pretend a
predilection for outdoor living
even if the only exercise performed is running down to get
more tonic water. Sports show
the Preppy's casual pursuit of
simple, healthful entertainment, with, of course, the correct, costly, athletic equipment.

S E V E N
DISCIPLINE

The credo was handed down
straight from John Calvin.
Daddy often proclaims he got
where he is through hard
work, sacrifice, and denial of
immediate pleasure for future
good and that grandfather's
trust fund is no reason to slack
off. Preppies believe that Latin
in Prep school builds a sound
English vocabulary and that a
coat and tie build character.

E I G H T
PUBLIC
SPIRITEDNESS

Once connected to a proper
organization, there's nothing a
Preppy, particularly a woman,
wouldn't do: lend her woody
wagon to the Girl Scouts, pin
little flags on strangers for the
Red Cross, purr reassuringly
over the phone for Suicide
Hotline—anything, as long as
it doesn't conflict with Julia
Child & Co. The same dictum
that teaches modesty about fi-
nancial status also insists on
generosity, if only out of guilt
for a lifetime of debutante seasons.

MAKING AN ENTRANCE

The Debutante Scene

The debut is one of the cornerstones of Prep life, though it has, as an institution, seen its heyday pass. Originally intended to introduce young girls of Good Family to society, the debut is now little more than a series of wonderful parties and a chance to be queen for a day without ending up with a husband. Somewhat downplayed in the Northeast, the debutante scene is still elaborate and very important in the South. While few debutantes take a year off from college (as St. Louis girls used

NOVEMBER 14, 1938   10 CENTS

The most famous debutante of them all: Brenda Diana Duff Frazier in 1938.

to do) the season can be exhausting and all-absorbing. Every debut involves the following ingredients:

1. The invitation. You have to be invited to come out by the debutante committee in charge of each ball. This is the hardest part, because you have to have the right parents (and the right grandparents) to assure eligibility. If you are of Anglo-Saxon descent, if your father is a stockbroker or a lawyer, and your grandfather was governor of the state, you are a shoo-in. If you are not invited by the committee, don't even bother appealing the decision. The more fuss you make, the more definite the rebuff will be.

2. The escort. Once you know you are going to make your debut, you will have to find an escort. This can be embarrassingly difficult—especially if you have gone to a single-sex Prep school. Brothers, cousins, and virtual strangers are pressed into service—many debutantes have gone to balls on the arm of Mummy's college roommate's son. Ideally, of course, your escort is handsome, charming, and a good dancer.

3. The dress. It has to be white, and since this is your chance to play princess, you want it to be as pretty as possible. In New York, a debutante shopping at a store such as Saks or Bendel's is assured by the store that she will be the only girl at a given ball in the dress she has chosen. With this white dress you will need long white kid gloves, white shoes, and pearls. If you are being presented at more than one ball, you'll need a different dress for each one.

4. The season. It's different in every town, but the idea is the same. The parents of each of the year's crop of debutantes give their daughter a party of some sort—a tea, a dance, or a dinner. Friends of the family may do so as well, adding a luncheon or a picnic to the schedule. Whether the season is in June (common in some northeastern suburbs) or around Christmas (more usual in cities), it will be a whirl of nonstop parties for a few weeks or even months.

5. The ball. The ball is usually administered for the benefit of a charity—the Junior League, the local Boys' Club, a children's hospital. At the ball, the girls in white are presented formally to the assembly: "Miss Alden Jewett Worthington, presented by her father, Mr. Tifton Newell Worthington."

COMING OUT ACROSS THE NATION

Atlanta: Harvest Ball, Christmas Ball
Baltimore: The Bachelor's Cotillion
Boston: The Cotillion
Charleston: The St. Cecilia Ball
Chicago: Passavant Cotillion, Christmas Ball
Cincinnati: The Bachelor's Cotillion
Cleveland: Assembly Ball, The Cotillion Society Ball
Kansas City: Jewel Ball
Memphis: Holiday Ball, The Summer Presentation Ball
New Orleans: Debutante Club Ball, Le Début des Jeunes Filles de la Nouvelle Orléans
New York: Junior Assemblies, Infirmary Ball
Philadelphia: The Assembly
Raleigh: The North Carolina Debutante Ball
Richmond: Bal du Bois
St. Louis: Veiled Prophet Ball
San Francisco: The Cotillion
Savannah: The Christmas Cotillion

They may also perform some kind of cotillion or other elaborate dance (sometimes with props such as fans or chains of flowers). Some young women are presented at more than one ball; they may come out in their home states, then go to New York for the Infirmary Ball—or if they grew up in New York they might be presented at the Junior Assemblies, the Junior League Ball, *and* the Infirmary.

ETIQUETTE IN CONNECTICUT

Quiz # 1

The following questions are designed to clarify some fine points of the Prep sensibility—to spotlight decisions in four situations that only a Preppy would make. For those to whom the difference between good sense and good manners is not obvious, answers appear at the bottom of the page.

1. You are involved in a rear-end collision on I-95. You leave your car and . . .

a. Violently and rudely gesture at the other driver, using objectionable and threatening language.

b. Exchange license and insurance information as stipulated by state and federal law.

c. Discover that your law partner skippered other driver's older brother's boat in Bermuda Race of '55, and go out for a drink.

2. At a dinner party, a young guest drinks the contents of his finger bowl. You, as the hostess . . .

a. Ask, in a loud voice, if the young guest wouldn't prefer his refill on the rocks.

b. Ignore his gaucherie and continue talking to Trip Dunwhistle just back from Bar Harbor sitting on your left.

c. Without further ado, drink the contents of your own.

3. After you save a drowning youth, the local newspaper asks for an interview, which would also be accompanied by a photograph. You decline because . . .

a. You don't think you look good with wet hair.

b. You don't wish to receive acclaim for what was a noble, selfless act.

c. Your family believes that you should appear in print only three times in your life—upon birth, marriage, and death.

4. When setting the table for an informal dinner you will serve, among other things . . .

a. Ketchup in a bottle, salt in a shaker, Triscuits in the box.

b. Ketchup in a bottle, salt in a shaker, Triscuits on a plate.

c. Ketchup in a dish, salt in a dish, Triscuits in the box.

Answer in each case is *C*.

CHAPTER 2

THE ROOT
OF
ALL PREP

The Years at School

SECOND TO NONE
Origins of the Prep School

*Front cover of the original Deed of Gift and Act
of Incorporation of Phillips Exeter Academy in 1781*

M any, many years ago, before there was L. L. Bean, before there was The Talbots, before there was even a United States of America, there were no Prep schools on these shores. Young people wandered about aimlessly, with nothing to do. There was no recreational sailing, there were no BMW's, and it was impossible to get a squash court.

Then, in 1635, the Boston Latin School was founded. This was a step in the right direction, but there were still bugs to be worked out: The school was public (it still is one of Boston's public schools) and it had "Latin" in the name, a subject that gives the Preppy some of his or her most trying academic moments. Further attempts were made in 1638 with the Collegiate School in New York City, and in 1645 with Boston's Roxbury Latin School, both of which still exist as private Prep schools.

These early schools taught classics, essentially, and it wasn't until around the time of the Revolution that people began saying, "Aren't we missing something? What about the weird biology teacher? The corridor fights? The headmaster's lonely wife?" It was necessary that schools be opened that weren't just Prep schools. They had to be Preppy—the sorts of places that encourage fond reminiscences of painful years.

The schools that fit this order were the boarding academies, schools that taught a broader range of subjects. They began with Governor Dummer Academy in South Byfield, Mass., in 1763. Was it Preppy? Let it suffice to say that Governor Dummer Old Boys (alumni) helped to found Phillips Academy (Andover) just after the Revolution. A few years after that, Phillips Exeter Academy was founded in Exeter, N.H. This was an especially notable development, because—at last—there was a school upon which, more than a century and a half later, the book *A Separate Peace* might be based.

For the next hundred or so years, things stayed pretty much the same. The number of academies grew, as did the public school system. There was a civil war. The military schools were started.

By the last years of the nineteenth century, the number of schools was creeping upward as fast as the ivy they cultivated. In 1898 and 1899 there was positively a mad rush to found schools, everyone suddenly recognizing that a founding date in the previous century would confer instant hoariness on the youngest of institutions. Gothic and Cotswold-style quadrangles were carefully engineered to look centuries old in a few years. Notions of uniforms, of rigorous regulations, and of noblesse oblige were adopted. Schools looked to social qualifications as grounds for admission. The quality of the food suffered.

Prep schools began to compete with one another to gain admission for the largest number of their students to the prestige colleges. Trustees began to hear stirrings of what-should-we-do-about-people-who-aren't-quite-of-our-set—and began ignoring these stirrings. Many schools became systems for keeping Us from Them, for ensuring the perpetuation of the ruling class. And at the same time, schools were begun to ensure the democratization of the ruling class (See *Bohemia Academe*.)

With the 1920's came the heyday of deb parties and the glamorization of drinking, forever changing the nature of Prep. Social excesses were regularly committed, and Getting Thrown Out acquired its cachet.

Prep schools, as we know them, had arrived.

PREPARING TO PREP

Picking the School for You

Do you really want to go to Prep school? It's not a decision to make without serious consideration. Of course it will be nice to wear that Farmington ring or to drink out of an Exeter beer mug for the next twenty years, and the friendships you make will stand you in good stead all your life: we're talking about the famous Old Boy Network. But like much in Preppy life, private school requires some rather intense suffering (or at least travail) in pursuit of a rather distant advantage.

For starters, you really have to *work* at private school. Preparatory is the key word and they are, theoretically, preparing you for college. Students in private school have long hours of class and are assigned lots of homework; one school in Virginia estimates that its students prepare an average of four hours per course per week outside of class, and they usually take five courses per term. Moreover, class size (fifteen students at the outside, gener-

ally half that) in private schools assures that the slightest degree of laziness is noticed and, if not punished, at least corrected.

Laziness is discouraged because it's a slipshod mental habit, and it runs contrary to the entire ethos of Preppy life. In actual fact, Prep schools are as eager to indoctrinate their students with the Preppy Morality as they are to get them into the right colleges. Catalogs speak of teaching students self-discipline, responsibility, and a quality called intellectual rigor. These schools are forming good citizens as well as good students—or so they'd like to think.

The process, like most moral indoctrinations, has its uncomfortable aspects: rules, parietals, demerits, and disciplinary action. (There is a tale that the legendary Frank Boyden, long-time headmaster of Deerfield, had unruly boys hoe the potato field to "work off" their transgres-

BOARDING VS. DAY

After deciding to apply to a preparatory school, it is necessary to choose between staying at home, or going away. Both have their virtues, but either is a key commitment.

BOARDING

1. Living away from home. Mummy and Daddy become two people who feed you well on vacation. No more prying questions every day. No brothers and sisters to borrow your clothes. No more "Kip, are you doing your homework?"

2. Independence. You're on your own. If you decide to goof off, go right ahead. If you get permission to go to the movies, you don't have to take your little sister—she's four hundred miles away. Your authority figures may have changed, but your housemaster doesn't really care what you wear to class.

3. Smoking cigarettes. You can smoke your head off at boarding school. Assuming Mummy and Daddy haven't given you permission to inhale cancer-inducing tobacco into your lungs, the campus is lousy with woods and hideaways into which you can sneak. And since you don't have to kiss your dorm master/mistress hello, as you come in the door he/she will never know.

4. Drinking. After you befriend a senior who'll buy you a fifth of vodka or rum, which you mix with Orange Crush or Coke from the dorm's machine, you can get drunk nightly.

5. Boarding schools are Preppier. Many of them are older and more ritual-filled than day schools. Atmosphere mimics Mummy and Daddy's country club.

DAY

1. Keeping your own car. You can drive to school, to the mall, or just cruise. Pay for gas with the fortune you will save by not having to buy name tapes.

2. Talking on the phone for hours. Even though it drives Daddy absolutely *batty,* you can talk on the phone ad infinitum. No dimes needed. No jockeying for position in long lines. You can even talk on the phone while watching TV and listening to the stereo at the same time.

3. The food is better. Mummy or the cook whips up much better food than any school dining room. You can go for 'za, burgers, and ice cream without signing out.

SINGLE-SEX VS. COED

When choosing a secondary school, you will be immediately confronted by two looming possibilities: a coed or single-sex school. Both kinds afford separate sets of advantages that make them desirable.

SINGLE-SEX

1. Dirty Hair. You don't always have to look good. You don't even have to be clean. Members of your own gender may complain that your personal habits are disgusting, but they don't have to date you.

2. Dances are better. School dances aren't very exciting when their only attendees are the people you see every day in your Latin and gym classes. They can be more fun when boys or girls are imported from another institution—shampoo recommended.

3. Concentration. Studying and living with members of your own sex (except for an occasional faculty husband or wife) makes diligence in your spare hours much easier. Daydreaming about the cute English teacher is one thing, but when it's a boy you see every day, it can become more like sleepwalking.

4. Hairy-leg shows. The all-male chorus line is among the traditions that usually bite the dust when coeducation rears its egalitarian head. These are the rituals that prompted Mummy and Daddy to send you to private school in the first place.

5. Single-sex schools are Preppier. Like boarding, going to a single sex school is just plain more old-fashioned, and therefore Preppier.

COED

1. Sex. You might not engage in actual sex until you're twenty-five, but the atmosphere of boy and girl adolescents coexisting with fecund imaginations makes for one ripe environment. Sure you spend more time getting dressed in the morning, but Life After School tends to be coed, hence the situation is more real. And if the dances aren't as momentarily dramatic, coeducation gives rise to real relationships between the sexes. You can observe firsthand that members of the opposite sex are just like you, with the same needs, fondnesses, and insecurities. They can buy you cigarettes and booze. You can be friends with them—you no longer have to live in fear that someone cute is a rotten human being. After a while, you should be able to study in the library without too many distractions . . . but let's hope you won't have to.

sions.) To quote another catalog, "Absolute permissiveness leads to chaos, whereas controlled and disciplined living can lead to a sense of real freedom."

If you do decide that you can stand the strain, it's important to choose the right school for you. Formative influences such as what sports you learn to play and to whom you lose your virginity can depend on where you prep. Choose carefully; you're stuck with a Prep school for longer than you're stuck with a spouse. Some of the basic considerations are:

Coed or single-sex. Even in these days of rampant coeducation, a few of the best schools (Madeira, Farmington, Deerfield) are still single-sex. They must know something. Though coeducation provides exposure to the opposite sex, some students prefer to be sheltered for just a while longer and to be boys or girls together, without opposition.

Boarding or day school. If there is a good day school in your town, you might prefer to stay at home and defer dealing with roommates, sex and drugs, and doing your own laundry until college. On the other hand, boarding school provides indubitable prestige. Leaving home before other children in your community confers instant adulthood and worldliness.

School character. The reputation a school has among students of other schools is probably accurate. Some, such as Kent, are known as prisons because of their strict rules. Others, such as St. George's, place a strong emphasis on the spiritual life. Special factors (Milton's proximity to Boston, Millbrook's zoo) may influence a student's decision as well. Is a school faintly Bohemian (such as Putney) or rather proper (such as St. Mark's)?

Location. If you're going to spend three years in a place, you want to be sure you like it.

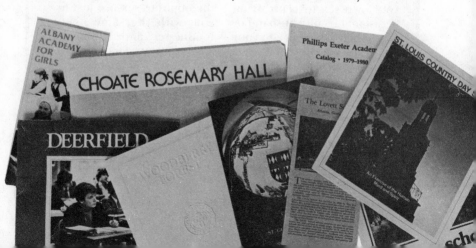

Proximity to cities, ski areas, boys' or girls' schools, your parents, an airport—these will affect your happiness more than you may think. The cold winters in Exeter will cause a nonskier nothing but chilblains, while the rural remoteness of Hotchkiss could drive a city-bred student crazy.

Plant. Some students make their choice on the strength of a school's physical facilities. While they aren't everything, they will make a difference. The arts center at Choate Rosemary designed by I. M. Pei is a major attraction, while the old yellow quadrangle building at Westover is something of a disadvantage. Foxcroft's riding facilities, the leafy suburban campus of Lawrenceville, the spectacular library at Emma Willard—each has persuaded at least some students that this is the school for them.

Studies. Probably last on your list going in to the school, but much more important coming out. Part of your reason for going to this school is that you want to get into college, and you want to go to the best one possible so that you can forever after wave your handkerchief or beat your breast during the last stanza of certain songs. You may also have specific academic interests you'd like to pursue: Andover is one of the few Prep schools that offers Russian, while the Hill School (in Pottstown, Penn.) offers Marine Ecology. One easy way to gauge the academic asceticism of a school is to find out where most of its graduates go to college.

It is also a good idea to be sure that you can get into the school of your choice. Many a budding Preppy career has been blighted when the postulant was turned down at the gates of St. Paul's or Ethel Walker's. If you really want to get out of the house, you'd better apply to a couple of "safety schools" just in case you aren't as smart as you think you are.

THE PREP SCHOOL YEARS. These two Preps are at that magic age when they are passing from unself-consciousness to self-consciousness. They're dressed this way because everyone else at school is dressed this way. Soon they will be in college and, for the first time, will discover that what to them had always been Just Clothes is in fact a distinct Look.

candy-striped shirt, unironed

frayed colla

rep tie, fished out of the bottom of bookbag where it lives

navy blue blazer, 9 year-old hand-me-down brass buttons with older brother's Prep school insignia

pocket contents: contraband cigarettes, 2-week old letter to parents without stamp with a phone number from a girl at girl's school written on it

tartan boxer shorts

green book bag holding: 2 lacrosse balls; 1 notebook with papers folded in it; 1 green shetland sweater with holes at neck; Swiss army knife; Cliff Notes for Madame Bovary; *dog-earred* Penthouse; *recent* National Lampoon

khakis, sitting low on hips

pocket conten $6.75 and protec

belt embroider with map of Nantucket

pants are too short— outgrown over the summer

Top-Siders, green gaffing tape on left, red on right

PREP PERSONA
No. 2

blonde streaks from experimenting
with peroxide (Mummy had a fit)

gold button earrings
(ears pierced last month)

boy's shirt, white, used to be brother's

navy blue cardigan,
never buttoned all the way

school ring

men's Timex on grosgrain ribbon watch band

three silver bangles from parents'
last trip to Mexico

elephant hair bracelet

bitten fingernails

kilt, Fraser
tartan

white canvas book bag
with red and blue trim

book bag contents:
large ring binder with different section
for each subject;
Glamour magazine;
Flair pens in 5 different colors;
5 spiral notebooks, one for each subject;
travel pack of Kleenex;
Mason-Pearson hairbrush;
The Elements of Style

new Indian-head
hockey stick—
not yet taped to
improve grip

navy blue
cable-knit kneesocks

Bean blucher moccasins

KEEP OFF
THE GRASS

PREP WITH A CAPITAL "P"

The Primary Secondaries

At first glance, all Prep schools look alike. But then you notice a distinct *noblesse oblige* in Andover graduates, a decided Maine hunting chic in Miss Porter's alumnae, a distinguishing alcoholic *savoir faire* in Woodberry Forest Old Boys that make them stand out from the mob of Prep school graduates. For, you see, there are preparatory schools and then there are Prep Schools, those institutions that bless you with a certain luster along with your diploma. Any Prep school can provide a good education, but the primary secondaries groom you for true-blue Prephood.

DAY SCHOOLS
G I R L S

1. The Agnes Irwin School. Ithan Ave., Rosemount, Pa. 19010. Founded 1869. Grades K-12. 18-acre suburban campus, 514 students. Uniforms are required. Preference is given to daughters of alumnae. Very straight arrow behavior here; idea of good time is not sneaking cigarettes but singing school songs. Field hockey team plays for blood.

2. The Bryn Mawr School. 109 West Melrose Ave., Baltimore, Md. Founded 1885. Grades N-12. 26-acre suburban campus, including 6 tennis courts, 534 students. Uniforms are required. Preference is given to siblings and alumnae daughters. Finishing school for those interested in Southern gentility, lacrosse, and good manners. Interview required.

3. The Chapin School. 100 East End Ave., New York, N.Y. 10028. Founded 1901. Grades K-12. 588 students. Uniforms required. Also known as Deb City (and not because the girls are named Debbie). John Lindsay's daughters studied here. Students like to hang out at Collegiate. SSAT and interview required.

4. Mary Institute. 101 North Warson Rd., St. Louis, Mo. Founded 1859. Grades K-12. 40-acre suburban campus with 12 tennis courts, 540 students. Dress code. Need to know how to mix a mint julep to graduate. Sun dress heaven. St. Louis Country Day boys are always available for dates. SSAT and interview required.

5. The Winsor School. Pilgrim Rd., Boston, Mass. 02215. Founded 1886. Grades 5-12. 6-acre urban campus. 8 tennis courts, 350 students. Dress code. Top school for Boston nobility who can't stand to leave home town. Helps to have Mummy as an alumnae.

B O Y S

1. Collegiate School. 241 W. 77th St., New York, N.Y. 10024. Founded 1638. Grades 1-12. Urban, 1 building, 540 students. Dress code. Bastion of Old New York Society and world headquarters for bowl-haircuts. Close to Lincoln Center; students on first name basis with Luciano Pavarotti. Interview required.

2. The Episcopal Academy. 376 North Latches Lane, Merion, Pa. 19066. Founded 1785. Grades K-12 (Girls K-8). Suburban, 70 acres, 240 high school students. Dress code. Breeding ground for squash players. As much fun as you can have in Philadelphia. Interview required.

3. The Gilman School. 5407 Roland Ave., Baltimore, Md. 21210. Founded 1897. Grades 1-12. 67 urban acres, enrollment 905. Dress code. Preference given to siblings and sons of alumni. Gathering spot for Roland Park Preps. Lacrosse set beelines to Mt. Washington Tavern, sailors seen downing burgers at McGarvey's in Annapolis, the less athletically inclined congregate at Alonso's. Interview required.

4. St. Louis Country Day School. 425 N. Warson Rd., St. Louis, Mo. 63124. Founded 1917. Grades 5-12. 6 suburban acres, 13 tennis courts, 470 students. Dress code. Big on spectator

activities: football and theatre division draw appreciative crowds. Where to go if you want to date a girl at Mary Institute. Interview required.

5. St. Mark's School of Texas. 10600 Preston Rd., Dallas, Tex. 75230. Founded 1933. Grades 1-12. Urban, 40 acres, Chapel, 741 students. Uniform. Preference to siblings and sons of alumni. Every student has a Scout, a Labrador and a favorite hunting spot. Idea of fun is taking date to "Cowboy" (the ranking Dallas bar) and dancing the Cotton-Eyed Joe.

C O E D

1. Charlotte Country Day School. 1440 Carmel Rd., Charlotte, N.C. 28211. Founded 1941. Grades K-12. 60 suburban acres, 936 students. No dress code. Preference to siblings and children of alumni. Students carry golf bags to class. Safety net for those kicked out of Virginia boarding schools. SSAT and interview required.

2. The Dalton School. 108 East 89th St., New York, N.Y. 10028. Founded 1916. Grades N-12. Urban campus, 2 buildings, 4 gyms, swimming pool, 1,243 students. No dress code. Students wear free sweaters from their designer Daddies' warehouses. They all have their own phones, some with extensions in Vail. SSAT and interview required.

3. Hawken School. Box 249, County Line Rd., Gates Mill, Ohio 44040. Founded 1915. Grades K-12. 370 acres spread over 2 suburban campuses, 785 students. Informal dress code (no coat and tie). Yes, even Cleveland has its elite and this is where they spend their time when they're not at The Country Club at Pepper Pike. Interview required.

4. The Latin School of Chicago. 59 W. North Blvd., Chicago, Ill. 60610. Founded 1888. Grades K-12. Urban, 890 students. No dress code. Preference given to siblings and children of alumni. For denizens of Lake Shore Drive who see Chicago as a four-block town, the perimeters being I. Magnin on the South, Oak Street Beach on the East, Orphan's on the North, and the Latin School on the West. Interview required.

5. The Lovett School. 4075 Paces Ferry Rd., N.W. Atlanta, Ga. 30327. Founded 1926. Grades N-12. 100 acres, suburban setting, football stadium, 1437 students, 535 upper school. Uniform. Old-family kids who are known to abandon the football field and jump in the contiguous Chattahoochee river with an inner-tube and a six-pack. Rival school Westminster has slightly better academic reputation but less fun-loving students.

BOARDING SCHOOLS

G I R L S

1. Dana Hall School. 45 Dana Rd., Wellesley, Mass. 12181. Founded 1881. Grades 7-12 and post graduate. 40 acres suburban campus, indoor riding center, 440 students. Occupying the old campus of Pine Manor (they were once associated). Need we say more?

2. Foxcroft School. Middleburg, Va. 22117. Founded 1914. Grades 9-12. 515 acres, rural, stables and indoor riding ring, 209 students. Dress code. For girls who never fully recovered from their equestrian phase—stables rival dorms for luxury. SSAT and interview required.

3. The Hockaday School. 11600 Wesh Rd., Dallas, Tex. 75229. Founded 1913. Grades N-12 day, 9-12 boarding. 100 acres, urban, 2 gyms, 2 swimming pools, 767 students. Uniform. Preference given to siblings and alumnae daughters. No one admitted without a charge account at Neiman Marcus and Cutter Bill's. A graduate wears a white formal at commencement, then runs out to a forest where she is snapped by a photographer for a portrait to adorn Mummy's dresser—until her wedding picture replaces it. Interview required.

4. The Madeira School. Greenway, Va. 22067. Founded 1906. Grades 9-12. 381-acre campus with indoor riding ring, chapel, 323 students. No dress code. Sweaters tied around shoulders, three singing clubs, and fun hockey matches equal Cute Girl Paradise. Mixers are jokes, but grab a guy from Episcopal just to have someone to talk to on the phone for four years (it's his bill not yours). SSAT and interview required.

5. Miss Porter's School. Main St., Farmington, Conn. 06032. Founded 1843. Grades 9-12. 30 acres, suburban setting, 301 students. Dress code. Preference to alumnae daughters. Winterim session spent skiing. Girls here receive more mail from boys' schools than they do from Mummy and Daddy. SSAT and interview required.

B O Y S

1. The Cate School. P.O. Box 68, Carpinteria, Cal. 93003. Founded 1910. Grades 9-12. 180 acres, small town setting, chapel, 193 students. Dress code. In a world without fall foliage, the closest you can get to Prep. For those who want to enjoy the secondary school experience without being too far from the Pacific. SSAT and interview required.

2. Deerfield Academy. Deerfield, Mass. 01342. Founded 1797. Grades 9-12 plus post-graduate year. 250 rural acres, planetarium, 566 students. Dress code. Students learn good sportsmanship which makes them everybody's favorite tennis opponents in later life. Graduates tend to get nauseously misty when reminiscing about the good old days. SSAT and interview required.

3. Episcopal High School.

Alexandria, Va. 22302. Founded 1839. Grades 9-12. 130 suburban acres, field house, football stadium, 280 students. Dress code. Nightly shuttle to Clyde's in Georgetown. For southern boys who want a taste of city (D.C.) in buccolic setting and don't want to go to Woodberry. Interview and SSAT required.

4. The Lawrenceville School. Box 6008, Lawrenceville, N.J. 08648. Founded 1810. Grades 8-12, plus post graduate year. 360-acre campus, small town setting, chapel, 717 students. No dress code. Preference given to siblings and sons of alumni. Looks like a junior Princeton—in fact, acts like one, too. SSAT and interview required.

5. Woodberry Forest School. Woodberry Forest, Va. 22989. Founded 1889. Grades 9-12 (includes day boys and girls). 1000 acres, rural, field house, 365 students. Dress code. Isolated country estate atmosphere. Dining room serves fresh milk from school dairy. For Southerners who don't want to go to Episcopal. SSAT and interview required.

C O E D

1. Choate Rosemary Hall. Christian St., Wallingford, Conn. 06492. Choate founded 1896, Rosemary Hall founded 1890, merged 1971. Grades 9-12 plus post-graduate year. 500 acres, suburban setting, chapel, 927 students. Dress code. Preference to siblings and children of alumni. Boy-girl ratio—3-2. Memorable school cheer. Still trying to live down the phrase: "If you can't get a girl, get a Choatie." SSAT and interview required.

2. Groton School. Farmers Row, Groton, Mass. 01450. Founded 1884. Grades 8-12. 285 acres, small town setting, chapel, hockey rink, 304 students. Dress code. Home away from home for Boston Brahmins. Fun dance program. Celebrated woodworking shop to occupy those who

wish to ignore sex until college. SSAT and interview required.

3. The Hotchkiss School. Lakeville, Conn. 06039. Founded 1891. Grades 9-12 plus post graduate year. 480 rural acres, skating rink, 491 students. Dress code. How to Prep without really leaving the crowd from New York. Library compensates as social center. Hotchkiss men go to graves thinking their time at Lakeville was the happiest years of their lives. SSAT and interview required.

4. Phillips Academy. Andover, Mass. 01810. Founded 1778. Grades 9-12 plus post graduate year. 600 acres, small-town setting, art museum, archeology museum, 1142 students. No dress code. So Prep it hurts. SSAT and interview required.

5. Phillips Exeter Academy. Exeter, N.H. 03833. Founded 1781. Grades 9-12, post graduate year. 200 acres, suburban setting, art museum, 972 students. Dress code. Preference given to alumni children. Almost as humorlessly Prep as Andover. Saving graces: presence of gentlemen jocks, proximity to New Hampshire shore. SSAT and interview required.

6. Middlesex School. 1400 Lowell Rd., Concord, Mass. 01742. Founded 1901. Grades 9-12. 350 acres, small town setting, chapel, 290 students. Dress code. You'll need a season train pass to Boston if you want to keep up socially. School even *makes* you take art appreciation (making college courses all the easier). Must carve a wooden plaque to get a diploma. SSAT and interview required.

7. St. Paul's School. Concord, N.H. 03301. Founded 1856. Grades 9-12. 1700 acre campus, small town setting, hockey rink, 497 students. Dress code. Loose academic requirements and insane electives ("God's Spell in Literature"). Liberal weekend privileges for seniors on the understanding that the ability to have a good weekend is a vital part of college life. SSAT and interview required.

GETTING IN
Interview Dos and Don'ts

The most significant element of the Prep school entrance application is the interview. You're smart and you've done well on the SSATs but so have other applicants, and the administration needs to get a look at you to see if you're right for student life pictures in future catalogs. It helps if a campus building is named after a family member—an endowment fund is better—but even without these assets you can shine in the interview by adhering to a few cardinal rules.

DOs	DON'Ts
1. Dress conservatively. Boys must wear a blue blazer, gray flannels, Weejuns, a white shirt and a red-and-blue rep tie (unless you're applying to a Bohemian Prep school, in which case sport white corduroys, a flannel shirt, and an incongruous tie). Girls have no choice but to wear a plaid kilt, button-down shirt, plain stockings, and loafers.	1. Wear Lacoste shirts, khakis and sneakers—implies an untrustworthy casualness. Absolutely no polyester or pens in pockets. (Sure, they want to groom you, but not *that* much.) Girls should stay away from short skirts, low-cut blouses, and platform shoes. Any suggestion of sartorial eccentricity should be reserved for impressing fellow students *after* you've been accepted.
2. Your parents should be jovial and well-dressed. Rehearse Daddy on his hearty laugh and firm handshake. Make sure Mummy clasps her hands in her lap.	2. Allow parents to talk about the trouble they've had with you at home and in school. They should not speak until spoken to (or they may overshadow you).

DOs	DON'Ts
3. Tell about your epiphany (SSAT word) of the human need for salvation while reading *The Catcher in the Rye*, your favorite book.	3. Discuss the *Communist Manifesto* and how it raises some unsettling questions about capitalism.
4. Check ahead to uncover which is the school's perennially bad team and stress your prowess in that sport. ("Except for my trophy in track, I don't feel I've reached my potential.")	4. Groan when the interviewer outlines the school's compulsory athletic program or let him know you were impeached by your Little League team.
5. Name-drop all siblings, cousins, and close friends who went or go to the school and "looooove it." This suggests that you'll fit right in and not become a loner who reads Sylvia Plath.	5. Admit to being second cousin to the student who tear-gassed last year's commencement ceremony.
6. Feign interest in the school's curriculum, emphasizing the courses not offered in your day school. ("I saw in the catalog that you have classes in modern theology and ....")	6. Go into your interest in music or art—this makes you sound like the type who won't respect the school's "classic" curriculum. *Never* mention TV.
7. Ask about extracurricular programs and react with enthusiastic fervor to every activity.	7. Inquire about the number of overnight or weekend leaves.
8. After campus tour, remark on the beauty of the grounds, the modernity of the facilities, the handsomeness of the buildings.	8. Query the whereabouts of cigarette machines, liquor stores, and sister or brother schools. Don't ask if the school fence extends through the woods at the back of the campus.

Rev. James "Jimmy" Penick School chaplain. Interprets Grateful Dead records for religious relevance in Chapel. His mandatory theology course, "God and Modern Man," has the easiest term paper at school. Wife invites the class over to tea. Son expelled from school two years ago in marijuana incident. Coaches varsity tennis. Delightful, ribald raconteur at fund-raising parties. Drives a Mercedes. *Nickname:* Rev. Panic.

Mr. Paris Marasonick Art and Music Appreciation teacher. Studied at Sorbonne, once met Alexander Calder—is working on a series of mobiles, examples of which litter the art studio (the school's old wrestling cage). Married to bohemian-dressing wife (Indian-print skirts over black leotards) and father of unruly eight-year-old son, Pablo. Has never set foot in the football stadium. *Nicknames:* Gay Paree, Mr. Moronic.

Mrs. Katherine Kingsley Konger Head of the English Department and College Admissions counselor. Fond of revamping the curriculum and inventing new electives ("The Tragic Flaw"). Daughter of former headmaster, considers herself more capable than present one. Married to an athletic-equipment retailer and Old Boy. Lives in Tudor house off-campus but comes to breakfast every morning. *Nicknames:* KKK, King Konger.

THE STAFF

Mr. Adam "Flash" Huxley
Headmaster. Ex-college athlete, tells same story at annual athletic dinner. Votes down student movements to abolish dress code, compulsory chapel, limited overnight leaves. Knows names and attendance dates for every Old Boy but can't remember current students' names. Sons off at school founded by great-uncle. *Nickname:* Flush.

Mrs. Phyliss Bagley
School nurse. Lives in infirmary. Students like to spend nights there as it's the only place lights-out is not enforced. Good-natured, trades wise-cracks, wears crumpled Kleenex in her cardigan sleeve, has hot line to hospital for any injury involving more than a Band-Aid. *Nicknames:* Bag Lady, Bonkers, Barfage.

Mr. Mark Smacklie
American History teacher. Head football, winter soccer, and lacrosse coach. Graduate of military academy and Notre Dame. Hero is Teddy Roosevelt. Toughest grader in school. Conducts dormitory inspection. Can repeat sports statistics on every game and player off the top of his head— which he does all through meals. Has tow-headed five-year-old son who always garners eight pictures in yearbook. Wife usually eats at home. *Nicknames:* Smackers, Marked-Off.

A TOUCH OF CLASS

The Curriculum

In the course of your years at secondary school, you will, on occasion, have to pay attention to studying, the ostensible reason your parents have sent you to such an expensive institution in the first place. There is little difference between the curricula at Prep and non-Prep schools—your basic History, English, Math, Science, and Language—except in Prep schools you don't get Health or Home Ec. Instead are electives with fancy titles like "Satire," "The Woman in Literature," and "Red China Today."

While Prep school is preparing you for college, both in terms of high SAT scores and proper study habits, it also endeavors to shape you for Prep Adulthood. The school hopes that, upon graduation, you will be a well-rounded young Prep, familiar with the right vacation spots and customs, articulate and witty in conversation, understanding of literary and historical references, proficient in the Prep vocation you pursue, capable of making at least one astute comment on any given subject—in short, everything necessary for membership in a good country club. As far as your Prep school is concerned, you are representing your alma mater after graduation—so it's important to its reputation that you know that Nietzsche is not the name of a German catering service.

In addition to these long-range benefits, Prep school nurtures the skills that will enable you to slide effortlessly through college. You learn never to read books all the way through since you can get the gist from reading the first and last chapters and the appropriate *Cliff* or *Monarch Notes*. You learn always to paraphrase your teacher's lectures on the exam. You overcome your fear of term papers and write them only the night before they're due, a habit that will stand you in excellent stead in college, where fast writing is a prized skill. Most important, you realize how to budget your time—one-eighth of it for academics, the rest for social life.

PREP I
The Basic Reading List

Every school specifies reading lists for various courses in its curriculum, but to gain a fuller understanding of the world of the school itself—and the sort of life for which it prepares you—try the below-listed fare: books about Prep schools, books read in Prep schools, books by Preppies, books about the joys and miseries of being Prep.

REQUIRED

THE CATCHER IN THE RYE
J.D. Salinger

A SEPARATE PEACE
John Knowles

A GOOD SCHOOL
Richard Yates

**THE PRIME OF
MISS JEAN BRODIE**
Muriel Spark

**TOM BROWN'S
SCHOOLDAYS**
Thomas Hughes

GOODBYE, MR. CHIPS
James Hilton

TEA AND SYMPATHY
Robert Anderson

THIS SIDE OF PARADISE
and anything else by
F. Scott Fitzgerald

LOVE STORY
Erich Segal

DECLINE AND FALL
and anything else by
Evelyn Waugh

THE HEADMASTER
John McPhee

RECTOR OF JUSTIN
Louis Auchincloss

GOOD TIMES/BAD TIMES
James Kirkwood

**THE STORIES OF JOHN
CHEEVER**
and anything else by
John Cheever

LAWRENCEVILLE STORIES
Owen Johnson

**THE BELLES OF
ST. TRINIAN'S**
Ronald Searle

OPTIONAL

THE DUKE OF DECEPTION
Geoffrey Wolff

**THE WORLD ACCORDING
TO GARP**
John Irving

Anything by
George Plimpton

Anything by
William F. Buckley, Jr.

CORPORE SANO

Photo courtesy Choate Rosemary Hall

I t is a commonly held notion that all Preps are athletes. Though perhaps not entirely deserved, this sporting reputation is the result of the stress laid on athletic activities throughout the Prep upbringing. This stress is nowhere more evident than at secondary school. Even if a child is hopelessly uncoordinated, he or she will be obliged to participate in strenuous sports every afternoon five or sometimes six days a week in hope of fulfilling some important tenets of the Preppy Creed.

Mens sana in corpore sano (a healthy mind in a healthy body). This is such a popular principle that every child under the age of nine can quote it in impeccable Latin. The connotations (faintly masochistic when taken to the limit) of *corpore sano* include regular subjection to cold salt water, very hard beds, and wind sprints.

Competition. Our capitalist society, young Preppies learn, is built on Competition. And competitive urges are encouraged on the playing field in order that Preppies will be better prepared to thrive on Wall Street, in the courtroom, at the club.

Sportsmanship. One of the most endearing things about a Preppy is his ability to say "nicely played" when he has just sprawled on his face and narrowly missed a shot, and to sincerely congratulate the winner of a game he has just lost. (Sportsmanship is also the reason why, despite their competitive training, Preppies do not actually run the world.)

Teamwork. Another principle that will be important on Wall Street or Madison Avenue. Whether or not passing to your wing will really teach future executives about delegating authority is a moot point—the concept is not questioned by the junior varsity lacrosse coach.

Physical hardship. Anything unpleasant builds character. Moreover, it is well known that if you keep the boys running around the playing field hard enough, they won't have energy left to think about girls.

On the whole, Prep sports are distinguished by a number of curious features. The balls they are played with (squash, hockey) are generally smaller than the balls non-Preps use (basketball, volleyball). Prep sports also require elaborate impedimenta such as sticks and racquets. A ball in flight is Preppier than a ball rolling along the ground.

SIGN UP FOR:	AVOID PARTICIPATING IN:
Soccer	Football
Rugby (men only)	Track
Field hockey (women only)	Folk dancing
Tennis	Basketball
Skiing	Volleyball
Squash	Synchronized swimming
Paddle tennis	Wrestling
Lacrosse	Archery
Crew (men only)	Baseball
Ice hockey	

FOR EXTRA CREDIT

Outside Activities

M any a Preppy, at college application time, has saved him or herself from the ignominious fate of being accepted only by county technical institutes or the Peace Corps by filling in the box marked "Outside Activities" with the entry: "See attached pages 2 through 24."

PRESTIGE ACTIVITIES

Monitor or prefect. Requires what the faculty calls "leadership abilities," which means that you don't laugh if someone breaks wind in chapel.

Honor committee. Requires a mournful visage as fellow students explain that the family doctor suggested taking Quaaludes to help them sleep.

Yearbook staff. Requires getting all the other committees to pose for their picture.

Newspaper—editor and news editor. Requires finding properly serious—but non-controversial—subjects for editorials and articles.

Student curriculum committee. Requires an ability to design a new curriculum that perfectly duplicates the old one.

Athletic advisory board. Requires knowing a football from a lacrosse stick.

EFFORTLESS ACTIVITIES

Debating society. Allows you to talk about sex and drugs under the pretext of resolving nonproductive trends in society.

Social activity, or hop committee. Allows you to get out of classes to set up for dances in the gym and to have access to a list of telephone numbers of girls' (or boys') schools.

Literary magazine. Allows you to write sarcastic short stories and poems under the excuse of artistic license.

Newspaper—features editor or cartoonist. Allows you to poke fun at everyone else in the school, particularly if you add things at the printer's before the faculty adviser gets a chance to edit them out.

Drama club. Allows you to miss all the rehearsals and then be the hit of the play when you ad-lib unmercifully.

Cheerleading or pep squad. Allows you to lead students in destructive pranks and bawdy cheers all in the name of school spirit.

THE BIG SLEEPOVER
Boarding School Life

Photo: Robert Phillips

Prep school is very much like summer camp, each a regimented series of activities that occupy you from waking to retiring—which are also monitored. From 7:30 A.M., when you are rudely awakened by the campus bell and a freshman running down the hall of the dorm shouting "First bell for breakfast," until lights-out at 11:00 P.M., when a faculty member prowls about checking to see that every room is dark, the school expects you to be where you've been assigned. And as long as you're where you're supposed to be, no one bothers you. As demanding as administrators may appear, they don't pry as parents do and you're free to develop your own political beliefs (if you have any), to start over with a whole new personality (since your classmates don't know the old you), and to pick up a liberating set of bad habits.

Dorms. The first major difference between home and campus life is that you'll no longer live in Mummy and Daddy's comfortable house with your own bedroom, but in a building similar to a poorly managed hotel with a roommate instead of a color TV.

Your room will soon resemble a maze, because you and your roommate will hang concealing blankets and place your desks and bunk bed at obstructive angles in order to give you time to extinguish a cigarette should an interloping instructor make an unannounced appearance. You must also resign yourself to the fact that there is no maid service and you will be expected to clean your room for inspection, a tactic the school uses to confirm that you've been in your room sometime in the past week.

You should know right away, especially if you're shy, that there is no such thing as personal privacy in a dorm. While it's true that girls' schools tend to have less barbaric bathroom layouts than boys', don't expect to be able to camouflage cellulite or embarrassingly located birthmarks in either. All the sinks are in a row like open palms at communion, the shower is a vast tiled room with dozens of nozzles hanging out of the walls like the heads of expectant vultures, and, in some of the older schools, toilets sit face to face in stalls that may not always have curtains.

Meals. Mandatory. The way to tell which meal you're eating is to see if it's chipped beef (breakfast), grilled cheese sandwiches (lunch), or fruit salad Jell-o with meat loaf (dinner). The dining room evokes a restaurant or a warehouse, depending upon your school, with long, rectangular tables arranged in lines. The freshmen sit in the middle of the tables where they stack plates and pour water for the upperclassmen and teachers who sit at the ends. An instructor often brings his family, unless it's a boys' school in which case he orders his teenage daughter(s) to eat at home. Meals are always started with a

prayer and only the class dullards bow their heads along with the faculty. Only seniors are permitted to have coffee and they exercise this privilege even if they can't stand the stuff.

On those fortunate occasions when the faculty member chooses to stay home, the students at the unsupervised end of the table are free to engage in ribald discussions and inventive tricks with their food. Inevitably, someone makes the mistake of throwing the bread too far or laughing when the headmaster announces during the end-of-meal messages that balls are missing from the athletic department, and the rowdy corner is censured if not fined with demerits.

Chapel. The little time-waster squeezed between breakfast and classes every school day. If you're attending an overtly religious school, bring along a magazine to get you through the fifteen-minute church service. If you go to a school that considers itself "progressive" enough to encourage students to sponsor their own chapel programs, chapel can even be amusing, especially if some wag attempts to adapt biblical parables to school life, e.g., a Philistine becomes a teacher, and Moses a student, etc.

Classes. These take up the day from 9:00 A.M. to 2:00 P.M. Some of them may prove diverting, but a course's interest depends on whether your teacher is a young instructor who feels (wisely) that students need a bit of entertaining to be absorbed in the material, or one of the school's beloved old fogeys, the Mr. Chips or Miss Dove whose sparkle diminished in 1952 and whose senility set in not too soon afterward. In general, French teachers are the most eccentric, history the most obstinate, science the most soporific, English the most profane, and math teachers (who usually double as coaches) won't give you an inch in the classroom or on the field.

Athletics. They dominate your afternoon. You may revel

Photo courtesy Choate Rosemary Hall

in sports, but be forewarned: both single-sex and coed schools have inordinately long athletic practices—exerting all that energy is cheaper for the administration than buying saltpeter. The need to have a few capable teams for Homecoming and Parents' Day tournaments explains why any other extracurricular activity is unwelcome during the afternoon.

Free time. Doled out warily and rarely. You have a few minutes after breakfast and before chapel to brush your teeth and clean up your room for inspection (which goes on while you're in class). Afternoon freedom depends upon the generosity of your coaches—a quality not frequently associated with them. After dinner you are awarded with a hour and a half of free time before you are to attach yourself to your place of study, but often this is the period in which all clubs and student publications vie for your participation. The post-dinner "lull" is perpetually broken by pep rallies where you are to express your faith in the school team by yelling yourself hoarse, or by mass meetings where the assistant headmaster explains why a number of students have been dismissed or fled from school.

Study hall. Often, quite literally, a hall—a long, Dickensian room with miles of wooden desks where alphabetically seated lowerclassmen are forced to study under the watchful eye of an unlucky bachelor teacher who is assigned the post one night a week. In many Prep schools today, study hall is a philosophical concept, a period when you are *supposed* to be in your room studying, or at the very least, not listening to your stereo. The school does its best to run you around all day so that the only time you have left to study is in the interval between 8:00 and 10:00 P.M. But, since it is the nighttime, and most of the faculty, except for the fascist instructors (nicknamed "Snake" or "Snoopy") who thrive on lurking around in the dark, are pooped too,

they leave you alone to do almost anything you want.

Lights-out. Revolves around your class standing. If you're an underclassman, you're commanded to be in your room with the light off by 10:30. If you're a senior, you have to be in your room at 10:30, too, but you get to keep your lamp burning for another half hour. One senior is chosen every week to oversee his dorm floor and to verify to a wandering instructor that everyone is in their room. As you might guess, this senior knows more secrets than Mata Hari.

Weekends. Privileges that are stingily granted. The student leaders are recompensed with the largest number—perhaps six per semester—

Photo courtesy Phillips Exeter Academy

while the more plebeian underclassmen have to make do with three. Before you can even think about packing your suitcase, you have to supply the faculty with a multitude of written permissions, invitations, and itineraries. Saturdays and Sundays are traditionally free, although they are the first liberty to be denied if your demerit tally is too high.

Oddly enough, most students don't jump at the chance to rejoin the rest of the world on the other side of the school wall. The isolation the school imposes all week inspires a camaraderie with your classmates that you don't want to surrender by mixing with the foreigners in town. After you've all crammed for an American History quiz, plastered the hall of your dorm with wet toilet paper, kicked a soccer ball for fifteen hours, and staged a satirical revue where you mimicked the faculty, why would you want just anybody to join your little group? The only outside trips you take are nocturnal drinking expeditions (shared experiences) and assignations (which become shared experiences through recapping).

Life in a boarding school is so (to use a favorite Preppy word) intense, that you don't want to lose that twenty-four hour, seven-days-a-week identification you and your buddies share.

LEARNING TO SMOKE

As its name suggests, a preparatory school should instruct its students in the customs they will encounter after graduation. One such tradition is smoking. The school can never officially endorse this practice on the grounds that it's "unhealthy," both in terms of character building and the illegality of selling cigarettes to minors. On the other hand, the noticeable consumption of butts by faculty members and alumni at fund-raising parties proves that the social cigarette is a necessary requirement for admission into Polite Society.

In many schools, smoking (tobacco, that is) is permitted only if the student has (a) reached a certain age (usually sixteen); (b) had Daddy send his written consent; (c) maintained a designated grade level (no lower than a B−); and (d) agreed to smoke only in the restricted student smoking area, invariably a four-foot-square corner behind the kitchen. Supposedly, athletic training rules prohibit students, even those with approval, from indulging in the "killing weed" during the three sport seasons that comprise the school year, but the crowd that bunches together in the tiny smoking spot (always dubbed "Egypt" or "Sahara" in homage to the camel on the pack of Camel cigarettes) confirms that the cigarette is as essential as the slide rule to a high school education.

One of the first tricks the debuting Prep smoker must master is the Underhanded Hold. Since Preppies accustom themselves to cigarettes before they are the "right" age, they must learn how to hide a lit cigarette quickly when a teacher suddenly appears—simply throwing the butt in the bushes would be wasteful, not to mention unmanly. Instead, the dextrous student must speedily turn the palm toward the ground and roll the burning 'rette from first and second fingers to the thumb and index finger. The downward palm thus acts as a shield, obscuring the cigarette from the intruding faculty member. A good trick, but one that has sent more than one young tyro running to the infirmary claiming a rope-burn injury.

Once the Prep Smoker feels confident about concealing the cigarette, he or she can get on to the more showy stunts, such as blowing smoke rings and French inhaling. Each school has its one smoking genius, a lad or lass who can do more with a cloud of smoke than Simone Signoret. Their achievements are recorded for posterity through cryptic comments under yearbook pictures ("Mr. Vesuvius" or "Head Pharaoh").

BREAKING THE RULES

The importance of getting kicked out

Never ones to rest on their laurels, inspired Preppies know that the first thing to do after getting into a prestigious school is to work on finding an imaginative way of getting kicked out of it. It's the Horatio Alger principle in reverse: Only those who continually fail to strive and to succeed are rewarded with the respect reserved for the upper crust. No one is more boring than the person who goes to Prep school to *study*.

Many Preppies consider their grade point averages to be their best ally for a quick dismissal. How glamorous it is to be able to point out that a busy social schedule is responsible for a negative GPA. What a lark that your class standing is so low that the school secretary assumed that it was your zip code.

If you can't bring yourself to flunk, you can always test your ingenuity by cheating. Imagine the pats on the back when classmates discover that you kept excusing yourself during the history exam because the Bill of Rights was scribbled on the bathroom wall. Think of the congratulations when they learn that you had the future and subjunctive tenses of the verb *être* taped to the tongue of your Weejuns during the French quiz. The faculty may not appreciate your cleverness, but friends will.

If you have hang-ups about Integrity and Honesty but still want to go out with style, there are lots of lively behavioral antics that can get you out as quickly and as spectacularly as Houdini. Fill your dorm room with so many Budweiser cans that the faculty room inspector can't get in the door. Permit the school post office worker to deliver the contraband from Jamaica addressed to your box. Borrow the brand-new Sony Trinitron from the audio-visual department for your room for the first semester. Practice with your 9-iron in front of the rose window of the school chapel. Organize a nude marathon during the board of trustees' annual meeting. Show your chemistry teacher the highly combustible nature of nitroglycerin by blowing up the squash courts just before he's due to play a match.

And then there's sex. For the female Preppy such preve-nient signs as a tower of birth control pills stacked on the dresser or a diaphragm left dangling from the shower noz-zle will generally do the trick. Due to Mother Nature's whims, the male Preppy has to be virtually caught in the act before his sinful efforts can be acknowledged. If you can't seem to persuade a young lady to assist you, then resort to a more public display of libidinal frenzy, such as pole-vaulting over the wall of a nearby girls' school after lights-out.

Don't be fooled into think-ing that any minor aberration will get you into the charmed circle of the dishonorably dis-charged. If you don't have the nerve to commit a single au-dacious act, then you should

CAMPUS TROUBLE SPOTS

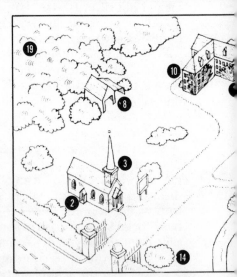

The secondary school campus provides a rich source of places where its students may pursue their own interests.

1. Hill. Faces west, great view of the sunset, good for illicit activity of any sort. People can be seen coming for miles.
2. Chapel, side door. Use to sneak in if late.
3. Chapel, choir loft. Excellent nook for necking.
4. Footbridge. Good place to waylay latest crush or prank-victim-to-be on way to dinner.
5. Field house. Girl's locker room door occa-sionally propped open.
6. To Town. 1½ miles to cigarettes, 1¾ to beer.
7. Pond. Ideal after-dusk rendezvous, natu-ral extinguishing agent at hand.
8. Maintenance shed. Useful during incle-ment weather—smoking, smooching, drink-ing—no more than three at a time.
9. Tall hedges. Shields not only the delin-quent, but also delinquent's smoke.
10. Ivy-covered wall. Makes post lights-out visit to friend in another dorm possible.

11. Laundry rooms. Accommodations for smokers, drinkers, the occasional card game.
12. Science storeroom. Many handy ingre-dients for the manufacture of destructive or just illegal sources of teen joy.
13. Computer room. After-hours use of equipment for managing gambling network or figuring stock market takeover.
14. Bushes. Waiting area for 3:00 AM cab to

plan on accumulating an extraordinary number of demerits over a period of time. This method involves doing nothing at all. For example, if you should miss breakfast, skip chapel, avoid classes, forget lunch, shun athletics, evade dinner, and ignore study hall, the number of demerits you will have amassed by the end of a single day will equal the figure Daddy pays for tuition. Multiply this total by the number of days in the week and you'll see that this tactic may be the most thorough—

and relaxing—means of expulsion of all.

Believe it or not, your biggest obstacle will be the faculty members who persist in feeling that kicking you out will cause your social downfall—and give you every chance for redemption until you force them to their breaking points. Remember, in the heart of every private school teacher lies the belief that all youth is fundamentally good and interested in learning. Your task is to convince them otherwise.

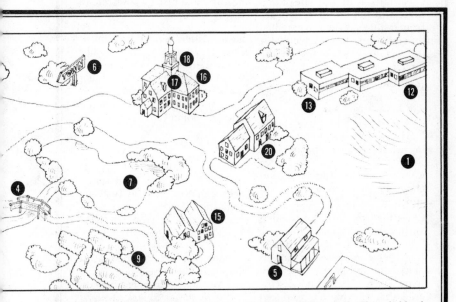

boys' school. Cab will round-trip you in time for 7:00 breakfast.
15. Lunchroom, back door. Can be pried open to allow off-hours food supply.
16. Main building, outer office. Window may be propped open to permit access to WATS line for long-distance calls.
17. Main building, inner office. Administration files on students are kept here.

18. Main building, wall. Where ladder is placed when the annual cupola painting takes place. "Legalize marijuana" logos are popular.
19. Woods. Outing cabins located here. A long trek for a smoke, but useful for serious beer fests.
20. Library. Porn film screening is held in basement. Senior uses baton to instruct underclassmen on significant points.

REAL-LIFE
HOLDEN CAULFIELDS

There's no adolescent Preppy who hasn't at one time identified with the sensitive but self-loathing hero of *The Catcher in the Rye*. Herewith a salute to those celebrities who, for some reason or another, shared Holden's fate of not making it all the way through.

Humphrey Bogart. Actor. Frequent co-star with Bette Davis (see below). Believed to be the first to utter quintessential Prep phrase, "Tennis, anyone?" in a Broadway show. Also remembered for film appearances in which he wore a trenchcoat. Won Oscar for role in which he didn't. Left Andover in 1918. Unconfirmed story says he was expelled for smoking, a habit which later became his trademark on the screen.

John Cheever. Author. Expelled from Thayer Academy in 1928 for smoking. At seventeen, moved to New York City to begin literary career by scribing a stinging tirade against Prep school life for *The New Republic*, but later wound up subsisting on stories about Preppies in Connecticut and New York.

Christina Crawford. Best-selling authoress. Left the Chadwick School in 1954 when her mother, Joan (who was then a famous movie star and later co-star with Bette Davis—see below) discovered that she hadn't prepared her Christmas card list before Thanksgiving. Christina got another chance to prep at Sacred Heart Academy, but missed the prom, thereby missing the whole point of prepping.

Bette Davis. Actress. Winner of two Academy Awards, the last one for *Jezebel*, in which she portrayed a headstrong debutante who didn't wear white to the ball. Left Northfield in 1924 after a mere four-month attendance. Rumor has it she was caught heading to a nearby boys' school after curfew.

Steve Miller. Singer and musician. Head of the Steve Miller Band. Left St. Mark's School of Texas in 1960. Didn't have what it takes, unlike fellow singer Boz Scaggs, who graduated from the same school in 1962.

J. D. Salinger. Author of short stories and novels, some dealing with Prep school life. At his interview at the McBurney School in New York in 1932, he said his favorite things were "dramatics and tropical fish." Flunked out in 1933.

Brenda Vaccaro. Actress. Best known for her Oscar-nominated role as a libidinous magazine editor in *Jacqueline Susann's Once Is Not Enough*. Left Hockaday in 1956 to attend public school. Her hoarse voice was inappropriate for saying key "pretty-sweet" words, like "cute," "love," and "fun."

BOHEMIA ACADEME

Education for the Organic Preppy

Odd though it may seem, some Preppies do not want to go to a school with restrictive parietal rules, rigid dress codes, and enforced etiquette. These are the Bohemian Preppies, and for them there is a small number of prestigious (and occasionally notorious) schools catering to their somewhat freer spirits.

The appearance of the Bohemian Prep school is deceptive. While the students and campus may suggest a 1968-vintage commune, it is nevertheless probable that these are the children of society's First Families—albeit the less-mentioned branches. The guiding principle is that in a relaxed atmosphere the student is freer to pursue his own initiatives, to develop creatively. The atmosphere is generally rustic; the manners casual in the extreme. Here are some hallmarks of the Bohemian Prep school:

1. Faculty members are called by their first names.

2. Students have names like Heather, Phoebe, and Anna with a soft "A."

3. Students have long, fuzzy hair and long, fuzzy sweaters. Both have leaves in them.

4. The arts are emphasized. Boys take dance. Girls take carpentry.

5. There is a working farm on campus.

6. The dining hall serves organic food, as well as the usual mystery meat and turkey tetrachloride.

7. Nearly everything is elective. Students may invent their own courses.

8. Faculty-student liaisons are not necessarily grounds for dismissal. They are grounds for discussion.

9. Those people repairing

the roof as you drive in for an interview are students. If you are accepted, you too will be required to do manual labor.

10. On vacations you go cross-country skiing or rock climbing, not downhill skiiing or beach-hopping.

11. There are lots of dogs on campus. There is a black Labrador retriever with a red bandanna around his neck. The students have given him drugs.

12. Half the students have been thrown out of other schools for infractions of the rules, but they are brilliant and are expected to blossom in the less repressive atmosphere. In fact, they end up getting kicked out of the Bohemian school and are then accepted by a traditional school which believes that they only need a little discipline.

13. One-third of the students go on to Ivy League colleges. One-third go to experimental colleges, where they relive their Prep school experience. One-third go to Montana to repair cars.

14. The headmasters of prestigious, traditional Prep schools send their children to Bohemian schools. (Incidentally, it is considered unwise for children ever to attend the school where their father or mother is headmaster or headmistress.)

15. Coed dorms, solar-heated dorms, and yurt dorms are not unheard of.

THE LEADERS IN BOHEMIA

While these schools don't necessarily fit the above description to the letter (after all, they wouldn't be Bohemian if each school weren't different) they are distinctly looser, freer, hipper than most schools. In a word, Bohemian.

Buxton School
Williamstown, Mass.

The Cambridge School
Weston, Mass.

Cranbrook Schools
Bloomfield Hills, Mich.

Darrow School
New Lebanon, N.Y.

Fieldston School
New York, N.Y.

The Hyde School
Bath, Me.

The Meeting School
West Rindge, N.H.

The Key School
Annapolis, Md.

The Mountain School
Vershire, Vt.

The New Lincoln School
New York, N.Y.

Palfrey Street School
Watertown, Mass.

The Park School
Brooklandville, Md.

South Kent School
South Kent, Conn.

The Walden School
New York, N.Y.

Woodstock Country School
South Woodstock, Vt.

any Friends (i.e., Quaker) school

TIME OFF
Holidays and Summers

The academic calendar determines all holidays; tradition determines how the holiday is spent.

Thanksgiving. First major break of the year. Almost everyone goes home by Wednesday afternoon, humming "We Gather Together."

Winter vacation (Also called Christmas break). Two to three weeks long. Skiing predominates, with most families making tracks to the slopes on December 26 and staying till January 1.

Spring vacation (Easter break). Two to three weeks, sometimes encompassing Easter and/or Passover. Palm Beach, Colorado, or Bermuda. Some students stay at school but may end up enjoying the most freedom, since nobody bothers to keep an eye on their activities.

Summer. A great many Preppies are happy to simply sit, sail, swim, play tennis, ride, picnic, sleep, eat, and go to the movies at and around their family's cottage. Traveling is another option and is fun because you can send postcards to all your friends who are doing nothing at home. Possibilities include the Experiment for International Living, which allows you to live with families all over the world, or bicycle trips to Nova Scotia, France, or Britain.

The socially eager Preppy may choose from an impressive array of prestigious Prep schools that open their doors wider in the summertime. Andover, Exeter, Choate, and Northfield-Mt. Hermon all offer extensive curricula during their six-week programs.

For the Preppy who is longing to satisfy the Puritan spirit, a working summer is perfect. Daughters of city parents often check in with the Anne Andrews Employment Agency in New York, which specializes in placing Preppies with families who summer in the Hamptons, the Vineyard, Nantucket, etc., as mothers' helpers. Mothers' helpers have a great social life, because they have an exclusive franchise on all the guys who teach tennis at the clubs, as well as teenage house painters and busboys.

THE SKI VACATION

The ski vacation is a standard feature of Preppy life, especially at Thanksgiving, midterm break or spring vacation. And, mystifying though its appeal may be to non-skiers, skiing is one of the cherished Prep sports for the following reasons:

1. It's expensive. Hundreds of dollars' worth of complex equipment (utterly unadaptable to any other purpose), lift tickets, lodge fees, transportation, all add up.

2. It's next to impossible to master completely. The best skiers have been doing it all their lives, and look supremely at ease on long boards on steep snowy mountainsides. Those who come late to the sport (say at age ten) are doomed to mediocrity.

3. It's uncomfortable, and that

HOW TO GET THERE

As a rule of thumb, the farther you have to go and the more rustic the lodgings (and the more difficult the mountain), the more satisfying the experience is. If you can get to a ski area in just one plane flight, it's not a true Preppy ski area. If you're driving, it has to take at least three hours.

By plane: Pack your clothes in as many small, olive-colored duffel bags as possible. Take at least two pairs of skis—one for powder snow, one for ice. Do not allow enough time between connections for your luggage to make it from one plane to another. When you are told that it went by mistake to Indianapolis, get drunk in the airport bar.

By car: Drive along Interstate 91 in the East or Interstate 70 in the West in a Volvo station wagon with initial license plates and a college decal on the back window. Drink beer. Eat pretzels and peanuts (to be left scattered inside of car). Tune the radio to the top-forty station as you drive north. Stop every half hour to make sure the skis are all right on top of the car.

warms the Prep heart. Sitting in an icy puddle on a chair lift seventy-five feet above the ground really makes a Preppy feel alive.

4. It's inconvenient. Places where people ski are never near places where people live. Moving the bodies and the equipment from one spot to another requires the organizational skills of General Patton. Such skills exist in many Preppy women.

5. It's dangerous. Chances are more than good that in an average skiing career a number of bones will be broken. A cast and crutches are as good as a Henley blazer in the hierarchy of Prep prestige.

WHERE TO GO

In the United States, there are basically two places to ski: the East and the West. (Europe is just a wee bit ostentatious.) Though the West almost always has better snow, the East is, well, Preppier. It's colder, more inhospitable, and you have to work harder to have fun. The snow is often terrible and it gets very cold.

In the East: Stratton, Stowe, Mad River Glen in Vermont, Sugarloaf in Maine. Not Mt. Snow.

In the West: Aspen and Vail in Colorado, Snowbird in Utah. Not Mammoth Mountain (too close to L.A.).

Moriarty hat. At least one stripe is navy. From Stowe.

The layers. Thermal underwear inherited from Daddy; cotton turtleneck, never worn folded down; Lacoste, of course; oxford cloth button-down—for emergency business meetings on the slopes; wool crewneck sweater, perfect for après ski, in contrasting color to parka; down parka—pockets hold Blistex and car keys.

Silk glove liners. Glittery fabric looks un-Prep, but they do add warmth.

Lift ticket(s). All-day pass for all lifts. Clipped onto parka's zipper.

Heavy leather gloves. Quilted on the outside, and lined with a fabric that nature never knew existed.

Silk socks. Fruity-looking but appreciated.

Mirrored sunglasses. To hide fear while going down slopes completely hung over.

Yellow ski goggles. Necessary piece of equipment, usually worn backward around the neck.

Wool knit scarf. Striped, school colors. That it stays on is a testament to gravity.

Straight-legged Levi's. Even though he drives to ski resort in heated Saab with tape-deck and stays in family's lavish ski house, he can rough it in cotton leggings, which don't really segue into boots.

Skis. Fiberglas. Accorded more love and respect than own sister. With name and hometown engraved above the binding.

Poles. To go with skis.

Plastic ski boots. These are Nordicas, but many acceptable brands available. It's hip to clomp around the lodge in these, unhooked.

Geared Up

QUO PREPARAVISTI?

The first great behavioral alteration in the life of a Preppy occurs just before graduation from Prep school. Before this point, life is a party—but when the party's over, it's time to realize that survival depends upon the safeguards of tradition. Having a Prep school's reputation to cling to gives the courage to face impending adulthood.

PHASE ONE: *Conversion*. Begins after final exams are finished and the Preppy has to bide his time until commencement. This period permits the Preppy to wallow in sentimental appreciation of the school and faculty that have been taken for granted and at times mocked for the past four years. The campus may have seemed like a prison since freshman orientation, but now it has the comforting aura of the house in the country. Even the most vociferous dissidents write pious editorials for the farewell issue of the school newspaper, advising underclassmen that "you get out of this school what you put into it."

PHASE TWO: *Assimilation*. Begins when the Preppy discards idle reminiscing for action. He or she double checks with the class alumni secretary to make sure a home address is on record. A knuckle-bruising effort is made to sign every classmate's yearbook, dredging up any silly memory from as far back as the first week of school ("You were the first person I met at the Parents' Tea.") and promising to do everything humanly possible to keep in touch ("We'll get together at the beach this summer and drink some brew and raise some hell and P-A-R-T-Y!"). They find themself unconsciously buying clothes with the school colors and loading up on all the gym shorts, socks, sweat shirts, windbreakers, and ties, emblazoned with the school insignia, that can be unearthed at the school supply store.

PHASE THREE: *Symbiosis*. The concluding step to school devotion, following the commencement ceremonies as good-byes are said. There is a sudden understanding about why the alumni always come back to the Homecoming Game. The rest of life starts to be planned around the school's alumni weekends. You even turn to dreaming about sending your own kids to school there one day—and when that degree of allegiance has been reached, you have arrived at the Preppy Point of No Return.

Sloan Hughes Atkinson
"Sloppie"
Mme. Presidente . . . Skip, Sam, Steve . . . MG fanatic . . . "Gross—How can you eat that?" . . . Glee Club will absolutely meet today . . . cute brother at Hamilton . . . Cuffy's confidante . . . "I am *not* an alcoholic!" . . . Nantucket summers . . . latest curfew . . . I only did it once . . . Hello Poughkeepsie.

Timothy Taylor Benton, III
Another 3-sticker . . . ski bum . . . First one to be legal . . . "I'm old enough to be your grandfather" . . . waiting for Williams. Astronomy I,II; Glee Club II,III; Ski Team I,IV; Social Committee I,II,III; Student Council II,III,IV, Treasurer IV.

Mary Gregory DeBreul
"Muffy"
Those long legs . . . our own Chris Evert . . . "you fruitcake" . . . "I don't care if he's cute, he's a junior" . . . raids the fridge with Becky . . . phone bills to Wallingford . . . a regular at Wimbledon . . . Frankie told me . . . her dumb look . . . "It's not my fault I can't gain a pound".

Julia Brooke Fairchild
"Brookie" "Bootsie"
"Quel Dommage!" . . . "Sorry, girls, I'm on a diet" . . . blue eyes . . . regular cut-up . . . A.R. van M . . . "Yale lock" . . . Shelly Hack look-alike . . . always having nic fits . . . Hobe Sound . . . hates men one day, in love the next . . . "Can I borrow a dollar?" . . . dancer par excellence . . . class radical . . . [. . . .]y says" . . . 'bye Kitty.

Kyle Manning Van Dorr, Jr.
Squash I,II,III,IV.

Archibald Suffern Weeks
Under the Clock . . . "What time *is* it, Buzz?" . . . "I left it in the dorm" . . . the scourge of Dobbs . . . Dartmouth legacy. Student Affairs Committee IV; Library Committee I; Newspaper III,IV; Lacrosse II,III,IV; Track I,II; Water Polo II,III.

CLOSING REMARKS

Quiz # 2

Prep schools teach you how to take tests, but do they ever test you on Prep schools? It's not likely. To correct this unfortunate lapse on their part, a multiple-choice quiz on various aspects of these institutions is provided below. Answers for those who don't "test well" are at the bottom of the page.

1. When Virgil wrote, "Forewarned, let us take the better path" in *The Aeneid*, little did he know that he was writing the school motto for:
a. *Hotchkiss*
b. *Eaglebrook*
c. *The Latin School*

2. "We Go Forth Unafraid" is the fearless motto of:
a. *Miss Porter's*
b. *Dalton*
c. *St. George's*

3. Attempting to live up to the motto, "Be Worthy of Your Heritage,'' are the graduates of:
a. *Bryn Mawr*
b. *Deerfield*
c. *Riverdale*

4. The unofficial motto for Madeira is:
a. *"Don't think, do!"*
b. *"Knowledge is a gift, kindness a must!"*
c. *"Function in disaster, finish in style."*

5. A "Greyhound" is a student at:
a. *St. Bernard's*

b. *Gilman*
c. *Foxcroft*

6. Caroline Kennedy attended a Prep school whose mascot is a:
a. *Squaw*
b. *Horse*
c. *Chameleon*

7. A "Daisy" is a:
a. *New boy at Saint Alban's*
b. *School symbol of Hewitt*
c. *Team member at Hockaday*

8. If you are a "Hilltopper," you attend:
a. *Darlington*
b. *Providence Country Day*
c. *Worcester Academy*

9. The school with twenty-three tennis courts (three indoors) is:
a. *Oldfield*
b. *Hotchkiss*
c. *Middlesex*

10. If you find yourself skeet shooting, chances are you go to:
a. *Mercersberg Academy*
b. *Woodberry Forest*
c. *Groton*

Answers: 1.a; 2.b; 3.b; 4.c; 5.b; 6.c; 7.c; 8.c; 9.b; 10.a.

CHAPTER 3

THE BEST YEARS OF YOUR LIFE

The College Years

GETTING IN
The Application Form

You've decided to go to college—if only because everyone else has. Now you've got to persuade a college to accept you. The easiest route to the halls of higher learning is to apply to the school that everyone in your family attended. It hardly matters that Daddy was kicked out in the legendary cheating scandal twenty-five years ago—as long as he keeps contributing to the alumni fund drive every year, the school will cherish the family name.

If you don't have relatives to count on and your SAT scores weren't all that astronomical, you'll have to resort to other means—athletics, for instance. If it's beyond your skills to win a varsity letter, then at least play the same sport for four years. When the truly Prep colleges see this measure of consistency, they'll be glad to accept someone who may be willing to forgo the Homecoming sideline festivities to play in the actual game.

Another oft-used tactic is to list an array of extracurricular activities so awesome that the admissions officer will think you were second in command to the headmaster. A little gratuitous padding is acceptable—jot down a claim to membership in the school's Bike Club when all you did was show up for the first meeting knowing well that your Raleigh was in Mummy's garage.

The essay is frequently a stumbling block. The key is to pander to the college's image of itself—to humble yourself before the school as it were—while still maintaining the unmistakably Prep tone (correct syntax is not necessary) that lets the admissions people know you wear J. Press button-downs and sport a peerless Locust Valley Lockjaw.

You may not know anybody at the college, but there's always one teacher per high school who can get any student into the college of their choice. Find out who that teacher is, and do *anything* to become his or her pet. Remember, it's much better to mow a faculty member's lawn all senior year, than to wind up mowing others' on a permanent basis.

THE COLLEGE
OF YOUR CHOICE

College is, in itself, a Prep concept. But not all colleges are outstandingly Preppy. Following are profiles, in alphabetical order, of the top twenty institutions of higher Prep learning, with admissions information. And, for your complete edification, a list of the ten *least* Preppy colleges—all of them superb institutions academically, but none of them up to the standards of Prep.

THE TOP TEN

1. Babson College. Wellesley, Mass. 02157. Coed business college, founded 1919. 33% from private schools. No one here got into Harvard, so they claim Babson's better (for their purposes, of course). For rich kids who have to wait four years to go into Daddy's business. Enrollment: 1,300 undergrads. SAT's: V475, M566.

2. Hamilton College. Clinton. N.Y. 13323. All-male school, founded 1793. Tried to make a go with Kirkland College for women, but students hated each other too much. Enrollment: 950, 33% come from private schools. An unusual proportion of them under 5'10". SAT's: V590, M630. Nine frats.

3. Hampden-Sydney College. Hampden-Sydney, Va. 23943. Presbyterian men's college, 7 miles from Farmville. Founded 1776. Enrollment: 750. 51% from private schools. *The* finishing school for Southern gentlemen, Hampden-Sydney issues its own etiquette book, *To Manners Born, To Manners Bred* for all incoming students. SAT's: V490, M545. Eleven fraternities.

4. Hollins College. Hollins, Va. 24020. Women's college, founded 1842. Enrollment: 980 women, 15 men. You need a dozen cableknit cardigans to get in. 63% come from private schools. These gals marry well. SAT's: V467, M480.

5. Lake Forest College. Lake Forest, Ill. 60043. Socially impeccable coed school founded 1857. Presbyterian. Private school graduates comprise 30% of student population. Known as "The Enchanted Forest," but only 57% of freshman class stays four years. You need a car so you can dine on Lake Shore Drive, 30 miles away. SAT's: V510, M520.

6. Pine Manor College. Chestnut Hill, Mass. 02167. 55% private school graduates. Conveniently located near the Chestnut Hill Mall (good Bloomingdale's), the students are the scourge of Wellesley women. Crudely referred to as "Pine Mattress" by its patrons. Cross-registration with Babson. Everyone (enrollment: 425) has a nickname. Can go for two or four years.

7. Princeton University. Princeton, N.J. 08540. Founded 1764. Coed, enrollment numbers 5,900. 40% from Prep schools, but by graduation it feels more like 100%. Most southern in spirit and accent of Ivies. Lots of legacies, clubs, and house parties. Must write thesis. SAT's: V636, M672.

8. St. Lawrence University. Canton, N.Y. 13617. Founded 1856. Enrollment: 2,200, private school representation 25%. Distinguished by unusual number of students who can mix drinks comfortably in their stomachs. Frats and sororities are popular, as are ski weekends. Everyone has a Norwegian sweater and a brother who made the Olympic trials. SAT's: V545, M600.

9. Sweet Briar College. Sweet Briar, Va. 24595. Women's school, founded 1901. Enrollment: 700, 50% private school graduates. Origin of the stockings-under-pressed-jeans look. Very pretty girls, all of whom aspire to speak French so that they may spend junior year in Gay Paree. SAT's: V510, M520.

10. University of Virginia. Charlottesville, Va. 22903. Coed, founded 1819. Total enrollment: 14,346, 23% from private schools. 40% are in fraternities, hence a lot of serious drinking. Annual highlight: Mud Day. Don't ask. SAT's: V589, M613.

THE RUNNERS UP

1. Amherst College. Amherst, Mass. 01002. The "h" is silent. 1,113 men. 408 women, all competing with Smith and Holyoke for attention. 43% from Prep schools. 18% go to law school. The Fair Isle capital of the northeast. Every student excels in winter sports. Heavy frat action. SAT's: V650, M670.

2. Colby College. Waterville, Maine 04901. 1,671 students, 27% of whom go on to business school, 12% to law school. 30% are from Prep schools. Near Sugarloaf for good skiing. People come here to ski and to be in the same state as L. L. Bean. SAT's: V570, M600.

3. Colorado College. Colorado Springs, Colo. 80903. Coed, 1,942 students, 30% of whom are Preppies. Need skis to be admitted. Campus newspaper runs daily ski report. Everyone loves to get ripped. Constantly. Close to Aspen, Vail, Taos. SAT's: V600, M600.

4. Connecticut College. New London, Conn. 06320. Née Connecticut College for Women, but there are 772 men now, in addition to 1,181 women. For students who didn't get into Wesleyan or Brown. They retaliate by getting Preppier, although 41% do originate at private schools. Big Art, English, Dance departments—'nuff said? SAT's: V550, M570.

5. Georgetown University. Washington, D.C. 20057. Used to be Catholic. 6,533 men, 4,515 women, who love D.C.'s cosmopolitan flavor, and the shops of Georgetown. 48% from private schools. Southern feeling with dash of diplomatic corps. Painter's pants, Lacostes, and Top-Siders are musts. SAT's: V607, M618.

THE IVY LEAGUE DILEMMA

Officially, the Ivy League is nothing more than an athletic conference, comprising eight colleges: Brown, Columbia, Cornell, Dartmouth, Harvard, Penn, Princeton, and Yale. These schools are not entirely the oldest, the best—or even ivy-covered. But in the public imagination, they are something very special.

Before the term "Preppy" was popular, "Ivy League" was used to describe a certain kind of person. Like the school he went to, he was steeped in tradition. He was smart, rich, well-educated— or at least he presented himself that way. The Ivy League schools became the mythic focus of the American notion of the young elite.

But, because the Ivy League colleges are generally large and wealthy, they can afford a diversity of students that goes far beyond the merely Preppy. Students are selected largely for academic achievement, rather than on the basis of whether they will fit in with a campus "mood." Students at Prep schools are often carefully groomed for the Ivy League—they stand a very good chance of admission, and they enjoy a large representation there, but they no longer dominate the colleges.

The feminine equivalent of the Ivy League is the group of colleges known as "The Seven Sisters:" Barnard, Bryn Mawr, Mt. Holyoke, Radcliffe, Smith, Vassar, and Wellesley. Of these schools, two have been annexed to their Ivy League brothers, one has gone co-ed, and the other four are seriously devoted to women's education. They, like the Ivy League colleges, are not the Preppy havens they were a generation ago.

Still, the Ivy League is widely perceived as the cream of the elite schools, and as the Preppiest of places too. But there is a paradox. While there is no Preppier credential than to have gone to an Ivy League college, there are many schools far more exclusively Preppy in appearance and atmosphere than these eight.

What is Columbia next to, say, Hollins or Pine Manor? The pink-and-green scale tips in favor of the more homogeneous smaller schools. Yet because of the public image of the Ivies they remain the ideal fantasy—or real-life—credential.

Thus, the Ivy League: in Preppy terms, it can mean nothing at all, or everything.

6. Reed College. Portland, Oreg. 97022. Bohemian Prep college, but Oregon's a hippie state anyway. School for rich carpenters-to-be. Has own ski lodge. 732 men and 500 women, all dress androgynously. SAT's: V622, M635.

7. Trinity College. Hartford, Conn. 06106. 1,185 men, 893 women. So what if they didn't get into Yale? Uniformly Preppier, students here embody good-looking, devil-may-care-ism. Lots of regatta winners. 40% from Prep schools. SAT's: V570, M610.

8. Vassar College. Poughkeepsie, N.Y. 12601. 1,370 women, 1,000 men. 43% Preppies. Still has imprimatur of Jacqueline Bouvier Kennedy Onassis. Even though there's nothing to do in Poughkeepsie, students always dress up. Cute school ring. SAT's: V563, M578.

9. Williams College. Williamstown, Mass. 10267. 1,138 men, 780 women, 35% Preppies. 45% go to "B" school. Not only does everyone ski, they compete at it, too. Isolated, so lots of (foreign make) Prepmobiles on campus. Must slalom to graduate. SAT's: V610, M645.

10. Wheaton College. Norton, Mass. 02766. 1,323 women. 35% from private schools. Best departments are English, Art, and History. Students who take junior year abroad never return. "Wheaties" hanging around Harvard and Brown on weekends are distinguishable by their pink-and-green Bermuda bags. SAT's: V500, M500.

OUT OF THE LEAGUE

1. Columbia University. In a depressed area of Manhattan. Engineering is very popular, and its majors are concerned about professional future. Even English majors here are concerned about future. Political campus. Barnard women love to discuss poetry. SAT's: V670, M680.

2. Cornell University. Not the place to quaff D.P. Best schools are Agriculture, Labor Relations, and Hotel Management. People get depressed in the winter and kill themselves. Enrollment is so large (15,000) you can't guarantee you'll be able to inbreed. SAT's: V580, M650.

3. Massachusetts Institute of Technology. How Prep is any school whose average student scored 730 on the math SAT? (V625). Best for sciences, Engineering, Urban Studies. Wear shortish pants to interview and buy Pocket Protectors. Geniuses do not make good dancers.

4. New York University. One of the largest private universities in the United States, NYU boasts a high number of transients. It's where you go if you just got engaged to a guy who works in New York, or where you go if you want to get engaged to a guy who works in New York. Undergrad enrollment is 8,000. Ethnic restaurants prevail. SAT's: V540, M560.

5. Oberlin College. Midwest's bastion of artistry, Oberlin is the place for people who are *serious* about music. Classical music. Very casual, girls wear scarves over their dirty hair. 1,396 men, 1,374 women. SAT's: V607, M620.

6. Sarah Lawrence College. Boho city. There are no grades. Students take just three courses a year, and spend most of their time looking for fun in Manhattan. Leotards and fur coats prevail for both sexes. Located in Bronxville, a Prep community, but rumors have it the college is really situated in adjacent Yonkers. 205 men, 758 women. SAT's: V600, M580.

7. University of California at Berkeley. Where we get hippies from. Can major in Rhetoric, Chicano Studies, Slavic Languages. 85% of enrollment from California. Men wear beards. Lots of tortured intellectuals. SAT's: V553, M585.

8. University of Chicago. Trimesters mean six exam periods a year. Windy, rainy, cold city. Students here love to work—75% go on to graduate or professional school. Everyone carries slide rules on dates. SAT's: V617, M639.

9. University of Michigan. It's not just that there are 40,000 students (30,000 undergrads), or that they still have an ROTC unit, or that 80% of Michigan's enrollment is from Michigan. It's that not only do students care if their football team wins—they actually pay attention to what's going on on the field. SAT's: V520, M590.

10. University of Wisconsin. Highly politicized, and in the Midwest to boot. Site of early campus sexual revolutions. Students are down-to-earth, half of them earning their tuition via on-campus jobs. SAT's: V534, M582.

THE
FOUR-YEAR PLAN
Collegiate Life

College, for most Preppies, is their closest brush with democracy. Since they've taken pains to go to the right college, they feel secure enough to indulge in most of that college's activities, even with the non-Preps (who must be tenable if they were admitted). Thus, the Preppy is eager to behave just as moronically as the graduate from Abraham Lincoln High during Homecoming parades, the Christmas party, midwinter bashes, Greek Week, and finals.

In terms of daily existence, college life is like Prep school life, except you don't have to adhere to any schedule or set of rules and a shower of de-

merits is no longer a threat. These may be the best years of the Prep life—no job, no family, no responsibilities other than to store up a wealth of

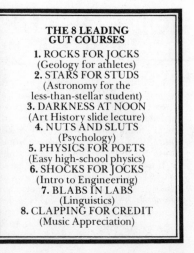

THE 8 LEADING GUT COURSES

1. ROCKS FOR JOCKS
(Geology for athletes)
2. STARS FOR STUDS
(Astronomy for the less-than-stellar student)
3. DARKNESS AT NOON
(Art History slide lecture)
4. NUTS AND SLUTS
(Psychology)
5. PHYSICS FOR POETS
(Easy high-school physics)
6. SHOCKS FOR JOCKS
(Intro to Engineering)
7. BLABS IN LABS
(Linguistics)
8. CLAPPING FOR CREDIT
(Music Appreciation)

fond memories to last a lifetime. The collegiate years are a final opportunity to sow wild oats, a chance to live the carefree life to the hilt, a license to be Prep with a vengeance.

When the four years are over, you will be expected to assume the duties of Prep Adulthood, so remind yourself while you're waiting for your fraternity brothers to open that fifth keg of beer that college is a once-in-a-lifetime experience.

The first and most essential factor you should consider in planning your campus modus vivendi is the academic schedule. Morning and evening classes are out of the question for the obvious reason that the latter prohibit you from enjoying happy hours and the former prevent you from recovering from them. A couple of hours in the library on week nights are mandatory: Apart from the necessary social scene, the library furnishes you with a quiet spell to shore up resources for the next drinking engagement while you scan *Othello* for choice references to be flaunted in class the next day. (Preppies *love* to contribute to class discussion.) But, as important as the library is during the week, there's no excuse for being stuck there on the weekend when everyone else has gone skiing.

DISCOVERING PREP

Although you may have been accepted as a show of the school's Jeffersonian democracy, a move to Hamiltonian elitism may be necessary if you wish to join the ranks of Prep. While a diploma from Exeter is not absolutely required, knowledge of some crucial points of the Prep Ethos is.

1. Learn your geography. The East includes: Georgetown, but not Washington, D.C.; Duke but not Durham; Nantucket but not Pawtucket. "The Cape" is not a fashion fad; Wheaton is more than a suburb of Chicago.

2. Figure out whether Newport is a cigarette, a town, or a jazz festival someplace else.

3. Stop confusing Olympic years with America's Cup years.

4. Order a cabinet without the slightest thought of carpentry.

5. Forget all about Corvettes, *real* college football (Michigan vs. Ohio State), and sober moderation when enjoying a good time. Favor BMW's, fake college football (Williams vs. Amherst), and drowning in a whitecapped sea of Molson, Becks, and Heineken (light or dark).

Residence is very important to your collegiate well-being. First and foremost, you want to be always near campus in case an impromptu party pops up. There are those who would stray to off-off-campus apartments, but they are not Prep and never will be. Secondly, the dorm room assigned to you by the housing office should quickly become a Prep Palace. If the Greek life appeals to you (and it certainly should), you may move into the frat house sophomore year, and then junior year move into the best room in the house; senior year may find you moving into your own off-(as opposed to off-off-)campus apartment. But no matter where you're living, the authorized Prep interior-decorating scheme will make you feel you're only one small remove from secondary school.

Preppies with a serious athletic bent may choose to partic-ipate in varsity sports like squash or lacrosse, but most won't because of the unreasonable training demands. (They had enough of those in Prep school.) More gentlemanly intramural sports are favored—they allow you to prove your athletic prowess, drink your beer afterward and provide entertainment for the Prep women who spectate when they're not flinging a ball themselves.

Although shunning any efforts of their Prep schools to expose them to culture, Preppies are quick to show off their superior breeding in college by partaking in clubs like the glee club, choral society, and philanthropic organizations. They may also attend art openings, classical concerts, and film festivals, not out of any real passion, but just to see each other—a sort of warm-up for the Junior League and the Racquet Club. Any highly specialized club is desirable for added social security.

Generally, college is an occasion to be with other Preppies, whether they are from your Prep school, from your rival schools, or simply passing for Prep. Except for the minimal forays into scholarship, you enjoy an uninterrupted stream of parties, rather like a four-year debutante season. But then again, as any self-respecting Preppy will tell you, college is just another Prep club itself.

---

13 WORDS FOR THE PERSON WHO *IS* WORKING

1. GRIND
2. SQUID
3. PENCIL GEEK
4. CEREB
5. GRUB
6. WEENIE
7. THROAT
8. TOOL
9. WONK
10. GOME
11. NERD
12. SPIDER
13. CONCH

THE GENTLEMAN'S "C"
or How to Choose a Major

Preppies, like everyone else, must choose a major from among the college's established list of courses of study (Beer Drinking is not one of these). Preppies know, however, that whether they go into banking, law, or business (preferably Daddy's) the specifics of the undergraduate career couldn't matter less.

This knowledge leads to three basic concerns when choosing a major—concerns that have established English, History, Economics or Classics (for the hard-core fringe), and Architecture (for the aesthetically interested) as the perennial favorites. These majors are:

Not too taxing, but still respectable. A Preppy cannot choose a laughably easy or "gut" major—Geology, Anthropology, Psychology. These are considered a tacky waste of Prep school cultivation. It's fine to be concerned about taking on too much work—no one wants undue distraction from social commitments—but there's no need to get obvious about it. Your major must have the ring of serious academic pursuit—and a "C" in History sounds a lot better than a "C" in Sociology. It is, of course, perfectly acceptable to satisfy distribution requirements with a "gut" course.

Not too esoteric, but still respectable. Out-of-the-ordinary concentrations—Comparative Literature, Philosophy, Linguistics—may not require any more work than English or History, but they smack of an equally undesirable effort: thought. These majors imply all sorts of unattractive qualities like intellectualism and curiosity about the universe that a self-respecting Prep wouldn't touch with a ten-foot length of ticker tape.

Not too obviously career-oriented, but still respectable. Professional majors—Engineering, Chemistry, Mathematics—all reek of practicality. They intimate concern for the future, worry about the post-collegiate life—concepts foreign to the Prep mentality, as they should be to anyone who would associate with Preps. Classmates in these fields of endeavor are also the most academically competitive on campus (the sort who booby-trap each other's lab experiments), so it is often necessary to swear off social activity altogether just to appear *somewhere* on the bell curve—and there's no such thing as a Gentleman's "F".

TRANSFORMING THE DORM ROOM

W hen first you see what will be home for the year to come, a desperate sense of disorientation and loss may overwhelm you. But with the following lists in hand, interior decoration becomes a breeze—in no time at all that little, spare room is a Prep Palace.

To Bring from Home:

1. Dirty laundry. Pile on top of bookcase.
2. Beer cans, empty.
3. Hanging plant from Mummy. Should quickly be put out of its misery.
4. Books from Prep school.
5. Sextant used by Daddy in the '53 Bermuda Race.
6. Record albums: Supremes' Greatest Hits, Beach Boys, Rampal "Suite for Flute & Jazz Piano," J. Geils, B-52s, Rolling Stones' "Exile on Main Street," "Elvis—The Golden Years," Arthur Fiedler "Best of the Boston Pops."
7. Map of Nantucket from older brother's bedroom.
8. Daddy's Dartmouth banner with year of graduation.
9. Towel stolen from Prep school.
10. Lobster trap from trip to Maine with girlfriend over the summer.
11. Clamshell ashtray from home (Mummy won't miss it).
12. Rag rug from parents' summer house.
13. Dad's varsity oar.
14. Banners from girls' Prep schools visited over the years.
15. Skis. For those all-important weekend forays into the snow country. Their decorative value can not be overestimated.

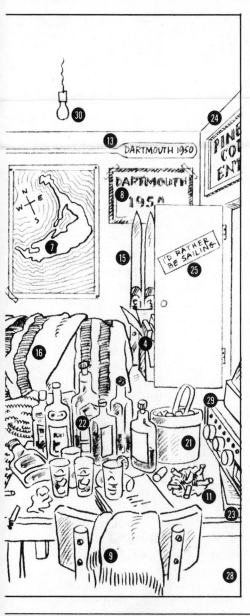

To Buy (or otherwise obtain as soon as possible):

16. Hudson's Bay blanket from L. L. Bean.

17. Beer cans, full.

18. Books: *The Social Contract*, *Norton Anthology of English Literature*, *Nostromo*, *The Iliad*, Samuelson's *Economics*, H.W. Janson's *The History of Art*, Northrop Frye's *Anatomy of Criticism*.

19. Sit-up pillow.

20. Linen service sheets. Even with the service, they'll be infrequently changed.

21. Ice bucket, set of highball glasses with school crest.

22. Booze—inexpensive scotch, vodka, bourbon.

23. Hamilton cartoon clipped from *The New Yorker*.

24. Entrance sign to popular women's college. May require forklift—the bigger the better.

25. "I'd Rather Be Sailing" bumper sticker. It's too much trouble to take the one you've got off the jeep.

26. Ceramic beer stein with school crest.

27. Bills. Pin on wall over bed and forget.

28. Typewriter. The seal need never be broken—professional typists are much quicker and can usually spell correctly.

29. Expensive stereo system reflecting your interest in technology *not* music.

30. Light bulb.

EAT, DRINK, AND BE EXCLUSIVE

Clubs at the Big Three

Maybe Harvard, Yale, and Princeton don't epitomize Prep colleges (theoretically, as the Big Three of the Ivy League, they have better things to do than to maintain Prep Purity of dress, thought, and activity), but in one important way they prepare Preppies for one of the great traditions of Prep life: clubmanship.

Harvard has the final clubs, Princeton the eating clubs, Yale the secret societies, St. A's and the Lizzie. And most of these organizations share important characteristics.

Togetherness. Membership in a club forms strong ties—the membership of each secret society at Yale is only fourteen seniors, and they meet twice weekly. Part of the secret activity is reading "biographies"— each member bares his soul and his inmost secrets to other members.

Facilities. With the exception of Yale's Elizabethan Club, all of these organizations can (and do) make liquor readily available to their members and allow them to charge it. This is probably more important than the leather couches, pool tables, backgammon boards, television, and libraries they also offer.

Exclusivity. Whether it's "Bicker" (at Princeton), "punching season" (at Harvard), or the traditional method of proposing members to a committee (the Lizzie at Yale), all of these clubs have ways of limiting their membership. However, members of the most exclusive clubs claim that they are very democratic, usually citing as an example a transfer student from Cornell.

Endowment. Many graduates are more loyal to their clubs than to their university, and they show their loyalty in material ways. Most of these clubs possess enviable (and enviably managed) securities portfolios, as well as investments in the real estate the clubhouse sits on, and the art and antiques that furnish it.

THE RIGHT CLUBS

AT HARVARD

PORCELLIAN. Members tend to be the most blue-blooded of old Boston families—and very rich. If your name is Peabody, you went to St. Mark's, and the interest on your trust fund is in the high five figures, "the Pork" is for you. The initiation fee is rumored to be fifteen hundred dollars.

FLY. Supposedly, Fly was founded by FDR when he couldn't get into Porcellian. The members see themselves as open to other forms of merit like intelligence, wit, and a pleasant personality.

DELPHIC. There were twenty Harvard graduates in the first-year class at the Harvard Business School in 1980. Of these, sixteen were men, twelve of whom had belonged to final clubs, ten of them to Delphic. The club attracts squash players, musicians, and big wheels in the Hasty Pudding Theatricals.

AT YALE

ST. ANTHONY HALL. St. A's is officially a fraternity, with branches at Columbia and UVA, among others. It appeals to the "cool element" of Preppies at Yale; this means Preppies who don't iron their shirts. It isn't rowdy: parties there conform to the intellectual self-image Yalies hold dear.

THE IMPORTANT PARTIES

Crucial to club image and—part of the very cachet of their existence—are the special occasions for revelry—and possibly debauchery—which they alone supply.

Samuel Johnson's Birthday Party. Given by the Elizabethan Club in September. There's a tent, and croquet on the lawn.

Princeton/Harvard/Yale Weekend. At the campus where the game is being held, the clubs give dances and elaborate parties. A genteel system of reciprocity assures, for instance, that a Princeton clubman or woman in Boston will be able to go to the dance at the Hasty Pudding.

Sign-ins Weekend. At Princeton, when Bicker is over. Climax is the initiation of new club members on Saturday night.

May Day Party. At the Elizabethan Club, featuring bourbon punch on the lawn.

Fly Club Garden Party. Big hats for ladies, seersucker suits for gentlemen. Held on the first Sunday in Study Period.

Houseparties Weekend. Princeton's spring parties; a whole weekend of elaborate events, often with themes like Gatsby or *Gone with the Wind.*

THE ELIZABETHAN CLUB. "The Lizzie," as it's fondly known, was founded for the purpose of furthering conversation about literature and the arts among professors and students. Its membership is strictly limited to fewer than forty members yearly, and old school ties are very important. Dues are ten dollars for life and entitle a member to tea at the club every afternoon. The contents of the tea sandwiches alternate: tomato one day, cucumber the next.

SKULL AND BONES. A "closed" secret society at Yale. Though no one knows quite what goes on at Bones and rumors are rife, it *is* public knowledge that the Bones members tend to be flamboyant—the great actors, athletes, stars of the senior class. Kingman Brewster is re-puted to have declined an invitation to join Skull and Bones. Ties with the CIA are very strong (all that secrecy, don't you know).

SCROLL AND KEY. If Bones is flamboyant, Scroll and Key is urbane. Also closed, but its members are supposedly New York Social Register types. Family tradition is very important: third-generation members are not uncommon.

AT PRINCETON

IVY. Other Princeton clubs have beer taps in their basements; Ivy has a wine cellar. Ivy members pride themselves on the intellectuality and the wide variety of interests found in their club members—lots of Classics majors discussing Vergil over backgammon. (It is not true that Ivy's endowment is larger than Brown's.)

COTTAGE. For the gentleman jock. The traditional club of swimmers, tennis, and squash players, it sometimes gets rowdy. Members tend to be large and blond and to enjoy throwing girls into their little fountain.

CAP AND GOWN. The only one of Princeton's big three clubs to take women, so the concentration of Preppy females is intense. (So is the competition to get in.) Male members are those with enlightened ideas about women at breakfast, or else those who didn't get in to Cottage or Ivy.

GONE BUT NOT FORGOTTEN

The Fence Club at Yale. Recently deceased and much mourned, Fence gave cocktail parties after football games, a dance on Harvard or Princeton weekend, a big spring dance. Bobby Short came up from New York to play the piano there, and they gave an annual Derby Day party where everyone drank mint juleps and dressed up to watch the race on TV.

FRATERNAL INSTINCTS

Frats and sororities range from national organizations to local chapters. There are some nationally established Preppy frats, where most of the members are from Darien and almost all went to Prep school in Massachusetts—Psi U and St. Anthony Hall fit this mold most consistently. But at every school, there will be a broad variety of types and, from one campus to another, a frat's or sororities' reputation will be different.

Straight arrow house. This is the club your parents will be proud that you joined—the house average is B+. Professors come to the cocktail parties and bring their wives. Any Preppy involved in student government lives here, and the frat claims the distinction of having all its furniture intact.

Ladies-in-waiting or bridal sororities. There's not much selection in sororities—either you join one of the popular chapters or you don't join at all. The highlight of life here is the sacred rite that comes to pass when a sister realizes her collegiate goal—getting engaged. The lights are cut off and the whole membership forms a circle. A lit candle is passed around the circle and the betrothed Preppy blows out the candle. Bridesmaids come with the house.

Gentleman jock clubs. Nearest to the squash and tennis courts. Girlfriends spend weekends here and often write homework for boyfriends who are on the field, in the shower, fast asleep, etc. Members are always practicing lacrosse on the front lawn.

Coed arrangement. Neither true frat nor sorority in spirit, nevertheless has advantages for Preppies who like to flirt with alternate lifestyles. Telltale traits include mixed bathrooms, loud stereos, potluck dinners, a Frisbee team, and a local dealer with two prices: "regular" and "in-house." Lasting romantic relationships are rare; one-night stands are regrettable. These houses attract stray dogs and vociferous audiences during televised presidential addresses.

The zoo. Only alumni loyalty keeps the building from being condemned. The house is part gym, part tavern-brothel, part war zone. Furniture burned and windows smashed on daily basis. Usually, this frat has the most extensive term-paper file and the worst class attendance record. Sued by the irate father of a harassed female party guest at least once a year, this frat is perpetually on probation.

THE COLLEGE YEARS. The boy is on the left; the girl, right. For the first time they are in a community of many different types of people, and this very functional uniform helps them to identify one another in the crowd. By now they have learned that they are different from everyone else, and they band together in a group even more tightly knit than their sweaters.

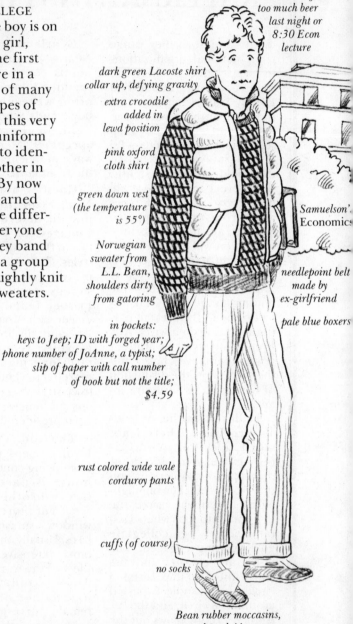

dazed look from too much beer last night or 8:30 Econ lecture

dark green Lacoste shirt collar up, defying gravity

extra crocodile added in lewd position

pink oxford cloth shirt

green down vest (the temperature is 55°)

Norwegian sweater from L.L. Bean, shoulders dirty from gatoring

in pockets: keys to Jeep; ID with forged year; phone number of JoAnne, a typist; slip of paper with call number of book but not the title; $4.59

Samuelson's Economics

needlepoint belt made by ex-girlfriend

pale blue boxers

rust colored wide wale corduroy pants

cuffs (of course)

no socks

Bean rubber moccasins, even though it's sunny

PREP PERSONA
No. 3

the bench has been stolen 5 times already this year, and is now bolted into the sidewalk

ambush for pouring beer on the unsuspecting

short hair (stays out of her eyes during squash games)

gold hoop earrings, concession to femininity

navy blue cotton Skyr turtleneck collar pulled up to chin

Fair Isle sweater, blue with yellow yoke — her mother's, bought in Edinburgh in 1962

yellow oxford cloth shirt, monogrammed on pocket — cuffs turned back over sweater

red down vest

with three sleeves, it's hard to bend your arms

old Timex men's watch with blue and green ribbon band

school ring, immediately recognizable from 25 yards

in pockets of khakis:
Trident gum, cinnamon flavor;
keys to room;
ticket stubs from an ice hockey game;
$3.62

khakis, men's, without a cuff because she let them down

Bean boots (also worn with kilts)

THE
SPORTING LIFE
What to Play, What to Watch

At college, the traditional Prep sporting proclivities continue unabated. Most truly Prep sports are played at all levels: varsity, intramural, and simply for exercise. Moreover, given the Prep fondness for turning any routine event into an occasion, many athletic competitions become social rituals. Even the sports that Preppies wouldn't consider playing are perfectly all right to watch.

TO PLAY

Soccer. Running up and down a field on a crisp fall day has lots of appeal. The sport is English, the uniforms are handsome, and it allows for some showmanship. A serious varsity sport, it's also often played by one fraternity or club against another. If you happen not to be hung over on Saturday morning of a football weekend, it's nice to go cheer the soccer teams. At least the game is easy to follow.

Field hockey. One of the ultimate Prep sports for women, hockey has a lot in common with soccer. Men, of course, love to watch the girls in those short kilts. When it's played intramurally, the teams are usually coed, and watching the men handle hockey sticks can be very amusing.

Rugby. Rough, rowdy, and very macho, rugby is most popular with large Southerners. Moreover, training rules are lenient, allowing for great and regular consumption of beer. Its spectator value is limited, however, to rugby players' girlfriends. Because it's so rough, it's only played by serious varsity-level devotees.

Squash. Squash is such an intensely Prep sport that general competence can be assumed to be part of the average Preppy's talents. You have to be *very* good to make the varsity squad, but that needn't stop you from playing every day. This is what Preps call a lifetime sport, which means that it makes sense to get good at it now since—unlike, say, lacrosse—it can be played at any

CREW
The Sport of Preps

KEY CREW LORE TO REMEMBER.

1. No one can row crew *and* study *and* party; guess what has to go.

2. Crew is capital-intensive. An eight-man shell can cost up to ten thousand dollars (there are eight-, four-, and two-man shells). A scull (for a single rower) can cost up to five thousand dollars. Hence only Prep schools can afford to buy these sleek, fragile things. The best Prep school for crew (men's and women's) is Kent. The best college is Harvard. Yale, Penn, and, *horribile dictu*, Wisconsin, are close runners-up. (Women's crew dates only from the opening of Prep school admissions to women; the best college for women's crew is Radcliffe.)

3. Crew jocks decorate their rooms with beer cans and the T-shirts of rival teams. A losing team always hands its shirts over to the winner. The losing team is usually Princeton (cf. below).

4. The Head of the Charles in Cambridge, Mass., is the great American crew event, athletically and socially. It occurs the second weekend in October; secondary schools and colleges send shells in all categories in the three-mile race up the Charles River. Drunken Preps line the banks and bridges at Harvard, ready to howl with glee as a coxswain rams his shell into a stanchion of the Eliot Street Bridge (where the river narrows and curves with treacherous suddenness).

5. The greatest crew event of all is Henley at Henley-on-Thames, England (June 30, July 1, 2, 3). Here you will find schoolboy crew, college crew, boat club crew. American crews often go; a varsity college heavyweight team would compete for the National Challenge Cup, a Prep school team

for the Princess Elizabeth. Viewing areas on the Thames are strictly class-linked. Aristos and the extremely rich view from the Steward's Enclosure, the middle-class from the Regatta Enclosure, the Great Unwashed from wherever they can. The surprising thing is that the Great Unwashed do attend.

6. In crew, contempt is important. In Boston, Boston University and Northeastern crew are treated with contempt by the college up the river. Intramural crew is treated with contempt. Nonathletic coxswains (Chinese engineering majors, poets) are treated with contempt. A true coxswain is a diminutive jock, raging against the pint size that made him the butt of so many jokes at Prep school. He runs twenty stadiums a day, his girlfriend is six feet one, and he can scream orders even when he has the flu (which he catches at least three times a winter).

KEY CREW LORE *NOT* TO REMEMBER.

1. A rich Catholic high school in New Jersey—Holy Spirit—produces the best rowers in the nation. This is embarrassing.

2. Columbia crew is a poor joke. According to rumor, one of its crew members disappeared in the East River.

3. Princeton crew is an expensive joke. Andrew Carnegie had an artificial lake dredged just outside the campus so that Princeton crew could reign supreme. Princeton crew has been consistently mediocre ever since.

4. The best crew in the world is always made up of blond, blue-eyed monsters from the East—East Germany, that is.

season and requires only one other person for a game.

Tennis. This is another lifetime sport, and it's marvelous for a tepid Prep date (you get to check out your partner's legs as a bonus). Watching tennis at college prepares women for a lifetime of doing needlepoint in the pavilion at the country club, watching their husbands double-fault in the quarterfinals of the member-guest tournament.

Lacrosse. By virtue of its very difficulty, lacrosse is limited to serious players. It probably wouldn't be Prep at all, except that lacrosse players traditionally come from Baltimore, and Baltimore is *very* Prep.

Crew. Crew is one of the Preppiest of sports, and its charm is puzzling. Training is rigorous—starving to "make weight," running up and down stadium bleachers, rowing in the tank all winter—and the athletes' glory, when it arrives in the spring, is sweaty and uncomfortable. But crew is an unquestionable character builder.

TO WATCH

Lacrosse. Saturday afternoons are for spending down at the lacrosse field with a coolerful of daiquiris. Lacrosse is a thrilling game to watch, and all those men from Baltimore are your friends so you wouldn't think of missing a game—if it's sunny.

Crew. Who needs an excuse to sit on the bank of a river with a picnic on a Saturday? Though few crew races (the Head of the Charles in October and the Red Top are exceptions) attract huge crowds, Preppies turn out in force. For one thing, those oarsmen are working so hard that they deserve some kind of cheering. For another, it's easy to tell—even through a haze of Bloodies—who's winning.

Squash. Though singularly ill-suited for an audience, Preppies nonetheless sit on chilly cement steps to watch two men chase a small black ball around a white box. (And there isn't even any liquor available!)

Football. Of course football games generate the greatest gaiety, drawing alumni back to the school, providing excuses for entire weekends of parties. Tailgate picnics, whiskey sours in the stadium, and the general complexity of the sport guarantee that nobody knows what is going on.

Ice hockey. After dinner on a winter night, taking a couple of beers down to the hockey rink is a good alternative to studying. The game is fast and fun to watch, and it doesn't matter that you can't tell who the players are, since they're all from Canada and you don't know them anyway.

PREP SEX

A Contradiction in Terms

Sex is as much affected by tradition as the rest of Prep life. There are certain habits and conventions that make the mating dance as predictable as the fox-trot—and as dull. While longstanding expectations and customs may make social intercourse polite, routine, and reassuring, they effectively stultify intercourse of the other sort. Sex roles for men and women are well defined, and while a bit of eccentricity may be dismissed in sartorial matters, deviation from the sexual norm is absolutely taboo.

What men want is sex, but they don't want it with other Preppies. Most Prep men suffer from the virgin/whore complex, and they only want to have sex with "bad" women. This is all very well for the non-Prep sexpots who oblige them, as long as they expect nothing but a good time and a polite thank you. Prep men will not marry these women; they will marry other Preppies.

Preppy men place Preppy women in two categories: women you might marry, and neuters. What a Preppy man looks for in a wife (or a girl-friend who might become a wife) is nothing less than perfection—as embodied in his mother. The woman he loves must be pretty, athletic, sweet, domestic, reasonably (but not startlingly) intelligent, and crazy about him. Sex is extra.

The neuter woman is one who, for one reason or another, the Prep man finds threatening. She's smarter than he is. Or she's ambitious. She plays better tennis. Or she is inescapably sexy and pursues men. Libido in a Preppy woman is so alarmingly contradictory that, however sought-after she may be by other cultural subgroups, the khaki crowd will shun her like Hester Prynne.

Preppy women as a group are not sexy. They aren't even all that interested in sex—at least they'd never let on if they were.What they want in a man is an escort, a Ken doll, a trophy. They want someone who is fun and handsome, someone who will squire them around and be witty and amusing at parties—and never lay a hand on them except on the dance floor. Sometimes they find this man; more often, they pretend that they have until he makes a pass at them. He will then be removed from the list of Acceptable Men for Dates.

The one exception to this general habit is the fling they may have in boarding school or early in college. After one or two Prep boyfriends, the Preppy girl may fall for someone of non-Prep background. (This is not a universal occurrence, because some Preppy girls simply don't have the opportunity to meet people of other backgrounds, and others don't have an adventurous turn of mind.) She will be intrigued by his exotic ethnic heritage, his warmth, his passion, his openness and emotional generosity. She will also be very curious about those funny underpants he

wears, and she'll secretly believe that she is very daring to sleep with a man who wears a gold chain around his neck. This romance, however, is guaranteed to end when she gets tired of taking him to parties where he objects to her dancing with Taylor or Worthington or Ames all night. The remainder of her beaux will be Preppies, and she will reflect fondly for the rest of her life on her fling with the outside world.

RULES OF PREP SEX

No PDA. (Public display of affection—i.e., hand holding, hugging, or kissing). This is the first and great commandment. You must never let on that you're sleeping with someone. If you have been "seeing each other" (the bloodless Prep phrase for a love affair) for a long time, everyone will assume that you *do* sleep together. They will be sure of it when you start having elaborate logistical discussions at the end of every party concerning how to get the Jeep across campus so your brother can use it early in the morning and then leave it in the club parking lot so you can pick it up right after class and drive to Vermont.

Girls do not sleep around. Word gets out remarkably fast and Preppy girls are not supposed to want to have sex at all. If they make overtures (or succumb to them) in any but the subtlest way, the story will be all over the back row of Psych 101 by 9:45 the next morning.

Men do not take advantage of Prep women. Unless a woman seems to want them to, desperately. (That in itself is unlikely, considering the prudishness most Prep women affect.) Prep men actually cherish the notion of a woman's honor, and are capable of apologizing after kissing her.

STANDARD OPERATING PROCEDURES

Certain stages of romance are, to be fair, made easier by the Prep lifestyle. The formality that persists in Prepdom pairs people up on dates, which guarantees ample opportunity to make overtures. Drinking also goes a long way to remove inhibitions, making it easier for men and women to forget that they are Preppies and remember that they're men and women. And then there's dancing, which allows both partners to check out the merchandise at first hand and respectably, while there's still time to back out. If a Preppy decides to go on with it, the steps to take are the following (this timetable may be accelerated if the encounter has definite boundaries—i.e., a

shipboard romance—or if one partner is not a Preppy):

Kissing. Some Preppies (mostly those who went abroad for their junior year) kiss a lot; girls kiss each other and men on all occasions. This is casual kissing, but it's not bad for practice and once you get used to it it can be very pleasant.

Real kissing. Rare on the first date, rare on the second. It usually takes place in a situation that has a built-in termination point; cab rides are ideal, and the presence of the cabbie is a reassuring guarantee that things won't get out of hand— it's almost like kissing with Nanny there.

First sex. This usually takes place when both are drunk, after a big party. It probably isn't much fun, and the man gets up before dawn to creep across campus to his room. If neither of the partners has a single room, they may go to someone's house in Vermont for the weekend, though that degree of calculation is rare.

Spending the night. At the girl's room, as a rule. This is a real coup for her, especially at a women's college when the man will be exhibited at breakfast, even if neither partner *ever* eats in the morning.

First Prep display of affection. She wears his jacket when she gets cold at a dance, or he allows her to drive his car. This means that they are practically engaged.

SOCIAL STUDIES
Parties for Preppies

At college, you learn everything you will need to know in later life. For Preppies, this is, as much as anything, how to go to parties. You get intensive training in this activity and you learn by doing, as it were. For a successful partygoing career, certain techniques are absolutely necessary, but you should have no trouble mastering them by the end of Freshman Week.

Dressing right. Always underdress. The goal is not to look as if you made an effort for the particular event. If you can dress for a different party (i.e., wear black tie to a cocktail party, or tennis clothes for lunch), so much the better. You give the impression of being much in demand.

Drinking right. You should be able to drink herculean quantities without being significantly affected. Choose a liquor and then stick with it— beer is always safe, white wine is for girls, gin is poison. Scotch is highly recommended for the serious drinker.

Part of drinking right is dealing with a hangover, and a Preppy knows that prevention is nine-tenths of the cure. Hence, aspirin before you go to bed. Another key technique: control the whirlies by going to sleep with one hand against the wall and one foot on the floor (tough to do if you sleep in a loft bed).

Talking to the right people. You have to learn how to slide gracefully in and out of conversations. Some men, for instance, always carry a drink in each hand, one for themselves and one for a mythical friend. If they want to exit from a conversation, they run off to find the person the drink is supposedly for. If they want to meet a pretty girl, they can say someone sent them over with a new drink. If they get engrossed in conversation with the girl, they drink both drinks.

For women, kissing can provide the necessary *entrée*: If you run up and kiss a man in conversation with other people, he has to introduce you around. Kissing a strange man by mistake never hurts.

Theme parties are a Prep entertainment favorite. Most often sponsored by the clubs, but often thrown by enterprising individuals, they feature specialized dress and drink ranging from formal to exotic.

Homecoming. Whatever it's called on your campus, Homecoming is the biggest football game of the season. If Daddy went to your school, he and Mummy will be there with a tailgate picnic. It's important to dress warmly since stadium seats can get chilly even in October. This means all the layers you can possibly fit under your herringbone tweed jacket. You should be comfortable with a turtleneck, a Lacoste, a button-down shirt and a Shetland sweater. Of course, you *will* be drinking large quantities of whiskey sours—much more warming than Bloodies. Liquor in the stadium is illegal, but that hasn't stopped a Preppy yet. Cider in a jug and bourbon in a hip flask solve the problem. Blankets are bush league.

Wassail parties. Held in any room with duck prints and a fireplace. Always overcrowd-

ed, these parties get very drunken because all they're serving is vile punch. Men wear ties with Christmas motifs, girls wear long taffeta skirts. Music is provided by tapes or records of the Beach Boys, and by midnight everyone in the room is jumping up and down to "Help Me, Rhonda." When the party is over the hosts are left with three identical chesterfield coats, some broken windows, and a carpet of cigarette ashes.

Casino Night. A long way from Monte Carlo, but further still from Atlantic City. Held in

20 WAYS TO EXPRESS DRUNKENNESS

As in other activities pursued assiduously by Preppies, drinking brings with it an extensive terminology, ever growing by sips and gulps. Admiration for excess in its multitudinous forms provides the linguistically lithe with an engaging glossary of euphemisms for being drunk.

1. *Bent out of shape*
2. *Blasted*
3. *Bombed*
4. *Faced*
5. *Gone Borneo*
6. *Loaded*
7. *Looped*
8. *Paralytic*
9. *Pissed*
10. *Polluted*
11. *Ripped*
12. *Schizzed out*
13. *Shit-faced*
14. *Smashed*
15. *Squashed*
16. *Tight*
17. *Trashed*
18. *Twisted*
19. *Wasted*
20. *Wrecked*

perhaps décolleté. We're playing for real money here, even though it isn't legal (the chance of police raids, though in-

frequent, adds spice to the proceedings). The hearty types drink beer, while real gamblers, intent on the blackjack game, have a glass of scotch (neat) at their elbow. Women don't gamble, though they are allowed to hold the chips.

San Juan Night. Always held in mid-February. Dress is "tropical," which means Hawaiian shirts on the men and long halter-top dresses in brilliant flowered prints for women. If you managed to go south during intersession, this is your chance to show off the tan. Music is island-related: watered-down reggae or steel drum. Drinks are based solely on rum, because someone made a deal with the promo-

one of the clubs or fraternities on campus and sponsored by several organizations, Casino Night is one of the highlights of a winter weekend. Again, black tie for the men, but the women are more likely to wear something a little slinky and

Very clever: sew a crocodile in the appropriate spot. If accompanied by a Roman-style dinner, these sheets may go home stained with red wine, though serious drinkers might switch to a grain alcohol punch around ten o'clock. Since dancing in a toga is impossible, getting drunk is the primary activity.

Rites of Spring. Invitations suggest that everyone is going to overcome their inhibitions, and licentious behavior will ensue. Girls try to look romantic, possibly with flowers in

tion department of Rums of Puerto Rico. The highlight of the evening is the drawing for a weekend in San Juan, with the flight leaving at midnight. Bring a toothbrush just in case.

Toga party. Girls wear designer sheets, men wear the kind from the linen service.

their hair. Men wear Grandfather's white linen dinner jacket. The party is held outdoors under a tent, with an open bar and a corny band. Everyone drinks gin and tonic to make them think it's summer, and the women take off their shoes to dance.

DEVIANT BEHAVIOR

To Preppies, a sense of humor is something to be acquired, like a Mercedes or a pair of loafers. When searching for the wit (or what passes for wit in the world of Prep) that will cause friends to label them with the ultimate Preppy laudatory adjective—"wild"— the smart Preppy will copy the accepted antics of his fore-Preppies. Many of these forays into zaniness actually wind up involving mayhem or destruction of property, but a Preppy doesn't worry about that; it's not for nothing that Daddy's a lawyer.

To the Preppy way of thinking, anybody can go to an afternoon class on Modern British Literature, but it takes a real *bon vivant* to steal a fire engine and hose down rival fraternity houses.

MOONING

Even though this practice was initiated by individuals who probably didn't make it through public high school, the Preppy finds this gag too rib-tickling to resist. Mooning is simply dropping one's drawers and pointing one's bare buttocks at an unsuspecting innocent—though Preppies have performed this exercise so often it's hard to find anyone who doesn't expect it. The favored locations for a quickly rising moon are swimming pools (because of the convenience of slipping in and out of bathing trunks) and moving cars (because a speedy getaway is possible, if necessary). Old ladies and frigid Cute Girls are beloved targets because of their shocked reactions, but a few of the gutsier Preppy women have been known to turn a moon into a goose.

GATORING

Gatoring is a sort of dance, but it frequently serves as an exit cue to those unimpressed with the Preppy idea of fun. At a terpsichorean function, one madcap yells "Gator!" and, like a Pavlovian pack of barking canines, all the Preppies will fall to the floor and commence imitating the movements of an alligator. After a while, the pseudo-reptiles wiggle together into a single pile of flesh. As this act begins to grow tedious, a Cute Girl who had just been standing around watching and fake-laughing is pushed into the pile. There is much excitement as the Cute Girl struggles to extricate herself from the writhing mass. It's mandatory that the Cute Girl at least give a show of embarrassment and effort—never is she allowed to wallow and enjoy the madness. There's little danger that she will experience much pleasure in being mauled, though, and more often than not the look on her face will not be forced timidity but sheer terror.

FOUNTAIN JUMPING

Possibly because the Preppies think they're being romantics along the lines of Scott and Zelda Fitzgerald by flinging themselves into a public fountain, this moronic custom is a perennial laff riot. The only real rule for this activity is that the fountain jumpers be dressed for another engagement—preferably a black-tie event. Thus, the plunge will have the charming spontaneity of a rocket launch.

WET T-SHIRT CONTESTS

This sneer-and-leer ritual proves that the 1950's female-breast fetish still lurks in the Preppy heart. A gaggle of game women in specially decorated T-shirts—meaning T-shirts ripped to shreds—parade in front of a hungry-eyed audience of expensively educated Prep males. The jocular, lewd-mouthed master of

---

THE TOP 10 DRINKING SCHOOLS

1. **Dartmouth College**
Hanover, N.H.
SAT's: V620, M665

2. **Bowdoin College**
Brunswick, Maine
SAT's: V550, M570

3. **Lafayette College**
Easton, Penn.
SAT's: V533, M626

4. **University of Colorado**
Boulder, Colo.
SAT's: V520, M570

5. **University of North Carolina**
Chapel Hill, N.C.
SAT's: V516, M564

6. **University of New Hampshire**
Durham, N.H.
SAT's: V477, M539

7. **Duke University**
Durham, N.C.
SAT's: V593, M633

8. **Southern Methodist University**
Dallas, Tex.
SAT's: V480, M535

9. **Holy Cross College**
Worcester, Mass.
SAT's: V575, M600

10. **University of Southern California**
Los Angeles, Calif.
SAT's: V545, M495

---

ceremonies invites each contestant to step forward and be doused by a bucket of water until her shirt (or what's left of it) clings to her body. The judging is nominally based on something like "Most Creative T-Shirt," but the real evaluation centers on what lies underneath. The audience decides, via an applause meter manned by the emcee, which shivering hopeful wins the tournament. The prize is either a lacy little thing from the Frederick's of Hollywood catalog or an even more colorful appliance purchased at a local "pleasure" shop. These contests are extremely popular entertainments—so much so, that the cops have dropped by on many occasions.

BEERITORY CONFINEMENT

This prank is a favorite for fraternity initiations, but is also common for Prep fun-lovers during the rest of the school year as well. A crowd of about five Preppies gather in the rec room of a frat where they are literally locked in by friends who nail plywood over the doors and windows. The intrepid quintet is not allowed out until they completely drain a keg of beer. When they have finally drunk the last drop, they, or at least the one among them who still retains his balance, hurls the empty keg through the plywood partition. This display of bravura would seem enough even for Hercules, but there's more.

The inebriated five are then blindfolded (as if the world weren't already spinning for them) and lead to a waiting vehicle. They are then driven to a field off campus, where an obstacle course (much like the

20 VERBAL EXPRESSIONS FOR VOMITING

There are some Preppies who do not consider an evening a success unless they have managed to divest themselves of all that day's meals. The best part being, of course, to be able to announce to your friends that you capped a romantic evening by vomiting. Using the accepted jargon. Which is extensive.

1. *Barf*
2. *Blow doughnuts*
3. *Blow groceries*
4. *Blow lunch*
5. *Boot*
6. *Buick*
7. *Drive the porcelain bus*
8. *Heave*
9. *Instant boot camp*
10. *Kiss the porcelain god*
11. *Lose lunch*
12. *Lose your doughnuts*
13. *Puke*
14. *Ralph*
15. *The technicolor yawn*
16. *Throw up*
17. *Toss your cookies*
18. *Toss your tacos*
19. *Upchuck*
20. *Woof*

ones found at Marine training camp) has been prepared for them. After attempting to climb fences, crawl under wires, and run through tires, the remnants of human beings are at last free to celebrate Most do so by retching.

GETTING OUT
Graduation and Beyond

Graduating is like being born—traumatic but inevitable. It means you have to decide upon a profession that you can talk about at future social gatherings. You can duck the issue for a while by taking the Grand Tour the moment you've handed in your cap and gown. But, sooner or later, depending on the amount of graduation-present money Daddy gave you, you'll be forced to return and get a job. So, while you're waiting in line in Victoria Station for your first InterRail Pass journey, consult the following list of careers to find the most painless way to pay for your dry-cleaning and Jeep repair bills.

Lawyer. Requires good grades in college, LSAT's, and three years in a tony law school, but is a satisfactory recourse for those who don't know what else to do. It gives respectability.

Stockbroker. Encompassing also bond and commodities trading. Requires knowing the best squash clubs, commuter neighborhoods, and traditional tailors.

Account executive. The only acceptable position in advertising.

Investment banker. Training programs provide smooth transition from college. The traditional chilliness of the female Preppy makes her particularly qualified for this.

Art dealer. Requires no knowledge of art, just conversational ability and a casual stance while holding a cocktail at gallery events.

Rare-book dealer, collector. Reading of the collected texts optional.

Editor. Prep attire and college English classes make you seem literate and well-read; once employed, leave the writing up to the authors. Publishing, in general, is a Preppy stronghold—training courses available in this field, also.

Furniture restorer. Bohemian, but still honorable.

Landscape gardener. For those who wish to live on the Cape or Nantucket.

College or Prep school admissions officer. Perfect way to keep up with friends and groom self for school presidency or headmaster post without bothering to get graduate degree in History.

Tennis pro. Live at country club; it's as if you never left campus.

Rancher. Huge ranch is mandatory if you want to remain stylish—otherwise, you may appear to be slumming.

Carpenter. Ph.D. is a must, preferably in Philosophy.

Nonprofit organization director. Any cause will do, since this job consists primarily of asking for money, something you've learned at Daddy's knee.

Yacht designer. At last, legitimacy for your Top-Siders—you need never leave the deck of a boat again.

Philanthropist. Necessitates wealth. Garners admiration while allowing plenty of time for golf.

Ne'er-do-well. Deceptively simple. Dictates ceaseless charm and the ability to sponge off others without ever appearing to be a bore or a burden. Brain surgery is easier.

THE FELLOWSHIPS

Although graduate school in the States is generally a don't (except for the magical MBA and JD degrees), study abroad after graduation adds nothing but luster to the Preppy résumé, especially if it's done on a fellowship. It's all very well to spend two years at Heidelberg examining the finer points of local beers, but it's even better if the research is paid for by the US government under the Fulbright-Hays laws. There are three that specifically attract Preppies.

Rhodes. The classic, the all-American fellowship. There are thirty-two American Rhodes scholars each year, chosen on the basis of leadership qualities and physical vigor, as well as intellectual prowess. Rhodes scholars usually spend their two years at Oxford studying Politics, Philosophy, and Economics. However, everyone knows that Rhodes scholars aren't really in Oxford to work, but to be exposed to England and to learn to call Europe "the Continent."

Fulbright. Fulbrights—which, like Monopoly money, come in several denominations—are granted for each country. The most common Fulbright for Preppies is a research grant for one year, for work on a specific project. Some countries are easier to get grants for than others: While France has only six full Fulbrights available, Germany has eighty. And naturally, competition for a fellowship to Belgium is considerably keener than competition for a fellowship to Lesotho. In recent years, ingenious students have gone to Europe to study pottery in Denmark and wine-making methods in France.

Keasbey. The best-kept secret in the grant world. Legend has it that Miss Keasbey, the heiress to an asbestos fortune, was accustomed in her youth to travel through England and greatly enjoyed the attentions of many eligible Rhodes scholars. As she got older, it seemed that the Rhodes scholars were less eligible (or simply less willing to dance attendance). So she set up her own grant, to allow charming young men (culled from the runners-up in the Rhodes competition) two years of study at Oxford or Cambridge. The stipend provides £100 more than the Rhodes.

THE
GRAND TOUR

It used to be that Preppies never saw the Eiffel Tower until they reached their twenty-first birthday or graduated from college, depending on whether they were girls or boys. Today, most have traveled overseas at least once (see *Holidays and Summers*) before commencement, but that trip was probably heavily chaperoned.

In order to raise the flagging spirits induced by leaving the collegiate womb, Mummy and Daddy offer to send their young alum to Europe without a monitor, but with a best friend. Even if the only destination is St. Tropez, the post-BA vacation is traditionally known as the Grand Tour. The duration of the trip is unimportant, but generally it will last between one and three months.

AUSTRIA
VIENNA

Voom Voom Club. Crowded disco, actual Viennese dance here, too.

SALZBURG

Stieglkeller. Beer garden. Go after music festival.

ENGLAND
CAMBRIDGE

Trinity College Buttery. Pub at Cambridge's most venerated college. Private. Nights only; beers and cider.

LONDON

Hardrock Cafe. Ivy League pennants on the wall, hamburgers on the menu.

OXFORD

The Grapes. Ornately victorian pub.

FRANCE
ANNECY

Père Bise. Beautiful restaurant, on Lake Annecy.

CAP d'ANTIBES

Eden Roc. Actual rock for sunbathing and diving. On premises of Hotel du Cap. Chic, exclusive, and expensive.

MONTE CARLO

New Jimmyz. Nightclub/disco owned by Régine herself. Caroline is a frequent visitor.

PARIS

Pub. St. Germain. Like an outpost of the Yale Club.

ST. TROPEZ

Hotel Byblos. Drinks are expensive, but the clientele is glamorous.

GERMANY
MUNICH

Alter Simpl. Dancing, drinking. Very in.

GREECE
ATHENS

Astir Beach Hotel, Vouliagmenis. There are Astir Beach hotels all over Greece, but this one, a short drive from downtown Athens, is where Greek tycoons frolic in the surf and eat lunch.

CORFU

Alexandros. Like being on the set of "Zorba the Greek". He'll invite you into his kitchen to see what's cooking.

MYKONOS

9 Muses. Waterfront cafe with good fish, bouzouki music.

SANTORINI

Yellow Donkey. Loud disco, playing year-old American hits. Large numbers of Preppies spotted here.

HOLLAND
AMSTERDAM

Melkweg. Multi-level club. Films, theatrical performances.

IRELAND
DUBLIN

Guinness Brewery. Drive the Buick to Borneo.

ITALY
FLORENCE

Harry's Bar. Right off 3rd Ave. Everyone drinks here after a hard day buying cute things in cute stores on the Ponte Vecchio. No one goes to Harry's Bar in Venice anymore.

ROME

Hotel Excelsior. Just sit in the lobby. Absorb atmosphere that's one hundred times nicer than where you're staying.

VENICE

Taverna da Pio. To slum in Venice means eating Chinese food in Italian restaurants.

PORTUGAL
LISBON

Lisboa a Noite. Popular for drinking, eating, and fado—melodramatic speech and song.

SCOTLAND
EDINBURGH

Cafe Royal. Pub, homey, frequented by people on Junior Year Abroad.

SPAIN
BARCELONA

Los Caracoles. Famous chicken roast outside. Touristy, but fun.

MADRID

Cuevas Sesamo. Good wall graffiti, piano, a tad rowdy.

MAJORCA

Cabala. Best nightspot. Calm, with a view.

SWITZERLAND
GSTAAD

Palace Hotel. Year round resort in town that gives "cute" new meaning.

GENEVA

Mr. Pickwick Pub. Feeling is American. Go from Georgetown to Geneva without skipping a beat.

ST. MORITZ

Palace Hotel. Related to Gstaad hotel. Preferably for winter.

ZURICH

Opfelchammer. This club has its own deviant behavior: swinging over ceiling beams and drinking wine upside down.

N.B. While the Scandinavian countries do provide plenty of fresh air and beer, they have never caught on among Preps. This may be due to the fact that no one has ever spent Junior Year Abroad on a fjord. Eastern European countries and Russia are not visited on the Grand Tour, although the Yugoslavian coast (Dubrovnik) is an occasional stopover from Germany to Greece.

HAIL, ALMA MATER!
Quiz #3

Alma Mater may be dear, her praises ever worthy of song, but often the exact wording of her celebration escapes even the most dedicated alumnus or alumna. To test your skill in this area, try matching the first lines on the left with the college names on the right (blanks in songs represent college name). Answer key appears at the bottom of the page.

1. "Oh proudly rise the monarchs of our mountain land."

2. "Hark, Alma Mater through the world is ringing, The praise thy grateful daughters bring to thee."

3. "To Alma Mater, _____ daughters, all together join and sing."

4. "Here's to old _____, a glass of the finest."

5. "_____, _____ flower fair, the rose that nestles in your hair."

6. "Dear is thee homestead glade and glen, fair is the smile that crown thy brow."

7. "Tune every heart and enjoy every voice, bid every care withdraw."

8. "Rise sons of _____, praise her fame and sing aloud her glorious name."

9. "Men of _____ give a rouse for the college on the hill."

10. "Set like a gem amid the waters blue, Where palms and pine their bright red incense brew."

11. "And he shall be like a tree planted by the rivers of water that bringeth forth his fruit in his season."

12. "_____ our dear Alma Mater, by Red and Black float proudly o'er us."

13. "Friends of wisdom, let us gather, We love beauty, but without display."

14. "Long ago the Pilgrims landed, high on a rockbound shore, They brought with them love and spirit, faith and ancient lore."

15. "Bright college years, with pleasure rife, The shortest, gladdest years of life."

a. VASSAR
b. HAMILTON
c. LAKE FOREST
d. WELLESLEY
e. BOWDOIN
f. SWEET BRIAR
g. PRINCETON
h. WHEATON
i. DARTMOUTH
j. HAMPDEN-SYDNEY
k. YALE
l. BRYN MAWR
m. CONNECTICUT COLLEGE
n. ROLLINS
o. WILLIAMS

Answers: 1o; 2a; 3d; 4j; 5f; 6b; 7g; 8e; 9i; 10n; 11m; 12c; 13l; 14h; 15k.

CHAPTER 4

DRESSING THE PART

The Basic Look

MADRAS

If there is one fabric that is quintessentially Preppy, it is madras. True madras, of course. The real thing is one of the oldest fabrics in the cotton trade, a fine, hand-loomed cotton that is imported from Madras, India. What sets true madras apart from imitations is that it "bleeds"; the murky colors—navy blue, maroon, mustard yellow—of its distinctive plaids are imparted by vegetable dyes that are guaranteed to run.

Since the colors are so unstable, madras has to be treated very carefully. Shirts, shorts, and items that are not going to be dry-cleaned must be soaked in cold salt water for at least twenty-four hours before they are washed the first time. This sets the dyes. Then they really should be washed separately for months thereafter, because the colors will still run. Old madras takes on a lovely soft look and feel with many washings (the crux of the fabric's appeal to Preps), though jackets, which are dry-cleaned, of course, maintain that sharp plaid.

FASHION FUNDAMENTALS

The Ten Underlying Principles for Men and Women

Amateur historians have speculated that Preppies all dress alike because they got in the habit from wearing school uniforms. Not so. Preppies dress alike because their wardrobes are formed according to fundamental principles that they absorb from their parents and their peers. And although the Preppy Look can be imitated, non-Preps are sometimes exposed by their misunderstanding or ignorance of these unspoken rules.

ONE
CONSERVATISM

Preppies wear clothes for twenty-five years and no one can tell the difference. The fabrics, the cuts, the colors are the same, year after year after year. A kilt from 1958, a ten-year-old tweed overcoat, a three-button suit bought in 1940 can all be worn until they fall apart.

TWO
NEATNESS

(Except for a brief period of rebellion during secondary school.) Preppies' shirts stay tucked in, through all kinds of strenuous exercise. Shoes are polished. Socks stay up. Sweaters are patched the moment holes appear in the elbows.

THREE
ATTENTION TO DETAIL

Subtleties of cut, weave, or color distinguish the merely good from the Prep. A small percentage of polyester in an oxford cloth shirt or a lapel that's a quarter of an inch too wide can make all the difference. Cuff buttons on a suit jacket that can actually be unbuttoned are the hallmark of the natty dresser. Everything matches—some Preppies go so far as to change their watchbands every day.

FOUR
PRACTICALITY

Prep clothes are sensible: rain clothes keep you dry; winter clothes keep you warm; collars are buttoned down so they don't flap in your face when you're playing polo. Layering is a natural response to varying weather conditions.

FIVE
QUALITY

Everything in the wardrobe should be well made. Fine fabrics and sound construction are taken for granted, hand tailoring is not unusual. Preppy clothes are built to last, since they certainly won't go out of style.

SIX
NATURAL FIBERS

Wool, cotton, and the odd bits of silk and cashmere are the only acceptable materials for Prep clothes. They look better. They require professional maintenance. They are more expensive. They are key.

SEVEN
ANGLOPHILIA

The British have a lot to answer for: Shetland sweaters, Harris tweeds, Burberrys, tartans, regimental ties.

EIGHT
SPECIFIC COLOR BLINDNESS

Primary colors and brilliant pastels are worn indiscriminately by men and women alike, in preposterous combinations. In some subcultures, hot pink on men might be considered a little peculiar; Preppies take it for granted.

NINE
THE SPORTING LOOK

Even if they've never been near a duck blind or gone beagling, Preppies are dressed for it. Rugged outerwear (snakeproof boots, jackets that will keep you warm at 60 degrees below zero) and hearty innerwear (fishermen's sweaters and flannel-lined khakis) are *de rigueur* in even the most sophisticated suburbs.

TEN
ANDROGYNY

Men and women dress as much alike as possible and clothes for either sex should deny specifics of gender. The success of the Lanz nightgown is based on its ability to disguise secondary sexual characteristics, while the traditional fit for men's khakis is one size too big.

THE
PRINT MANIFESTO

On some people's clothes, prints are blue cabbage roses, or modernistic geometrics, or necromancers' stars and planets. On Preps, they are little maps of Nantucket. Preps love prints—their own particular favorite prints. These prints fall into two distinct categories:

1. The splashy flower print. Based on bright green, with lots of hot pink, orange, white, or yellow. For women only, of course, and found on pants, dresses, and skirts. (For some unfathomable reason, considered a bit loud on shirts.) Prep women don't like delicate little flower prints. They think they're "ditsy."

2. The small, repeating-motif print. Possibly derived, at great distance, from men's foulard patterns. This is such a Prep favorite that it has a number of manifestations: it's

seen printed, appliquéd, woven, and embroidered on a wide variety of fabrics. Men and women alike sport prints

of this sort—sailboats, crossed tennis racquets, golf clubs, pigs, lobsters, maps of Nantucket—men usually limit them to motifs embroidered on ties, belts, and corduroy pants. For women, however, the possibilities are endless, and expanding every day. A new Prep favorite is the cotton turtleneck with a whimsical little print— hearts, turtles, frogs, acorns, butterflies, and elephants are some of the cutest. Skirts embroidered with strawberries, shirts covered with spouting whales, sweaters with daisies scattered all over; all are available in the key Prep primary colors. (Ducks, for the sake of verisimilitude, usually appear in a muted beige.)

THE POLITICS OF MONOGRAMMING

When Your Own Initials Will Do

Preppies have known it for years: who needs LV or YSL when you can lay claim to a discreet EBW III? In fact, most Preppies are so proud of their monograms that they put them on virtually everything in sight.

The monogram itself must be tasteful. Women may occasionally choose a rather loopy script, but its use should be confined to writing paper and—at the outside—sheets and guest towels. Linens, silver, and cocktail glasses are conventionally monogrammed by Preps and non-Preps alike. But Preppies also put monograms on wastebaskets. A classic Prep present is a monogrammed needlepoint tennis racquet cover.

Clothing, of course, is a natural for monograms, though the conventions of monogramming are very strict. Men's shirts, for example: they must be monogrammed right, or not at all.

Although men's monograms are usually rather small and discreet, women's tend to be more elaborate. Sweaters, turtlenecks, jewelry, and tennis clothes are all fair game. Women's monograms are usually larger, with the last initial centered. They tend to hover about the collarbone, and navy blue is the color of choice, regardless of background shade.

One of the most trying sartorial problems for Preppies is that of too many initials. What if you have four names? Or more? And what if one of your names has a complicated initial, like DeW? Sadly, no compromise will do. If it isn't possible (because of space limitations or uncooperative tradespeople) to use the correct complete monogram, the Preppy does without. If your own initials are enough, it's probably enough that only you know what they are.

Block letters: the masculine version

The diamond: ideal for linens

Art deco: for fashion-conscious writing paper

The single letter: on sweaters and tennis dresses

RULES FOR THE MONOGRAMMING OF MEN'S SHIRTS

1. You really should use your initials; it spoils the effect if you have "Duke" stitched carefully onto the cuff of your pink shirt.

2. The initials are small block letters, in the same order as your names. The monogram is always on the left side of the shirt.

3. Subtlety is the goal: the monogram should not show at all when you have your jacket on, and should be hard to find when you have it off. The breast pocket is the favored spot, if a little commonplace. Some men have monograms on their cuffs. Less often seen (but very creative) is the monogram on the body of the shirt, just below the rib cage. And a favorite for Preppies who fancy themselves as dandies is the monogram on the left sleeve at the elbow. Hardly anyone *ever* sees it there.

4. The monogram on a shirt gives a man the opportunity to express himself with color, and to make a real fashion statement. If he's the sophisticated urbane type, he may go for maroon on his pink or white shirts. Navy blue is for the true conservative. Bright red or bright green (matched to the webbing belt and the grosgrain watchband) denote the sportsman.

THINGS TO MONOGRAM

attaché cases
wallets
date books
address books
cuff links
key chains
circle pins
rings
pendants
ice buckets
place mats
lampshades
ashtrays
golf club covers
doormats
luggage
wastebaskets
sweaters
button-down
  shirts
polo shirts
  (initials where
  the crocodile
  would be)
turtlenecks
tennis dresses
tennis skirts
tennis racquet
  covers
  (needlepoint)
mailboxes
handbags
towels
napkins
tablecloths
cocktail glasses
hip flasks
cigarette boxes
coasters
stamp boxes
napkin rings
paper napkins
hooked rugs
aprons
bookplates
soap dishes
guest towels
soap
shower curtains
bath mats
silver flatware
pitchers
vases
handkerchiefs

pajamas
belt buckles
bathrobes
photo albums
small silver
  picture frames
door knockers
cushions
playing cards
blotters
blankets
quilts
blanket covers
sheets
pillowcases
Kleenex box
  covers

eyeglass cases
candlesticks
silver trays
baby spoons
baby rattles
porringers
tea cozies

THINGS *NOT* TO MONOGRAM

suits
cashmere
scarves
your dog's collar,
  (ostentatious)
your china (it
  will look like a
  hotel)
your car, unless
  you use
  nautical flags
  to signal your
  initials on the
  door

BASIC BODY TYPES

Although mankind is composed of a complex mixture of forms and figures, Preppies have ingeniously evolved into definite body types. Each sex offers three distinct models and each model has its correlate in the opposite sex forming three basic couples.

The most brilliant specimens are the Cute Guy and the Cute Girl. Clean-cut, blue-eyed, dark-

MALE

THE CUTE BOY	THE GOOD OLD BOY	THE AESTHETE
Pepsodent smile Moderate muscles, early-James Franciscus look	Beautiful eyes, spare tire Genetically attached beer can	Tortoise-shell glasses Absence of body hair Abundance of freckles
WOODBERRY FOREST	LAWRENCEVILLE	PORTSMOUTH ABBEY
UVA	HAMPDEN-SYDNEY	HARVARD
Should I call you for breakfast or just nudge you?	*Trading bonds is the most fun you can have with your clothes on.*	*In vino veritas.*

ly-tanned, they are both as wholesome and perfect looking as a freshly baked loaf of white bread.

And then there's the Good Old Boy and the Party-Hearty Girl, the Tweedledum and Tweedledee of the Preppy set. They may both be quite nice looking, but the spare tire they carry around their waists makes them a different species.

When the male and female traits seem to have switched genders, you have the Aesthete and the Amazon. The Aesthete often looks as if his voice hasn't changed yet but will any minute. Everything a man—or the Aesthete—could want, the Amazon has; mostly a torso that would make Steve Reeves jealous.

FEMALE

THE CUTE GIRL	THE PARTY-HEARTY GIRL	THE AMAZON
Slim hips, small bust Pretty but never voluptuous	Lovely hair, love handles Cigarette pack, lighter, and lit cigarette	Thick ankles Muscular legs Big-boned
MASTERS SCHOOL	OLDFIELDS	MIDDLESEX
PINE MANOR	HOLLINS	PRINCETON
How many colors does it come in?	*I really shouldn't, but . . .*	*Don't worry, I used to have problems with my backhand, too.*

MUMMY KNOWS BEST

The Look For Women

There is one sartorial goal for Preppy women: to look like Mummy. It starts with mother/daughter bathing suits and gingham dresses. Then daughter starts borrowing the clothes her mother wore in Prep school. Before long, they share a charge account at The Talbots, and their wardrobes are virtually interchangeable. They know what they like: the ultimate accolade for a piece of clothing is "useful" (with "cute" a close second).

1. Men's clothes. Either actual garments from the man's wardrobe (button-down shirts, Shetland sweaters, anything from L.L. Bean), or near imitations. The blue blazer, the khaki skirt, and the gray flannel suit are cornerstones of the female Prep's wardrobe. Some women go so far as to shop in the boy's department at Brooks, and have things (slightly) altered.

2. Navy blue. The new neutral, it is the automatic first choice for shoes, purses, suits, sweaters. It serves as the perfect foil for colors that do not exist in nature—shocking pink, poison green, brilliant yellow, Windex blue. Purple is not Preppy.

3. Don't wear black. With the exception of evening clothes (never say "gown") and the little black dress, black clothing (shirts, sweaters, bathing suits) make you look like a fast woman.

4. Someone else's clothes. Other people's things have inherited charm. Your roommate's needlepoint belt, your boyfriend's Lacoste, your mother's old hacking jacket are all very classy.

5. Underdressing. Always in good taste. Key advice from Mummy: "Get completely dressed for a party, then take off one piece of jewelry."

6. Layering. Turtlenecks, then oxford cloth shirts, then a Fair Isle with the three buttons undone. Women often dispense with the crocodile (Lacoste) layer, in the fear that it will make them look fat.

WOMEN'S

SHOES

Women's shoes are divided into two distinct categories: work shoes and play shoes. The play shoes are the ones without leather soles. Heel height is two and one half inches maximum (remember the practicality principle) and colors are conservative, as Preps understand the meaning of that word (for shoes, hot pink is conservative).

1. Classic pumps. In the basic black, navy, oxblood. Never purchased until college graduation, they are perfect for all indoor occasions.

2. Jacques Cohen espadrilles. (No other brand will do.) Never mind that they wear out in three weeks, never mind that they are ruined in one rainstorm. Available in a dozen shades.

3. Chris Craft foulweather boots. The Preppy-come-lately addition to mandatory footgear. Shearling-lined, Dayglo-colored in red, green, blue, yellow—to mix 'n' match with foul-weather gear.

4. Blucher moccasins. Bean claims that these never wear out—and it's true. They soak up water like sponges and the soles get slippery, but you love them anyway.

5. Pappagallo Blossoms. So pretty. And so comfortable. Little leather flats with big kid "blossoms" at the toes. Available in many colors. Signature Pappagallo mattress-ticking lining.

6. Gucci loafers. Variations on this theme of a metal bar or bit across the inseam may come and go, but the Italians make this show last and last. In stacked, low heel.

7. Weejuns. You weren't allowed to wear loafers for so long that there's still a thrill in it. To wear all weekend.

8. Tretorn sneakers. The only acceptable brand, with blue or green trim. For squash, for tennis, with shorts anytime. One toe should be worn down from being dragged while serving.

9. Clogs. For the younger Preppy. Clogs are a sixteen-year-old's idea of a dress shoe. Worn with knee socks and kilts, or with blue jeans. Made by Olofdaughters (pictured above), and Krön.

10. Sperry Top-Siders. These have been in Prep closets since sailing lessons started in sixth grade. The stitching is rotting, the sole is wearing out, but they're the automatic choice with khakis.

11. Bernardo sandals. They may not allow anything else at the country club. Thongs show off toenail polish and well-tanned feet. Must be worn in pastel colors or white.

12. Black Chanel slingbacks. Calf with patent leather cap on toe. Also popular in beige/black combo. If you work on the trading floor and have an active social life, you can't afford to be without them.

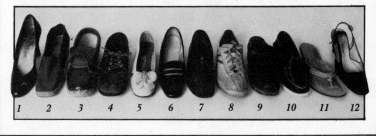

1 2 3 4 5 6 7 8 9 10 11 12

WOMEN'S

SHIRTS

Women's shirts, like men's, are all cotton. (There may be subversive silks in some metropolitan closets, but they're not the exclusive province of Preps.) Shirts are worn tucked in, *always*. Collars, if possible, are turned up, and cuffs are turned back over sweaters, buttoned at the wrist, or rolled below (*never* above) the elbow.

1. Cotton turtleneck. Comes in wonderful solid colors, yellow and blue and pink and—yes—green. Now available with whimsical flora and fauna (pink and green turtles, navy blue whales) motifs on a white background. The collar is never folded down.

2. Chemise Lacoste. (The crocodile). Big-boned flat-chested women can get away with the men's version, but the crocodile does tend to sit neatly on the left nipple. Closer cut, longer placket, and the tactful location of the reptile distinguish the women's shirts. Comes in all the good colors. Pink, after 6:00 P.M., is construed as dressy.

3. Tucked shirt. Dress for Prep success. Worn heavily starched by a Chinese laundry (who could iron all those tucks?) the bib is as good as a breastplate. In men's shirting colors (white, blue, yellow, pink), and sometimes worn with a foulard bow.

4. T-shirt. The scoop-necked ones with the piping are so feminine, and they come in all the nice, perky colors. These shirts look especially good with flowered wrap-around skirts, or sharkskin shorts.

5. Blouse with Peter Pan collar. Yes, Virginia, it still exists. Not seen much on young women, unless they're a bit naive. Available in broadcloth, but more likely to be a faded version in Liberty print that Mummy bought in Bermuda on her honeymoon.

6. Oxford cloth button-down. Just like Daddy's. Maybe it *is* Daddy's. Yours might be a little less voluminous, and his are monogrammed on the pocket, yours on the cuff.

WOMEN'S

DRESSES

A dress is less practical than separates: you can't change its look as easily as you can that of a khaki skirt. But it does have the unarguable advantages of being simple, neat, and comfortable. You may want, as well as these, a long black dress with spaghetti straps, for the most formal occasions.

1. Diane von Furstenburg wrap dress. Never mind that the print gives it away as four years old. Flattering on all body types, wearable for work or dress-up, comfortable—it's practically perfect.

2. Little black dress. You're not supposed to have one until you're thirty. Still, it may be the most useful garment invented, so if you're clever you can start wearing it at age twenty-five. Adaptable to anything from a day at the office (worn with a scarf) to a black-tie party (with pearls).

3. Lilly beach dress. For having lunch on the terrace at the club, when something is needed to put on over the bathing suit. What could be cuter than a Lilly print cover-up, with monkeys drinking champagne or elephants dancing the fox-trot, in brilliant unnatural colors?

4. Turtleneck dress. Really just an overgrown cotton turtleneck. Worn for work with a blazer and pumps, or a webbing belt and little tassel loafers (if you're in publishing). Navy blue, maroon, and dark green are the favored colors, since this is a winter dress.

5. Basic shirt dress. A Prep favorite since forever. Adaptable to just about any occasion from country club to Madison Avenue. All cotton, in standard shirting fabrics (pinstripes are cute), with grosgrain accessories.

6. Silk shirt dress. Most often seen in the city on the young professional type. Usually in bright colors, it's the eighties alternative to the Diane von Furstenburg. Goes from work to cocktails to dinner to Pedro's.

WOMEN'S

SKIRTS

Preppy skirts, like Preppy pants, tend to disguise rather than emphasize the female figure. Length is modest. No cinched-in waist, no long slits, no tightness outlining the derriere. Neat but not gaudy might be the best description.

1. Khaki A-line. Worn all year round, with anything from a Lacoste and espadrilles to a tucked shirt and pumps. Because it is an A-line, it is never really in style or out.

2. Wrap. Can be adjusted to compensate for a couple of weeks of hard living (read hard drinking). Often reversible, with strawberries on one side, polka dots on the other. Predominant colors: navy blue, green, red.

3. Calvin Klein jeans. The true genius of Calvin Klein is revealed in his design of a skirt that fits every female body comfortably, and succeeds in flattering them all. Preppies cut the label off the back pocket with nail scissors and wear this skirt with a gold snake belt.

4. Lilly. Typically, a golf skirt (above-the-knee length outer wear). No waistband and straight cut. It shows off those tanned legs to perfection.

5. Gray flannel. The winter version of the khaki A-line. May be pleated or gathered. Best worn with a navy blazer.

6. Kilt. Worn as the school uniform, official or unofficial, and a lifelong staple of the wardrobe. Originality is having a kilt in a tartan you can't buy in the States. Always worn with the kilt pin fastened.

7. Long kilt. Evening wear all winter long (even if it clashes with your escort's plaid trousers), but classic for Christmas Eve. Especially popular for dinner parties in the suburbs, with a cashmere sweater or a blouse and a velvet blazer.

8. Long black velvet. For those really special evenings. Almost always paired with a white stock-tied blouse and pearls, it is usually cut completely straight.

9. Long summer. Featuring an "unusual" motif. Patchwork Lilly fabric, appliqués of the house on the Cape, silkscreen design of ferns from the garden.

10. Optional: plaid taffeta. Dressier than the long kilt, and rather specific to Christmas. Usually worn in the city for slightly formal evenings.

WOMEN'S

PANTS

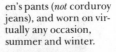

Preppy women would never wear the kind of pants that you have to lie down in to zip. Trousers should fit loosely, at no point emphasizing the figure. The standard cut is constructed like men's, with a stiff waistband, loops for the needlepoint belt, and pockets in the side seam. Legs are straight, not belled, not pegged. Another key style is the trouser without a waistband, which is popular for its comfort factor. Baggy pants are out. So are patch pockets.

1. Khakis. Supremely useful. Either men's khakis or women's pants made of khaki fabric.. The men's variety is best worn with a cable-knit sweater and Tretorns: the women's, with a navy blazer and espadrilles.

2. Wide-wale corduroys. Again, men's or women's depending on your figure. Women are more likely to wear navy blue or hot pink than rust or sage green.

3. Gray flannels. Worn with gold earrings, a turtleneck sweater and a shell belt for cocktail parties, or with a blazer for going to a museum.

4. Lilly. Perfect to wear for an evening picnic at the beach club, or for shopping in Southampton. In the suburbs, considered a bit exotic for everyday wear.

5. Very beat-up jeans. Only Levi's, and only straight-leg. Often worn without a belt, with a man's shirt tucked into them. Casual, but neat.

6. Patchwork. Low waistband, and the patches are often gingham or madras. Worn with espadrilles and a T-shirt.

en's pants (*not* corduroy jeans), and worn on virtually any occasion, summer and winter.

8. Sharkskin. No waistband, and no pockets. These are dress pants for resorts, and are traditionally worn with a wide belt with heavy gold double clasps, and sandals in the same color.

9. Embroidered corduroys. Adopting a style popular in men's wear. To be brought out on occasions like tailgate picnics. Your turtleneck and Shetland sweater must match the colors of your pants.

7. Beige corduroys. The workhorse of the wardrobe. Traditional wom-

WOMEN'S
ACCESSORIES

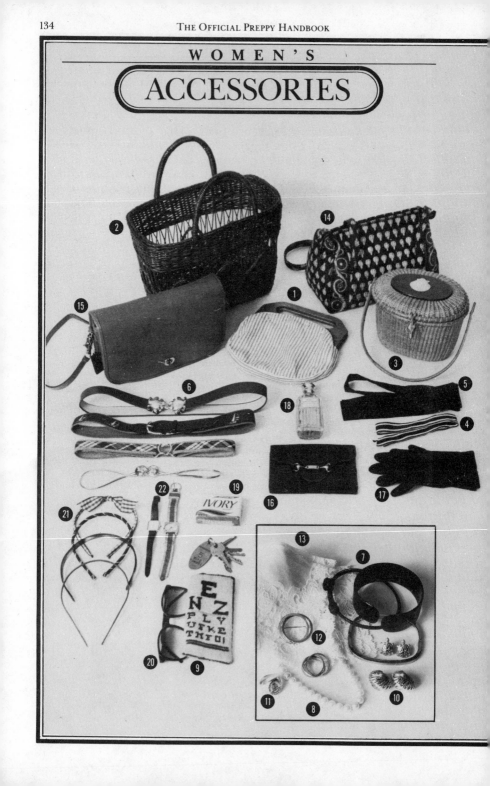

More is more, and it all matches. This is the one area where Prep women display their femininity, piling on accessories with utter disregard for fashion conventions. Note: Prep women never take off their jewelry—pearls on the squash court are perfectly acceptable.

---

1. Bermuda bag. The cloth covers for this bag come in essential Prep colors and button on and off so that your purse can match every outfit. Ideal for monogramming.

2. Straw basket bag. The purse for the woman who doesn't want to carry a purse. For that sporty look Preps love.

3. Lightship basket. Made by cottage industry in Nantucket. The best ones have real scrimshaw on the lids, and are signed and dated by the maker.

4. Grosgrain ribbon. Grosgrain comes in all the bright colors, with neat stripes and polka dots as well as solid colors. Headbands and watchbands should match. Make your own belts to match your favorite ensembles.

5. Foulard bow tie. A softer adaptation of the men's version. It gives that polished air, without looking entirely masculine. If the background of the tie's pattern is navy blue, it can be worn with anything.

6. Belts. Webbed belts have cute motifs such as strawberries and pink and green turtles. The belts with shell clasps have interchangeable leather strips, so they can match everything. Madras with shorts, gold snake belt to dress up.

7. Bracelets. All gold. Often worn in profusion, on the same hand as the watch (also gold). Bangle bracelets don't match, because they're presents from various relatives. Elephant hair is a passing fancy, but the tortoise-shell cuff will be worn until it breaks.

8. Pearls. Everyone has them, and they're usually real (grandmother's). A single strand, of a modest length, with a simple clasp.

9. Needlepoint eyeglass case. If you wear glasses (even sunglasses) the case must be needlepoint. If you can't persuade your aunt to do it, make the case yourself—with your monogram and little violets.

10. Earrings. Ears are pierced at age sixteen, but not a minute sooner. Whimsical shapes like turtles are often preferred in secondary school, while the professional set goes for the knot or shrimp models. They need not be real gold, but of course it's better if they are.

11. Rings. Worn on the ring and pinkie fingers of both hands (the fourth finger of the left hand is left significantly bare until it is decorated with a diamond). Rings are always real gold (in this case, imitations look tacky); favorites are the shrimp, the signet ring, the school ring (if it's flat and simple), and three bands of different colored gold.

12. Circle pin. For the lapel of the blazer, or the cable knit sweater.

13. Handkerchief. Never used, of course. But very lady-like.

14. Provencal print bag from Pierre Deux. These wear out quickly, and have to be replaced every season. Popular with over-25's.

15. Coach bag. Good materials, good workmanship, classic design. Navy blue or wine the best colors: last for years.

16. Gucci wallet. No G's, please. Fine leather, well made, and elegant without being vulgar.

17. Gloves. Leather, lined with silk or cashmere. The third pair this winter.

18. Eau Sauvage. Men's cologne, but that's all right. Perfume is a little *too* feminine for Preps.

19. Ivory soap. The cosmetic kit.

20. Sun glasses. Tortoise-shell frames, just like real glasses. Usually worn pushed up on top of the head.

21. Hairbands. To keep the pageboy in place.

22. Watch. The classic Cartier with a lizard strap, or a man's Timex on a grosgrain band. No stretchy Speidel watchbands, no diamonds.

MEN'S & WOMEN'S

SWEATERS

Apart from being useful in keeping the body warm, sweaters are part of layering, often British, and make dandy accessories. Tie them around your waist, tie them around your neck—great treatment for hand-me-downs (the size doesn't even matter). Sweaters are for collecting—you can never have too many.

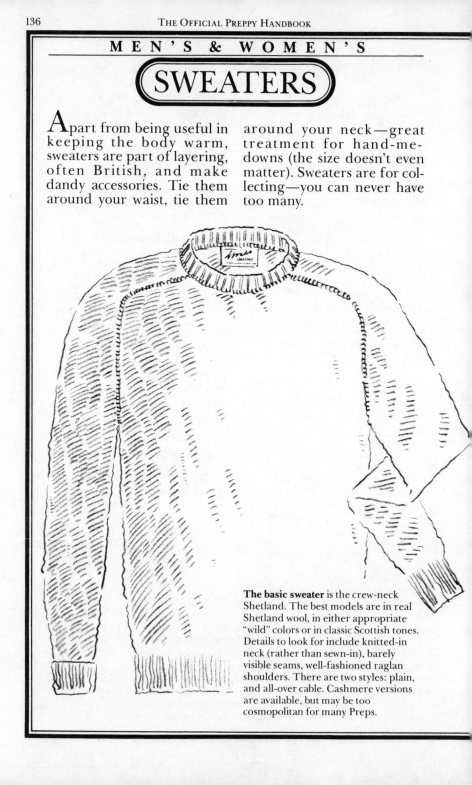

The basic sweater is the crew-neck Shetland. The best models are in real Shetland wool, in either appropriate "wild" colors or in classic Scottish tones. Details to look for include knitted-in neck (rather than sewn-in), barely visible seams, well-fashioned raglan shoulders. There are two styles: plain, and all-over cable. Cashmere versions are available, but may be too cosmopolitan for many Preps.

Ladies' Fair Isle cardigan or pullover. Shetland-type sweater with elaborate yoke, in pattern of contrasting colors, usually against white. In crew neck or Henley-style neck. The four-button neckline opening of Henley cut allows a lusher arrangement of layered collars to show.

L.L. Bean Norwegian pullover. The nearest thing to a Prep membership card. Outdoorsy types in general often have similar sweaters, but the L.L. Bean model is the real thing. Navy blue with white checks, "80 percent unscoured wool for water repellency and 20 percent rayon for strength." The collar will stretch out of shape, allowing plenty of room for layering. Very nice with a pink oxford cloth button-down shirt. For men and women.

Irish fisherman pullover. Must be hand knit in the Aran Isles. Heavy, cream-colored wool with distinctive raised patterns. Originally, each family had its own pattern, so when bodies of lost fishermen washed up on the shore they could be identified. This is a boon around the tennis club. For men and women.

Ladies' plain cardigan. A cardigan without cables. In Shetland wool, with a satin-ribbon facing on the placket. Cut longer than the cable-knit.

Men's cashmere V-neck. A luxury. Often worn under a jacket. Goes with a dress shirt, never with a jersey. Usually in camel, navy, or gray.

Ladies' cable-knit cardigan. Short-waisted with three-quarter-length sleeves. The cables are bountiful, running over the entire sweater. The buttons are knitted in the same color as the sweater. In all colors, wool or cotton.

Tennis pullover. V-neck, cable-knit sweater in cream-colored wool with navy-and-maroon stripes around cuffs, waist, and neckline. Smashing with white flannel trousers, it is also one sweater that looks well with shorts. For men and women.

FROM DESK TO DUCK BLIND
The Look for Men

Basic style for the man never changes because the man never changes. Elderly as a child, youthful as an adult, he is always a mixture of schoolboy and corporate president. One year the corduroys may be embroidered with little ducks, the next year with whales. But there is never, ever, a new look for the man.

1. Go sockless. Socks are frequently not worn on sporting occasions, or on social occasions, for that matter. This provides a year round beachside look that is so desirable that comfort may be thrown aside.

2. Most jewelry is taboo. Cuff links must be small and exquisite. One signet ring is allowed, either a family or school crest. Collar pins are worn, but no tie clips or tacks.

3. Careful grooming. Crucial. Clean shaven—no sideburns, beard or moustache. The hair should be cut conservatively short, but not freakishly so. Straight hair may be either slicked back in a rakish, 1930's gloss, or deftly windblown in a just-back-from-the-regatta tousle. Under no circumstances may a man's hair be combed down-and-across in front, covering the forehead.

4. Outerwear indoors. The Irish fisherman's sweater, hunting shoes, a down vest are all in order at cocktail parties.

5. Boxer shorts. The underwear of choice. Big, baggy, and long. It is not entirely ludicrous, in Prep circles, for the bottom of a man's boxers to peep out from time to time beneath his Bermuda shorts. The boxers are made of cotton. White or solid pastels. The man may be given tartan plaid shorts as a gift, but only by a woman.

6. Layering. Adding or subtracting a layer or two or three can take you from yacht club to board room; from desk to date. Layering means a tweed jacket over a Norwegian sweater over an oxford cloth shirt over a Lacoste. And a down parka over everything. And rubber foul-weather gear over that.

MEN'S

SHOES

When they're checking to see if you're Prep, the first thing they look at is your shoes. From there they go on to the rest of your wardrobe.

The Right Shoes give you a fighting chance. The wrong shoes will break you instantly. These are the Right Shoes.

1. Weejuns. Either penny loafer or tassel variety—both are acceptable. Leather heels, cordovan finish. Worn highly polished or decrepit. May be repaired by winding white adhesive tape around the front part of the shoe.

2. Bean's rubber moccasins. Many people find the moccasin more versatile than the hunting shoe, especially in warm weather. It is worn when other people would wear rubbers, and on any informal occasion in dry weather, too. Bean's Maine Hunting Shoes (not shown). A boot with the same foot as the rubber moccasin, but with the leather upper available in two-inch gradations of height from six to sixteen inches. Only Bean's has the true chain-tread outersole.

3. Brooks Brothers loafers. The grownup version of the Weejun.

Correctly worn in either brown or black with business suits.

4. Gucci loafers. Black. Glove-soft leather. Worn at the country club, never with socks. Definitely post-collegiate.

5. White bucks. Classic oxford style only, please. White suedes ("buckskin") with brick-red crepe sole. Strictly a late-spring and summer shoe. Appropriate for garden parties. Use a chalk bag, if a touch-up is necessary.

6. Bean's other moccasins: blucher, camp (shown here), and ranger oxfords. Ideal casual shoes. The blucher offers a secure fit, as it laces fairly high for a moccasin. The camp moccasin is easy to slip on and off; as comfortable as a bedroom slipper. The ranger oxford's thick sole adds height, making it suitable for long walks.

7. Sperry Top-Siders. The classic sailing shoe, now widely imitated. Sperry's shoe has razor-thin ripple cuts in the sole that give it terrific traction on wet decks. The more salt-stained, the better.

8. Sperry Top-Sider canvas deck shoes. For Preps who find the leather Top-Sider a Prep cliché. Perfect for tennis.

9. Tretorn sneakers. Along with the Sperry Top-Sider canvas deck shoe, this is the tennis shoe of choice.

10. Wing tips. The correct shoes for business dress are hand-constructed, carefully lined and finished, and *do not* have broad running-board soles.

11. Optional: patent leather opera pumps. They look like a cross between a bedroom slipper and a ballet slipper, and they're the one correct shoe for black tie.

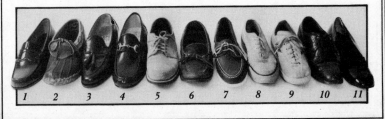

1   2   3   4   5   6   7   8   9   10   11

MEN'S
SHIRTS

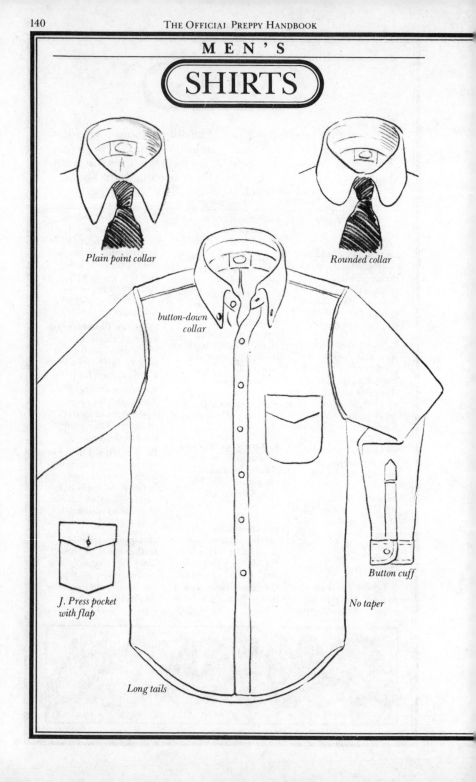

Plain point collar

Rounded collar

button-down
collar

J. Press pocket
with flap

Button cuff

No taper

Long tails

The classic shirt is the Brooks Brothers button-down all-cotton oxford cloth shirt. Pink is the most famous color, and it is widely supposed that no one except Brooks has ever been able to achieve that perfect pink or that perfect roll to the collar. One should have the shirt also in yellow, blue, and white—several in white.

The oxford cloth shirt is also available in a candy stripe on a white background in blue, a pinky-brick shade, yellow, gray, and brown. The candy stripe is especially favored at Prep school. These shirts are a bargain in the boy's department of Brooks Brothers, but the ultimate is the basic, first-floor men's shirt, which is cut fuller than almost any other shirt on earth. Voluminous luxury is the hallmark of the Brooks Brothers shirt. The prices are always reasonable. In warm weather, shirts of blue cotton madras with white collars are in order.

The adult businessman often moves beyond the button-down to a plain collar, with moderately short or rounded points. These shirts may be worn with a collar pin—the kind that looks like a safety pin but actually clips on so as not to harm the shirt. Business shirts (and shirts for relatively formal occasions) may be in a silky, light broadcloth of Pima cotton. A few delicate tattersall designs also belong in the shirt drawer.

Regardless of what the signs in the stores say, there is no such thing as a short-sleeved dress shirt. For jacket-less sportswear, it is far more desirable to roll up long sleeves.

The casual wardrobe should include some L. L. Bean chamois shirts—the cotton flannel that gets better with each washing, and some plaid Viyella shirts in neatly tailored models.

The sport shirt of choice is the Lacoste. Only the all-cotton model will do, the one with cap sleeves with the ribbed edging, narrow collar and two-button placket (never buttoned).

The Lacoste

A couple of polo shirts in even, narrow, horizontal stripes (red and navy, navy and white, yellow and white) are worth owning.

Velour is not Preppy, and should never appear anywhere in the Prep wardrobe.

MEN'S

TROUSERS

There is only one cut for men's trousers—straight leg, neither tapered nor flared. Belt loops should be slim and, ideally, should not drop below the waistband. Side pockets may slant slightly, but it is better if they open along the side seam of the pants. Unless a pant is of a very heavy material, it should be cuffed. The cuffs should be one and one quarter inches wide. Flaps over the rear pockets are a nice touch, as is a watch pocket on the right front. *Pleats are wrong.* One wears the pants a little short—especially khakis.

1. Khakis. Also called chinos. Pure cotton only. Tempered by washing and wearing to a soft finish.

2. Wide-wale corduroys. In soft, country colors or loud party colors. At least one pair of embroidered corduroys is a must—the specific motif may vary according to region and, to some extent, taste.

3. Gray flannels. A must. For college and Prep school interviews. For lunch at the Palm Court with Grandmother. For any occasion when you just don't feel up to putting on a suit—or when you don't own a suit. The flannels are worn with a basic blue blazer.

4. White ducks. For lawn parties. Worn with summer jackets, tennis sweaters, and/or white bucks. Popular on deck. Keep them meticulously clean.

5. Poplin and canvas. In whoopie colors. Nantucket Reds fit into this category. Worn anytime.

De rigueur at country- and yacht-club affairs, with a blazer and club tie.

6. Seersucker. Usually part of a suit, also cool and pleasant for summer separate wear.

7. Four-panel. Each of the four large pieces of fabric from which the pants are constructed is in a different (Prep) color. Available in wide- and fine-wale corduroy, and in some poplins as well.

8. Oxford cloth. Like shirts, only pants. In the basic shirts colors; the best of these trousers are lined.

9. Lilly. Wild hard-core resort wear. Crazy, almost tropical prints, the name "Lilly" is always hidden in the print, which is hand screened on duck. Practically an admission requirement at many country and yacht clubs.

10. Wool plaid. Classic stadium wear for alumni. In authentic tartans, preferably connected to one's own family. Worn with a tweed jacket and an Irish fisherman's sweater, or with a tuxedo jacket for winter black-tie affairs.

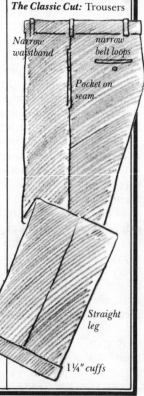

The Classic Cut: Trousers

Narrow waistband

narrow belt loops

Pocket on seam

Straight leg

1¼" cuffs

MEN'S
SUITS AND JACKETS

The suit jacket is a natural shoulder, three-button, single-breasted model. It is not a "fitted" cut; rather, it is cut free and easy for comfort and a baggy look. The pockets are straight and have flaps.

1. Wool worsted suit. For business. In a fine gray herringbone, a blue pin stripe, a gray chalk stripe.

2. Cotton poplin suit. For summer, in khaki or olive drab.

3. Seersucker suit. To justify the straw boater. Especially natty.

4. Optional: tweed suit—a nice luxury for the country gentleman. It should be worn in the company of a large dog.

5. The blue blazer. It is the wardrobe's backbone—or exoskeleton, really. If you could only own one jacket, this would be it. It has three buttons, is single-breasted, and comes in soft flannel for cool weather and hopsacking for warm weather. The double-breasted blazer is worn by larger men, especially on board large power boats.

6. Tweed. A couple of burly, country tweed jackets in the same basic blazer cut belong in the wardrobe. Herringbone, houndstooth, or Harris tweed, of course.

The Classic Cut:
Jacket

conservative lapel

natural shoulders

no shaping

3-button front

Regimental blazer button. Hardy brass buttons, bearing the insignia of real British regiments—although it rarely matters which. College insignia buttons are similar, with the addition of enamel in the school colors. It does matter which *college*.

Monogrammed blazer button. In gold plate, usually. Men's buttons have sturdy, block initials; women's buttons may be in a flowing cursive, although the more masculine style is, of course, preferred by Prep women.

MEN'S

ACCESSORIES

Know the man by the accessories he keeps. They are never flashy, always carefully crafted. Monograms are discreet, but ubiquitous. The most beloved accessories are inherited from male progenitors.

1. The silver belt buckle. Monogrammed, sterling silver, rectangular—it is bought without the belt at the best silver store in town. Plain belts without buckles may then be purchased separately (Brooks Brothers carries them) and easily attached.

2. Cuff links. The wafer-thin, two-button kind, never the swivel-backed version. Your initials go on them, or yours on one and your wife's or girlfriend's on the other. Simple, flat gold or silver designs.

3. Knot cuff links. The inexpensive alternative. Knotted silk cord, available in numerous color combinations.

4. Collar pin. In gold (or gold plate). The correct kind is designed to look like a safety pin when worn, but it doesn't actually puncture the shirt. Look for the shorter collar pin, if there is a choice.

5. Elegant lighter. Even if you don't smoke, useful for chivalrous gestures.

6. Cummerbund. Worn with a tuxedo.

7. Striped watchband. The band of choice is made from grosgrain ribbon.

8. Surcingle belt. Available with plain webbing, stripes, embroidered designs.

9. Ribbon belt. Grosgrain ribbon. Brass loops. You can never own enough.

10. Key chain. One more place for the duck, the sailboat, the tennis racket.

11. Garters. These are for men's silk socks. Used with formal wear.

12. Ring. Gold signet only. Either family crest or school crest. Worn one at a time only, on the fourth finger of either hand. Upon becoming married, a man may wish to wear a wedding ring (plain gold band) on the left ring finger.

13. Flask. In pewter or silver, often curved to fit the body. Monogrammed. Look for models with attached caps.

14. Eyeglasses. "Full-view" model, *light* tortoise shell only. Also, tortoise-shell-covered wire frames.

15. Straw boater. For the seersucker suit.

16. Tennis hat. Floppy, white cotton.

17. Umbrella. Just in case.

18. Scarf. In school colors.

19. Eau Sauvage. The his-and-hers cologne favored by Preps.

20. Needlepoint belt. Gift of a creative woman, always monogrammed.

21. Web-with-ribbon belt. Motif-embroidered webbing stitched to nautical webbing; brass rings.

22. Suspenders. With leather tabs for waistline buttons in trousers; never clips.

23. Long ties. The rep tie has diagonal stripes woven into ribbed silk. Club ties are Jacquard woven silk foulard with embroidered elements—club insignias, coats of arms, school mascots. Also acceptable are the printed foulard with diagonally aligned diamond figures, the cotton madras tie, and the blunt-ended (Rooster-style) knit tie. The standard width is three and one half inches at the widest part of the tie, but two and seven eighths is often seen. The *de rigueur* knot is the four-in-hand. The point of the tie should land at your navel. A Windsor knot may be used in order to give bulk to a tie of light-weight material.

24. Bow ties. Worn in two styles, straight or butterfly. The butterfly should not be more than two inches at the widest part. Rep stripes, polka dots, madras, and foulard are the preferred patterns. With a tuxedo, black silk or ribbed satin.

CUMMERBUND GEOGRAPHY

Men from the Midwest and the South favor bright colors. Their idea of black tie may include a Lilly cummerbund (possibly patchwork) and brilliant yellow pants. Or a cummerbund woven from pink ribbons in different patterns. Baltimore men particularly love needlepoint cummerbunds, which their mothers make for them. They correspond to everyday needlepoint belts, but the colors can be brighter and the design more festive. The best have significant little items on them such as crossed oars, sailboats, and ivy leaves. New Yorkers tend to keep black tie simple and restrained. Maroon silk (tie and cummerbund match) would be very creative, as would a bow tie that's so small that it has to have belonged to a great-grandfather.

MEN'S & WOMEN'S

SUMMER WEAR

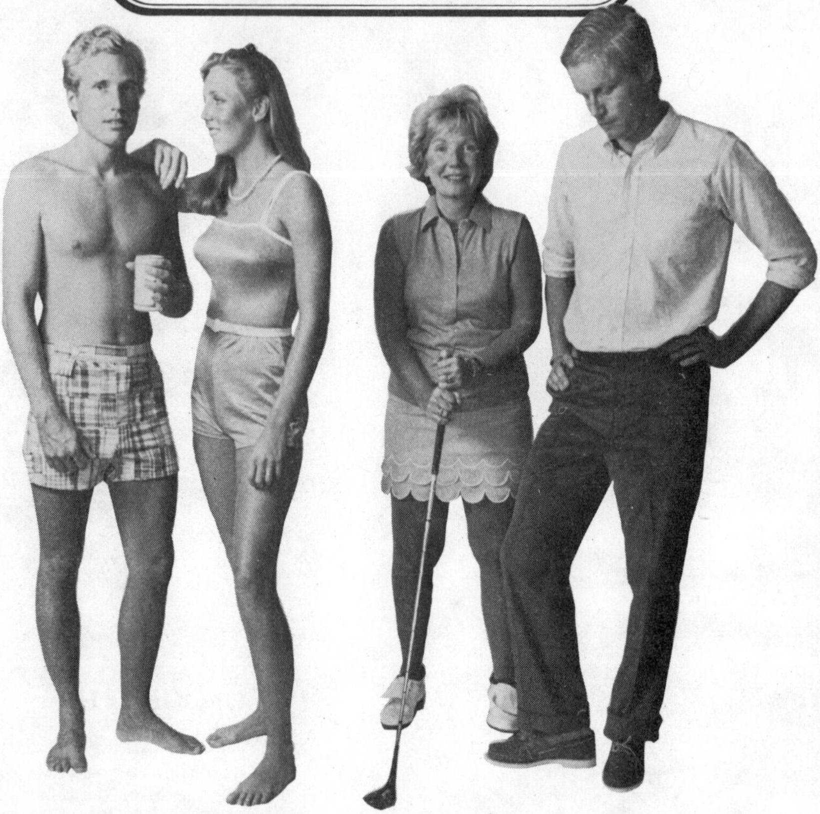

Madras swim trunks. Plain and boxy. The Prep man has no interest in looking daring or sexy on the beach. Because these are made of cotton, they never fully dry out if they are used daily.

One piece boy-cut bathing suit. Prep women are modest. No matter how firm their figures, five years after marriage they inevitably purchase the athletic, if somewhat sexless, one-piece bathing suits. This may be due to Mummy's urging that it just isn't *right* to wear anything a little more daring.

Golfing outfit. Golf clothes are popular among golfers and non-golfers alike. The skirts are short, and look super with kiltie-style golf shoes. Pastel colored sleeveless shirts are coordinated for the complete look.

Nantucket Reds. These well-loved Reds, originally a brick-red cotton canvas, have faded to the requisite cherry pink that only authentic Natucket-bought Reds can achieve. Can be paired with any top—our sailor chooses a white oxford cloth button-down. Shown here with Top-Siders.

Preppies couldn't let this most important of seasons go by with- out some wardrobe response all their own.

Khaki hiking shorts with button-down shirt. These shorts are comfortable for movement since they flare out, and they can be dressed up with a leather belt, as shown here. Worn with monogrammed striped shirt and Tretorns.

Bermuda shorts and Lacoste. An integral part of the man's wardrobe. He wears them cut like dress trousers, only hemmed just above the knee. Solid cotton duck (shown here) or madras. Pictured with webbed belt, Lacoste, and Top-Siders.

Tennis whites. The color revolution in tennis wear has not hit the Prep world. The shorts are old, and all cotton. The shirt is a Lacoste or similar cotton jersey. The shoes are Tretorns or Top-Sider canvas sneakers, worn with socks. The sweatband is optional. Everything is white.

Lilly petal bikini. Lilly Pulitzer, a major force in Prep resort wear, favors whimsical prints and four colors: Shocking (pink), turquoise, yellow, and lime. Her bikini is the ultimate swimwear for the young lithe Prep female.

MEN'S & WOMEN'S
OUTERWEAR

Camel's hair polo coat.
With its heavy-duty padded shoulders, loose-fitting body, and slim, no-nonsense collar, the camel's hair polo coat is the quintessential Prep winter coat for women. It evokes the Seven Sister schools in the 1950's. It's a classic: warm, functional, Republican.

Foul-weather gear. (For men and women.) This two-piece rubber or vinyl-coated rain suit is at its most functional on deck in a storm. For that very reason it is delightful city wear. It says that you've just popped in to that business meeting from your sloop. From Top-Sider in orange or L. L. Bean in yellow.

Field coat. (For men and women.) Preferably from Bean's, although competitors carry equivalent models. This is in light-brown, water-repellent canvas, with green corduroy trim. It looks (and is) exceptionally functional, especially for the tiny percentage of people who actually wear it for hunting.

In a way, according to Prep rules of layering clothes, there *is* no outerwear—there is just a continuing series of concentric garments. Outerwear for the Preppy is simply the last layer donned.

Tyrolean jacket. The only word to describe the Tyrolean jacket is cute. It is cut short—waist length— has no collar, has contrasting trim, darling print lining, and silver buttons. Fashioned of loden cloth, it warms a small portion of the upper torso and must be worn over a cotton turtleneck for full effect.

Burberry. (For men and women.) The full Burberry cotton trench coat. Equipped with grenade loops, a double-layered back to keep shoulders dry in the trenches, a camel's-hair wool lining that unbuttons, turns inside out, and becomes a robe. The belt is tied, *never* buckled.

Chesterfield. The most bankerly of coats. Right for all dress occasions. In gray herringbone wool, usually. Often with a velvet collar. A tartan cashmere or dotted silk scarf looks fantastic with it. Like a tuxedo, the Chesterfield makes any man wearing it look tall and handsome.

HOW TO TALK TO A SALESPERSON

You talk to a salesperson the way you'd talk to the tennis pro or the mailman—politely. If you know the person's name, use it. Always say "please" and "thank you" and phrase requests politely—in other words, noblesse oblige. When shopping in The Right Stores, remember the accepted words of praise are "divine," and "darling" for women, "super" and "outstanding" for men. Keeping the following dos and don'ts in mind will enhance the joy of building The Look into your wardrobe.

DOs	DON'Ts
1. Let the salesperson know immediately that you really do not have the time to putter about and will rely on him to find what you want quickly. If you have no intention of buying anything, say so without smiling.	1. Trust the judgment or look for approval from any salesperson who wants you to think he's your friend, or if he's a man, wears argyle socks with a suit.
2. Announce your preferred labels. (Men: Use the designer's last name or initials only. Women: You're on a first-name basis.)	2. Tell him your size. Let him guess—he'll remember it on your next visit.
3. Get the salesperson's first and last name and call him by his first.	3. Answer irrelevant questions about how much you want to spend, or ask what's on sale.
4. Make a casual remark that you regularly play golf with his boss—or remember when he was called Stinky—it can't hurt.	4. Listen to his stories about his friends or relatives, unless they're your neighbors.
5. Consider at length the various monogram styles available, but settle for the same you've always worn.	5. Let him touch you while fitting or follow you into the dressing room.
6. Ask about home delivery for future phone and mail orders, and pick up the store catalog for the bathroom.	6. Pay in cash or buy anything you can't return later, unless it's a gift you would like to forget.

WHERE TO SHOP
Stores

Part of the burden true Preppies must bear is that they cannot buy their clothes in just any department store or shopping mall. Only certain elite stores are recognized in the unwritten code Preppies live by. Luckily, however, these Approved Stores are plentiful throughout the country, making it possible for children to progress routinely from diapers to gray flannel without skipping a beat.

Of course, the Preppy look has a number of manifestations, and there are stores that cater to each. For instance, within a football punt's distance of any self-respecting college campus stands the College Shop. This establishment is often run by a middle-aged alumnus who was never able to leave his fraternity days completely behind, and who now lives vicariously through his young clientele by outfitting them in corduroys and cable-knits. Then there's the local marine supply store, always a good source for the sailing gear that's essential whether or not you ever actually get near the water.

Each of the Right Stores generally has its own loyal following, and many need no introduction. But should you ever be caught in unfamiliar territory, the following handy guide will see you through almost any emergency.

L. L. Bean, 6936 Casco Street, Freeport, Maine. Bean's is nothing less than Prep mecca. The showroom is open 24 hours a day, 365 days a year; consequently, a middle-of-the-night pilgrimage here is one of the Prep rites of passage. Record your trip by having your photo taken in front of the canoes downstairs.

The Country Store of Concord, 15 Monument Street, Concord, Mass. (main store). Branches all over New England. This is where the Pine Manor girls shop for their monogrammed sweaters, Skyr turtlenecks, and little-gold-turtle-buckled belts. Any Saturday at Quincy Market, this is the label most frequently sighted.

Murray's Toggery Shop, 62 Main Street, Nantucket. (Also in Vineyard Haven, Martha's Vineyard.) Murray's is the birthplace of the legendary all-cotton Nantucket Reds, and, especially since the store's recent expansion, a great place to spend a rainy afternoon. Official outfitters for all island activities: Cliff Road cocktail parties, Sankaty Head golf, Erica Wilson's needlepoint class, etc.

Hillhouse, 135 Thayer Street, Providence, R.I. One of the more interesting—not to mention, Prep—spots in Providence, Hillhouse is fairly hard-core and offers a good selection of the basics. Store windows often pay homage to Brown's football and hockey teams.

J. Press, 262 York St., New Haven, Conn. Branches in Cambridge, New York City, and San Francisco. J. Press has catered, since 1902, to the ultraconservatives of the Old Guard who feel Brooks Brothers is too trendy and women's departments are an abomination. While custom tailoring is a specialty here, the store also features accessories that complete the J. Press look: club ties with every imaginable insignia and blazer buttons adorned with the hallowed crest of your alma mater.

Brooks Brothers, Madison Avenue and 44th St., New York, N.Y. (main store). Branches in twenty-three cities and Japan. Established in 1818, Brooks Brothers ranks as the Oldest Preppy Store Still Alive. As creator of the Wall Street look and bastion of the narrow tie and collar, Brooks is the epitome of the very traditional Preppy store, and in many circles, shopping here is a religion. Trivia: Brooks gave Ralph Lauren his start—as a tie salesman.

Paul Stuart, Madison Avenue at 45th St., New York, N.Y. Right next door to Brooks, Paul Stuart has established itself in the more sophisticated Progressive Prep category. Excellent women's department upstairs.

The Bermuda Shop, Madison Avenue and 57th St., New York, N.Y. The Bermuda Shop specializes in pretentious salespeople and tailored Prep fashions for women. Always has J. G. Hook's current line. Particularly nice sweaters and beachwear room.

Burton Clothing Ltd., Fifth Avenue and 41st St., New York, N.Y. You might say this is the speakeasy of Preppy stores. In Burton's series of well-appointed rooms on the second floor of a midtown office building, you'll find a good selection of men's and women's Prepwear at cheaper-than-Madison Avenue prices.

H. Stockton, Lenox Square, Atlanta, Ga. Located in the heart of Southern Prep territory, H. Stockton is a popular spot with the hard core of both sexes for recharging their wardrobes with clothes in "100 percent" fabrics and no-shame color combinations.

Harold's, 88 Highland Park Village, Dallas, Tex. When Dallas women, in their off-the-ranch hours, want to look as though they've been shopping on Boston's Newbury Street, they head for Harold's, which features khakis and tweeds by J. G. Hook, Villager, and others.

Leslie and Co., 1749 South Post Oak, Houston, Tex. Leslie and Co. is Houston's Preppy stronghold and carries classic clothes with the store's own label, as well as such familiar names as Lacoste, Bert Pulitzer, and Cole-Haan for men; Ralph Lauren, Barry Bricken, and Evan-Picone for women.

Land's End, 2317 North Elsten, Chicago, Ill. On the shores of Lake Michigan, Land's End specializes in outdoorsy Prep and offers particularly wide selections of sweaters (of both wool and cotton), boating shoes (from Top-Siders to Sperry's fourteen-inch boot), and the store's own Square Rigger canvas luggage.

Molterer Sports, 520 East Cooper Street, Aspen, Colo. When Preppies feel an urge for a few weeks on the slopes, their go-for-it philosophy draws them to the ultimate snow country of Aspen, and to Molterer Sports for the latest and most expensive skiwear and equipment.

Cable Car Clothiers, 150 Post St., San Francisco, Calif. "San Francisco's British Goods Store Since 1939." Cable Car's clothing selection and the store's ads use of such terms as "handsome," "classic," and "superior fit" are dead giveaways that this is a West Coast clone of Brooks Brothers.

Trimingham Bros., Front Street, Hamilton, Bermuda. A major reason the pink-and-green island of Bermuda is such a popular Preppy vacation spot. Sales of reasonably priced Fair Isle sweaters, tartan kilts, and Bermuda bags by the gross are not unusual.

Sousa & Lefkovits, 2251 S. Sepulveda Blvd., W. Los Angeles, Calif. and 621 S. B Street, Tustin, Calif. These out-of-the-way, elegantly high-tech warehouses sell fine quality, natural-fiber clothes at 30% - 40% less than the usual prices. By locating away from shopping thoroughfares the stores keep the rent down—and enhance the sensation for customers of discovering a real "find."

R.I.P

The Late Great Stores

Best & Co. 641 Fifth Ave., New York, N.Y. and branches. A name synonymous with Harris tweeds and velvet hats, the store where a child's first haircut was documented with photographs and a ribbon-tied lock of hair. A source close to the deceased has been quoted as saying, "What killed Best's was a split personality in its old age. 'Stage Nine' was the final blow." Stage Nine, the renovated ninth floor for juniors got winded by the frenzy of the sixties, while the rest of Best stayed contentedly, stolidly Greenwich. Best & Co. finally succumbed to uncertainty—it is survived by Saks Fifth Avenue and Bergdorf Goodman. There was a special mourning service for nannies and grandmothers.

Peck & Peck. 54th and Fifth Ave., New York, N.Y. Long known as "old reliable," Peck & Peck was spoken of as "the sensible place to shop." In the 1950's a young woman would always check in at one of the New York stores before going off to college—now she has to rely on one of the remaining branches. It is survived by the Bermuda Shop and assorted specialty stores across the country. Services were held at the Cosmopolitan Club. Mourners were advised to wear something simple.

Abercrombie & Fitch. 46th and Madison Ave., New York, N.Y. Death came as a shock to the many patrons who'd purchased sporting, hunting, fishing, and "fashion" goods, originally on their parents' and grandparents' charge accounts. Unable to keep any of their signature English tackle bags in stock, the store passed away with dignity, with customers still awaiting the leather-trimmed canvas shoulder bags. The spacious store's most popular departments were the adult game and odd equipment floors, the top two of the main branch. Mourners who are expecting new shipments of the bags are invited to shop at Hunting World, 16 East 53rd St., New York, N.Y. 10022 where more expensive versions should be available indefinitely.

DePinna. 650 Fifth Ave., New York, N.Y. Just a vague memory, this austere store was where parents shopped for their children, ignoring the adult clothing departments. In its heyday, DePinna's enjoyed a bustling six-floor home. As its illness set in, it withered away to four and then part of four floors. Mummies adored DePinna. "It was so convenient, just across the street from Best's," whimpered one disconsolate mother of three. "I don't know where I'll ever find another loden cloth duffel coat with horn toggles for my sons." Many Mummies shopped at DePinna prior to a full Brooks Brothers engorgement, but it appears that they will have to start there earlier now. In lieu of flowers, mourners were referred to Brooks Brothers' boys department and Saks Fifth Avenue.

WHERE TO SHOP
Catalogs

Between tennis, Bloodies, backgammon, Bloodies, sailing, and Bloodies, even the most ardent Preppy may not have time to shop for the wardrobe he or she needs to maintain the proper lifestyle. And after all, you can wear Daddy's old shirts for only so long.

The answer to this dilemma is, of course, catalog shopping.

A tradition for over a hundred years, shopping by mail evolved as established stores' customers who moved away found they couldn't live without those suits old Joseph had been custom-making for them for years. "Please, Joseph," they would write. "You must get up one of those suits you've been custom-making for me for years and send it along right away." These retail stores soon began the practice of compiling illustrations and descriptions of their popular items into pamphlets. Thus, the catalog was born.

Today, Preppy catalogs are a common sight sandwiched between *The New Yorker* and *Town & Country* on many an elite coffee table. And catalog shopping is a multimillion-dollar phenomenon.

It's important to note that the major problem with shopping from ordinary store catalogs—not knowing what the item you've ordered will be like until it actually arrives—doesn't apply here. When ordering from a Preppy catalog, it doesn't matter that you can't examine these items because, true to the Prep status quo, they haven't changed in years. Just take a look in your parents' closet and you'll see exactly what UPS is bringing your way.

L. L. Bean, 6936 Casco Street, Freeport, Maine 04033. (207) 865-3111. A Down-East extravaganza, the Bean catalog is the biggest seller of the rugged New England Prep look. Never mind that you don't really need a game pocket in your back-to-school field coat. Home of the ubiquitous rubber moccasin and the Norwegian sweater. Let that label show!

The Talbots, 164 North St., Hingham, Mass. 02043. (617) 749-7830. Behind the red door on every Talbots catalog cover is the best selection of women's Prep fashions anywhere. Unlike the other catalogs, Talbots carries a lot of designer names so the clothes here are a rare combination of Preppy, tasteful, and sophisticated. It *is* possible. (Note: great sale at the store twice a year.)

Carroll Reed, North Conway, N.H. 03860. (603) 447-2511. The best part of the Carroll Reed catalog is always the beautiful New Hampshire landscape on the cover. Clothes here (mostly for women) fall into two categories—cute or matronly—though the store itself, which has a lot of nice skiwear, is better than the catalog. "Fun" prints a specialty.

The Tog Shop, Lester Square, Americus, Ga. 31709. (912) 924-9371. Need a pair of frog-print slacks or a terry cloth halter jumpsuit? This is the place, a bizarre hybrid of Carroll Reed and Frederick's of Hollywood.

Lilly Pulitzer, 8 Via Parigi, Palm Beach, Fla. 33480. (305) 655-0112. Shopping from the Lilly catalog is a Preppy's idea of walking on the wild side. The clothes here—men's and women's resort wear—are totally out of control in prints famous for their distinctively intense shades of lime green, shocking pink, and electric yellow. Count on at least four women at any yacht club gathering to be wearing one of Lilly's whalebone-bodiced dresses.

Jos. A. Bank Clothiers, 109 Market Place, Baltimore, Md. 21202. (301) 837-8838. With its very conservative Ivy League clothes—basically men's suits, shirts, ties, etc.—Jos. A. Bank is somewhat of a less-expensive, mail-order version of Brooks Brothers. Button-down oxford cloth shirt a real bargain.

Eddie Bauer, Fifth and Union, Seattle, Wash. 98124. (800) 426-8020. Camping, backpacking, and canoeing (especially if done in Vermont or Oregon) are popular activities among the outdoorsy Prep set. From sleeping bags to a combination stove/survival kit, and down clothing from head to toe, the Eddie Bauer catalog is *the* source.

Orvis, Manchester, Vt. 05254. (802) 362-1300. Touts its catalog as "the bible for serious fishermen since 1856." Originally, for fishing and hunting gear only, Orvis now also carries very traditional, tweedy clothes for men and women, and features such obscure but

necessary items as silk long johns and moleskin trousers. Big on ducks and dogs.

Chris Craft, Algonac, Mich. 48001. (800) 521-3230. Perhaps Chris Craft's biggest customers are landlocked Preppies who've discovered that they too can achieve the all-important yachting look by ordering sailing gear from Chris Craft that will never experience the ocean's spray. The catalog also features a variety of other Prep clothing for men and women, jewelry, nautical *objets de Prep* and gift-type items such as traditional brass pineapple door knockers, digital-clock pens, and gold-plated toothbrushes.

Gokeys, 84 South Wabasha St., St. Paul, Minn. 55172. (612) 292-3911. While Gokeys is best known for its distinctive $220 knee-high snakeproof boots, this catalog is also good for high-quality Harris tweeds, sweaters, corduroys, and hunting gear. Check out Gokeys' down comforter with the duck-and-pond print cover—a classic!

POSTAGE RATES TO FREEPORT, MAINE

If you're ordering, put a fifteen-cent stamp on the order blank stapled to the inside of the catalog. If you've made a tracing of your foot for them, check at the post office to see that you don't need more postage. If you're returning anything, use the box it came in. Third class rates from New York to Freeport start at $1.71 for a one-pound package. The catalog helpfully includes the weight of each item: the Heavy Duty Haversack weighs one pound nine ounces; a pair of Blucher moccasins, about two pounds.

THE VIRTUES OF PINK AND GREEN

The wearing of the pink and the green is the surest and quickest way to group identification within the Prep set. There is little room for doubt or confusion when you see these colors together—no one else in his right mind would sport such a chromatically improbable juxtaposition.

Not just any shade of pink and green will do. Seafoam green and girl-baby pink would be as unthinkable as a wide tie or Famolare wedgies. No, this is unashamed, outrageous go-for-broke hot-hot pink and hubba-hubba electric wild lime green.

To help in understanding the full potential of this color combination, we have prepared a little exercise. You will need a pink and a green crayon (Crayola yellow-green and carnation pink) or, better yet, felt-tip markers (Flair pink and green are acceptable, or Pentel numbers 111 and 109). Study the figures above carefully. When you have fully absorbed all the details, color them in. Color the areas numbered 1 pink. Color the areas numbered 2 green. Then color your friend's copy of *The Official Preppy Handbook* differently. The possibilities are endless.

CHAPTER 5

THE
REAL
WORLD

The Young Executive Years

THE CITY AS SUBURBIA

Most starting jobs don't pay enough for the young Prep to be able to afford a house in the suburbs right away. So you spend a few years in the big city.

There's a real air of adventure about urban living that makes the experience exhilarating. It also has a limit in sight: most Preps know that ultimately they will move to the suburbs to spawn—in the interim, the city is home.

One of the key characteristics of the best Prep schools is conformity, and this is a virtual requirement of Prep life in the metropolis. That, combined with the clannishness and the quasi-Masonic network of Prepdom, allows Preps even in the largest and—one would think—most democratic cities to keep themselves to themselves.

Ways to meet people present themselves as the Prep version of metropolitan life takes form. Your roommates, for example (even if they were your college roommates), will have new friends in the city, and you can meet *their* Prep school friends. You will naturally join a club, if only to have some place to hang out and play squash in midtown. Before long, the party circuit will have swept you up—whether you go for the hard-core black-tie charity ball routine, or prefer more modest dinner parties for twelve, there will be an unending source of new acquaintances. And, since you are all Preps, even if you haven't met before, you'll have a lot in common.

Gradually, the city becomes a small community. Everyone you know lives in the same neighborhood. They frequent the same Chinese laundries and subway stops. You run into each other at Gristede's; it's really just like the country. Brooks Brothers on a Saturday in the winter is as good for catching up on the gossip as a suburban post office any day.

Inevitably you will get married. It is a natural and proper step—most Prep social pursuits are undertaken with the choice of a spouse implicit. It is then, paired off two by two, just like Noah's animals, that the young Prep couple will decide that the city is no longer suburb enough. They move to Connecticut.

A HOME OF YOUR OWN (ALMOST)

The First Apartment

The move to the big city may represent the first time you sign a lease. But you are not alone in this—signing with you are the apartment-mates-to-be. This apartment is for each of you the great vehicle of transition—from college life to professional life, from adolescence to adulthood, from Mummy and Daddy's summer house to your living room.

The Kitchen

1. Waring blender for mixing daiquiris.
2. Toaster oven with crumbs and tin foil.
3. Silverware drawer. *Includes*: four corkscrews; two dull steel knives; silverware stolen from the college dining hall; chopsticks.
4. Sink. Full of dishes.
5. Dish drainer. Full of dishes.
6. Plenty of coffee mugs.
7. Glassware. Includes set of Old Fashioned glasses from Orvis with woodcocks painted on them.

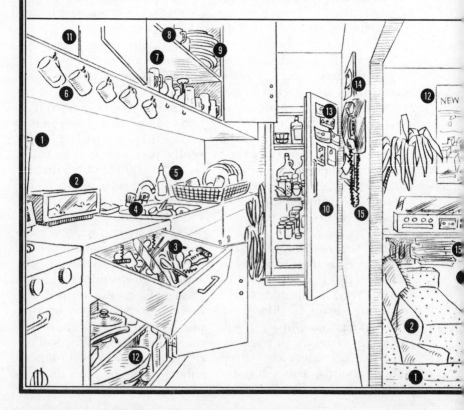

8. Leftover china from everyone's parents' summer houses.
9. Eight matching plates from someone's Mummy's first set of china.
10. Refrigerator. *Contents of freezer*: Absolut vodka, old Stouffer's French Bread Pizza, almost-empty trays of ice cubes. *Contents of refrigerator*: half-empty magnums of Folonari Soave; jar of capers; jar of olives; lemon with one slice cut out; Dijon mustard; horseradish; pint of sour milk; four cans of Miller; tin of deviled ham.
11. Food cupboard. *Contents*: instant coffee, Twinings Earl Grey Tea; Coffee-mate; little packets of soy sauce, duck sauce, mustard; opened box of spaghetti; Raisin Bran; can of tuna fish; bouillon cubes; a can of snails some dumb guest brought months ago.
12. Drano, extra garbage bags, booze (two bottles of Scotch; three of exotic rum from the islands; a premium gin).
13. On the refrigerator (held in place with magnets shaped like fruit): post card from Bermuda from former flame; post card from the Cape from one roommate on vacation; post card from Disneyland from roommate slumming on business trip; invitation to wedding of former flame; invitation to charity ball for the benefit of indigent Russian nobility.
14. On the bulletin board by the phone: phone number of the nearest pizza place that delivers; phone number of the nearest Chinese place that delivers; list of who owes how much money for staples; list (begun six months ago and abandoned after three weeks) of who is supposed to do which chores.
15. Phone cord stretched out from people walking to fridge to get out a beer while talking.

The Living Room

1. Haitian cotton couch (hide-a-bed) from Jenifer House.
2. Needlepoint pillows.
3. Glass and chrome coffee table with one rickety leg.
4. Bowl of matches from watering holes around the world.
5. Stubborn spider plant.
6. Three weeks' worth of *New York Times* and *Wall Street Journal*.
7. Dhurrie rug from Conran's.
8. Danish modern table from parents' first apartment.
9. Salt and pepper shakers from school cafeteria.
10. Plates from dinner.
11. Stereo from college on cinder block-and-plywood shelving.
12. Steinberg poster of New York.
13. Canvas director's chairs in designer color.
14. Books: Samuelson's *Economics*, E.B. White's *Letters* and *Essays*, complete Shakespeare, the *American Heritage Dictionary*, the complete works of Garry Trudeau; an atlas; two or three Sierra Club books, including *On the Loose*; complete short stories of John Cheever.
15. Records. *Collection should include*: Ella Fitzgerald singing Cole Porter; Ella Fitzgerald singing Jerome Kern; Frank Sinatra singing Cole Porter; Frank Sinatra's *Ol' Blue Eyes Is Back*; three Whiffenpoof albums; Mozart's 35th Symphony; Peter Allen; Elvis Costello; Beach Boys; *The Divine Miss M.*

PINSTRIPES IN THE P.M.

The best socializing in the Prep world is done at parties. And now that you're paying income tax, you'll start going to—and giving—grown-up parties.

Of all the important party-giving principles, the greatest is Never Run out of Liquor. (The corollary, Never Run out of Ice, gets more important when you are older and more discriminating.) Other important points for hosting Properly Prep Affairs:

More men than women. Most of the party-givers are women. They like being surrounded by men. However, since the men are quick to perceive an imbalance, it's best to keep the ratio near two to one.

Ostentation is out. If it looks as though you've taken a lot of trouble, everyone feels uncomfortable.

Innovation is optional. It is also usually wasted. It gets discouraging to serve homemade pesto at dinner for eight, when you realize they don't really like basil at all.

Always be prepared for dancing. If you don't have a stereo, someone helpful will walk ten blocks to get his. If your living room is minute but you have a porch or a terrace, they'll turn around the speakers and dance there. Move everything breakable.

THE BASIC PARTIES

The Large Cocktail Party. This is the party where you pay back all the invitations you have received over the year. You invite as many people as you can fit into your apartment, and they all arrive with friends. By eight o'clock no one can move, and six people are permanently wedged against the table where the food is: pretzels, hunks of supermarket Cheddar, and potato chips with onion dip. Drinks are jug wine and a refrigerator full of beer. At 10:30, everyone has gone off to dinner with someone they have a little crush on.

The Small Cocktail Party. More carefully planned. About twenty people come up after work, have two or four drinks, and leave. This is a close imitation of an adult's party; real glasses are used (every Preppy household, even those of recent college graduates, has three dozen cocktail glasses), real liquor is served (albeit house brands), and the food is a bit more elaborate than at the mob party. This means Knorr's vegetable soup mix in the dip instead of onion, and a piece of Jarlsberg on a plate with Triscuits.

The Dinner Party. There are two reasons for giving a dinner party: paying back and pursuing. Though the guest list for the former promises an evening of boredom, the latter is carefully planned to conceal from the quarry the reason for his (or her) being there. When guests are invited, they invariably ask, "What can I bring?" They are invariably told, "Wine." No matter how many bottles of wine are brought, all are consumed.

The House Party. Held at a house (usually owned by a relative of the host or hostess) which is equipped with a pool, a tennis court, and a croquet lawn. All kinds of activities are planned, accompanied by liquor at every phase of the day. Saturday morning arrivals are handed Bloody Marys the moment they surface from the pool. Cucumber sandwiches and whiskey sours accompany the croquet. After dinner, the rugs are rolled back for dancing to the vintage Glenn Miller collection. Sleeping arrangements are innocent: everyone drags sleeping bags together and tells ghost stories.

THE COOK'S REPERTOIRE

Boy Preppies usually can be counted upon for a decent omelette, a stiff and spicy Bloody, and, for special occasions, either coq au vin or lasagna. Girl Preppies are less reliable. They can open a yogurt container (strawberry to match her chemise Lacoste), and they often know how to burn a steak. In any case, Preppies as a group are not renowned for culinary talent—while they may be discriminating and demanding consumers in a restaurant, they display an Anglophiliac delight in bland, mushy, lukewarm food for their at-home dining pleasure. When dropping by unexpectedly on the Preppy household, you may expect to be served, in all its glory, at least one of the following foods:

SMOKED OYSTERS
CREAMED CHIPPED BEEF ON TOAST
WHITE TOAST
EGGS BENEDICT
BEEF STROGANOFF
CHEEZ WHIZ
TRISCUITS or RITZ CRACKERS
WELSH RAREBIT
CODFISH CAKES
ANYTHING PREPARED BY STOUFFERS
CREAM OF TOMATO SOUP

THE COCKTAIL PARTY

We found a special beach in Bermuda —just the pink sand and us. And the shops . . .

The natives tried so hard to explain cricket to us. Of course we'd had quite a few G&Ts . . .

Want to blow this firetrap? A couple of girls in the International Division are having this party . . .

You really ought to consider a money market fund. Call me at work—we'll have lunch. Or drinks.

Daddy's on my case to see some old friend of his at your bank, anyway. I think his name's Keynes or Smith or something . . .

Will there be dancing? Any cute guys? What are they serving? Am I dressed okay?

Banker, out of Vassar four years. Midwestern. Newlywed.

Account executive at huge ad agency. Still goes out one night a week with the boys. Bowdoin '70. Newlywed.

Volunteer worker, member of Junior League. Southern. Attended Pine Manor for two years. Looking for a husband.

Investment banker. Carries wrong squash bag. Babson grad. On the make.

Editor at small, dignified publishing house. Works long hours to assuage guilt about independent wealth. Wheaton alum.

Saleswoman at Brooks Brothers. Pine Manor grad, heavy drinker. Devoted horsewoman.

Was Eggy's party really wild? At St. Paul's he used to do the craziest things. What a great guy.

It was really excellent. Really. They had this punch—really excellent.

At the firm we call Eggy's parties "passing the bar . . . as often as possible." Trip came up with that one . . .

You'll have to come. My roommates rented the Republican Club and it's going to be completely out of control!

Stop! Stop! You're killing me! That's the funniest thing I ever heard in my whole life!

And our school nurse was so stupid she used to give out aspirin for a . . .

Crew member of the *Courageous*. Not at home in a suit—note poor hem job. Went to Trinity College for three years.

Interior decorator. Favors wicker and duck prints. Waitressed on Nantucket during summer vacations from Colby.

Lawyer at prestigious, corporate firm. Yalie. Voted "Most Likely to Succeed" in Prep school's yearbook.

Trainee at Sotheby's. Subscribes to *Town & Country*. Georgetown alum, and Chippendale fanatic.

Legislative assistant to state senator, fresh out of Smith. Fake laugher. Loaded and dumb.

Admissions officer at New England Prep school. Celebrates his own wit at homecomings and parties like this one. Hamilton grad.

WINDING UP TO WIND DOWN

The Prep Weekend

FRIDAY NIGHT
SLUMMING

Friday night is often left open, so drinks after work with a convivial crew may result in a clever suggestion involving what's known as slumming.

Slumming actually means performing activities that are perfectly normal to non-Prep society. Because of the very spontaneity of these events, Preppies don't have a chance to go home and change, so they end up in all these places in their work clothes, briefcases in tow.

Ethnic food: Chinese (Szechuan or Hunan, never Cantonese) is being edged out by Thai, with strong competition from Middle Eastern. Preppies claim to be real aficionados of the chosen cuisine, and drag their friends to restaurants whose decor is distinguished for its garishness. Be-cause the food is so cheap, they feel justified in having drinks afterward at the most expensive bar in town.

Baseball games: Going out to the ball park and drinking beer and eating hot dogs has a real appeal for Preps. They think it's very basic and American. Some Prep men are actually knowledgeable about the sport, but this enthusiasm is indulgently regarded as an eccentricity. Girls who go on these expeditions feel quite dashing—one of the boys, as it were.

MUSIC TO SLUM BY:
1. Motown
64 Greatest Hits
2. Earth Wind & Fire
Gratitude
3. Tammy Wynette
Greatest Hits Vol. I.
4. Donna Summer
Bad Girls
5. Blondie
Parallel Lines

THE PUNK-PREP CONNECTION

A subgroup of Preppies are connoisseurs of punk. Some of them simply read the music columns in the *SoHo Weekly News* in the subway on the way to work for shock value, and some just like to dance to punk music. But there are serious Prep-punk types who would dye their hair blue if they didn't work in law firms, and who spend their weekends in alphabet city (Avenues A, B, C, and D) on the Lower East Side of New York wearing oversized hand-painted T-shirts and black sneakers, prowling through thrift stores searching for thin-lapeled jackets and harlequin sunglasses. They know not only all the clubs, but also all the groups, and can tell you everything about how the Talking Heads sounded at their last concert.

Urban working-class bar: (This is not to be confused with fake slumming, like going to Pedro's.) In a rundown section of town, frequented by vaguely threatening-looking characters, this bar has a jukebox full of Donna Summer hits and locals who resent the invasion. Preppies try to dance in very little space using the all-purpose, freestyle Lindy, and protest ineffectually when the women are whisked away to dance with the large and frightening habitués. They get kicked out for gatoring.

Cruising: Cars in the city are rare, so driving around aimlessly has tremendous appeal. Everyone drinks beer and the radio is tuned to the Motown sound. This makes Preppies feel as if they're in high school. Additional hilarity can be provided by performing the Chinese Fire Drill in the middle of town—at a stoplight, everyone leaps out of the car and runs once around it, then gets back in.

Punk rock clubs: Especially in New York. On any given night at the Mudd Club, there are several pairs of Pappagallo flats on the dance floor, and not all are worn with plastic miniskirts. The appeal is partly the music (rock 'n' roll is wonderful for Prep-style dancing) and partly avant-garde cachet. Bouncers are probably confused by the sartorial similarity between punk and Prep.

SATURDAY NIGHT
DANCING

Preppies love to dance, and spending Saturday night doing just that is their idea of bliss. Three or four men and the same number of women, all friends, meet for dinner at the apartment of one of the women—these evenings are almost always planned by the females—and drink lots of wine, or champagne if it's someone's birthday. After dinner everyone piles into a cab and they go off to a nightclub. Ideal dancing conditions consist of a roomy dance floor, cheap drinks, and swing music. The preferred Preppy dancing style is a hybrid of a discreet two-step and an animated jitterbug, with various eclectic influences thrown in. It may be the influence of dancing school, it may be watching Mummy and Daddy fox-trot, it may be practice in college, but most Preppies seem to know the rudiments. Southerners and Princetonians excel.

It's easier for a Preppy woman to be a good dancer than it is for a man. All she has to do is follow and hold on tight. It's the man who is actually doing all the work, deciding when to spin and when to reverse; deciding when something fancy is in order and how to recover if she misses the cue. Unfortunately, she is the more often injured of the couple, and trodden-upon toes are the least of it. There are four specific types of Prep male dancers—each with his own distinct style.

Angel wings. This man thinks it's debonair to dance

MUSIC TO BOOGIE BY:

1. Beach Boys
   Surf's Up

2. Duke Ellington
   Take the "A" Train

3. Widespread Depression Orchestra
   Boogie in the Barnyard

4. Glenn Miller
   Greatest Hits

5. Frank Sinatra
   A Swingin' Affair

with his arms out from his sides. Despite constant injunctions (polite and gradually less so) to keep his elbows in, he cannot control them. They are always sharp, and usually make contact at about the solar plexus of other dancers.

The yo-yo. He has very long arms. So does his date. The female spun out to their combined arm length goes a long way, fast, and he manages to clear the floor with her. Then he reels her back in, and they dance cheek to cheek until everyone is relaxed. Then he spins her out again.

The perpetual motion machine. This man is very energetic. He is also afraid of really touching the girl he's dancing with, so he keeps her in motion at all times. Very exotic moves are called into play here, the pretzel being the least of them. As they warm up, his hands may get sweaty, and he may let go of her. She makes a fairly dangerous missile.

The Rudolph Valentino. If he has on black tie at a semiformal party, if there's a rose in his lapel, if he slicks his hair, he's dangerous on the dance floor. His two favorite tricks are the tango step (which involves knifing through the crowd with hands outstretched) and the dip. The dip, to be stylish, requires that the woman kick her free leg up in the air. To about chin level.

SUNDAY
THE BRUNCH

Sunday brunch was invented to give people an excuse to drink during the day. Even the Puritanistic admit that the whole reason to go to brunch is to drink Bloodies.

Time: Given on weekends of general festivity—after a big dance, for instance, or after a wedding—or as an alternative to a dinner or cocktail party. You see people at brunch that you've seen mere hours before, and all you have to talk about is your hangovers, so conversation centers on that topic. A thorough post-mortem of the previous evening is also sure to amuse. The hour is late (imagine asking anyone to get up before eleven!); one o'clock is standard.

**MUSIC TO DRINK
BLOODIES BY:**

1. J.S. Bach
The Brandenburg Concerti

2. The Beatles
Rubber Soul

3. G.F. Handel
Water Music

4. Joni Mitchell
Court and Spark

5. Vivaldi
Four Seasons

THE BLOODY TRUTH

Bloodies are the centerpiece of the Sunday Brunch—they are also, perhaps, the #1 Prep mixed drink. There is some question as to what makes the perfect Bloody—is gin better than vodka? Is Aquavit better than either? Tomato juice is traditional, but V-8 adds some punch. Pepper is a must, Worcestershire sauce no less crucial, but Tabasco may be optional. And there are a good many Preps who like to throw in a touch of horseradish. Or celery salt. Lemons are preferred by some, limes by others. Sticks of celery are fun to play with, but too crunchy and aggressive to eat early in the afternoon. For those who can't make up their minds:

1. Place ice cubes in large glass
2. Pour in two fingers of vodka
3. Fill glass almost to top with V-8
4. Season with:
   2 drops Tabasco
   4 drops Worcestershire
   ½ tsp. horseradish
   1 tsp. lime juice
5. Add wedge of lime, stir and drink
6. Repeat as needed

Food: The breakfast variety, easy on the stomach after a night of hard drinking and dancing. Eggs, rolls, orange juice, coffee, fresh croissants, aspirin. Dress is cozy—when you're hung over, your oldest shirt and softest khakis are somehow comforting.

Activities: Kind hosts provide Sunday papers for those who are obsessive about keeping up with the news or for those who simply can't speak. Guests may loll around as late as five o'clock—if the vodka doesn't give out and there are enough sections of the newspaper to go around. If the host possesses a complete pack of cards, a few guests may perk up enough to play clear-minded and competitive hearts or gin rummy. This lucidity may not, however, extend to cogent conversation. If the weather is good, and the hangovers not acute, the energetic may drag the lazy out for a walk—across the park, down to the lake, around the block. There are Preppy fiends who believe that a day without specific Activity is wasted (these people were usually proctors in Prep school), and they'll corral everyone into going to a museum or (if it's near Christmas) to evensong. Since Preppies can't bear to be alone, they may end the day by seeing *Casablanca* together.

VACATIONS
A Seasonal Guide

One of the most difficult adjustments Preps have to make once they're out of school is losing two weeks at Christmas and three months in summer for vacation. Most jobs allow only two weeks of paid vacation per year, so those weeks must be spent in the Right Places, at the Right Activities. Before you leave, get introductions to friends of friends, especially in foreign cities. Use them. This is what being a Preppy is all about. After the college years, backpacking and youth hostels are all wrong when you can carry a suitcase and stay in a hotel.

Spring/Fall: the physical activity vacation. Gains prestige in direct proportion to the hardship required. Skiing the headwall at Tuckerman's Ravine in May is better than skiing the Lift Line at Stowe in April (although the latter is more than acceptable). Lots of arcane gear and ghastly weather conditions are part of the fun. Sailing a small boat single-handed across the Atlantic is a logical extension of this vacation. Take the first week for exercise, spend the second recovering in Bermuda.

Winter: the resort club vacation. In a subtropical climate. Resort clubs—the Lyford Cay Club in Nassau, the Mill Reef Club in Antigua—offer the same amenities as northern country clubs, with the addition of reliably clement weather. Tennis, golf, swimming, and paddling around in small boats are the daytime activities. The evening parties are familiar, but the drinks are made of rum. A variation on this theme is chartering a boat and cruising around the Bahamas or the Virgin Islands. This provides the illusion of physical activity without any of the hardship. Bermuda, unfortunately, is a touch chilly in the winter.

Summer: the cultural enrichment vacation. Interpreted loosely—this is not a week listening to Wagner at Bayreuth, or tracking down Wordsworthiana in the Lake Country. Culture is found in any foreign place—that can mean California for Preps who grew up in Maryland. (Northern California, of course. Los Angeles is strictly slumming material.) A European vacation is spent where you *didn't* go when you were at school abroad. While you might stop in Paris or Florence to see some friends, you'll spend most of your time driving through Burgundy or Tuscany. Save a week for Bermuda later in the year.

THE YOUNG EXECUTIVES. The Preps here are learning that charming Preppy excesses have no place in a bank—it is a boon to their careers for them to cultivate being boring. Right now the corporate ladder is the focus of their lives; the sporting life will have to be put aside for a few years. Still, they do manage the hour of squash a couple of times a week. All their physical energy goes into the game and they are formidable opponents.

squash racquet
for lunchtime game
terrycloth on handle
to absorb sweat

short hair, cut by Joe
the barber for
$3.00

round
tortoise-shell
glasses (20/20
vision)

signet ring on pinky

white linen
hand-
kerchief
(no
starch)

maroon ribbon
watchband (tomorrow,
a green band)

white broadcloth
shirt, mono-
grammed in
maroon below
the ribcage

striped tie that he
got as an usher in
someone's
wedding

first business suit—
2-piece gray pinstripe
from Brooks'
"346" shop

monogrammed boxer shorts,
present from an ex-girlfriend

attaché case
(graduation present)
monogrammed below handle
contents:
this week's Sports Illustrated;
1 legal pad; calculator;
box of macaroni and cheese
(tonight's dinner)

Church's shoes
(cost almost a week's salary)

PREP PERSONA No. 4

growing her hair to be more executive
navy blue grosgrain hairband

gold knot earrings

well-scrubbed look (makeup reduces credibility)

Barron's; always carried, not always read

pale pink tucked front shirt, extra starch

blue single-breasted blazer from Brooks Brothers golden fleece brass buttons

wine-colored Coach bag (she's going to take the tag off the moment she gets to the office)

school ring, still recognizable at 25 yards

gold cuff bracelet
Swiss watch with lizard band (graduation present)

oxblood briefcase with retractable handles and shoulder strap

contents: file folders that she never got to because she went to Tap-a-Keg instead

khaki dirndl skirt

thick ankles from too much field hockey

too-dark stockings; L'Eggs "Suntan," bought in the drugstore at lunchtime

navy blue Gucci pumps with gold buckle

CONTENTS OF THE PREPPY PURSE

comb
lip gloss
wallet from Gucci with no G's; in it, $12.98 and one subway token
Mark Cross credit card case, monogrammed; Citibank card, Saks charge plate, Brooks Brothers charge plate
Tiffany key chain—the kind you throw in a box and the post office sends back to Tiffany's
checkbook from Morgan Guaranty Trust
timetable for ferry to the island
Swiss Army knife with corkscrew
matchbook from Bailey's Beach
leather bound date book and matching address book
invitation to the Rugby Ball
ticket stub (orchestra seat) from "A Chorus Line"
one shrimp earring
Chinese laundry ticket
receipts from cash machine

WHERE THE PREPS ARE

A City-by-City Going Out Guide

	Monday	Tuesday	Wednesday
ANN ARBOR	**Liberty Bell**. S. University St. *Half-Pitcher Night. University people, frats.*	**The Pretzel Bell**. 120 E. Liberty St. *Dinner. Lunch. Bar.*	**The Count of Anti Pasto**. 1140 S. University St. *Dinner.*
ATLANTA	**Lenox Square Shopping Center**. *Neiman Marcus, ritzy shops.*	**Limelight**. 3330 Piedmont Rd., N.E. *New disco. Transparent dance floor. Closest thing to N.Y.*	**Houlihan's Old Place**. Lenox Square, 3393 Peachtree Rd., N.E. *Bar/restaurant. Very Prep.*
BALTIMORE	**Mount Washington Tavern**. 5700 Newbury St. *Lacrosse hangout. Preps live here.*	**Alex Brown & Sons**. 135 East Baltimore St. *Oldest brokerage house in U.S. Everyone's Prep and all Preps work here.*	**Alonzo's**. 415 W. Cold Spring Lane, Roland Park. *Great pizza.*
BOSTON	**Oxford Ale House**. 36 Church St., Cambridge. *Brewskis from all over. Caroline Kennedy spotted here.*	**Quaffer's**. 84 Beacon St. *Clubby, library atmosphere, with the requisite backgammon tables. Private club, but flexible, especially for ladies.*	**Lulu White**. 3 Appleton St. *Live, mostly black jazz. Supposed by Preps to be funky; often it is. Smoky and dark.*
CHICAGO	**Fritz That's It**. 1615 Chicago Ave., Evanston. *Restaurant. Lots of wood and plants. Salad bar.*	**New York Bagels and Bialys**. 4714 W. Touhy Ave., Lincoln Wood. *Non-Jewish Preps take out bagels. Open late.*	**Wrigley Field**. *Preppies go for Cub games, not White Sox. Take Daddy's box.*
CLEVELAND	**D'Poo's**. 746 Old River Rd. *An eclectic crowd; where Preppies slum.*	**Night Town**. 12383 Cedar Rd., Cleveland Heights. *Quiet, romantic dinner.*	**The Hunt Club**. Old Mill Rd., Gates Mills. *Just the guys playing paddle on health night.*
DALLAS	**Greenville Bar & Grill**. 2821 Greenville Ave. *Monday night there's live jazz. Cajun dishes.*	**The Hofbrau**. 3205 Knox St. *Austin Preppies who feel lost in Dallas come here for dinner, since the first one appeared in Austin. Steaks.*	**Greenville Avenue Country Club**. 3619 Greenville Ave. *Bar with swimming pool in the back. Casual.*

I f the phrase "free time" suggests wild adventures to most people—exploring and carrying on in uncharted territory—to Preppies it means going to that night's anointed club, restaurant, or bar. Here, then, for the uninitiated or the Prep on the road, is a daily guide for going out in cities coast to coast.

Thursday	Friday	Saturday	Sunday
The Whiffle Tree. 208 West Huron. *Dinner. Nice, not too expensive.*	**Second Chance**. 516 Liberty St. *Live music. Get there around 9:30.*	**Dooley's**. 310 Maynard St. *Best after football games.*	**Mr. Flood's Party**. 120 W. Liberty St. *Country rock. Loud and rowdy. Slumming potential.*
Phipps Plaza. *Most expensive shopping in Atlanta. Saks.*	**Billy's**. 3130 Roswell Rd. *Says in neon "The Place to be seen." Young execs.*	**Good Old Days**. 3013 Peachtree Rd., N.E. *Bar, sandwiches.*	**Piedmont Driving Club**. 1215 Piedmont Ave., N.E. The *country club. So restricted that Preppies may not be admitted.*
Harborplace. World Trade Center. *Baltimore's Quincy Market, just opened. One pavilion is food, the other Prep clothing.*	**Peter's Pub**. 21 S. Calvert St. *Where you go for cocktails after every work week.*	**The Crease**. 523 York Rd., Towson. *An abundance of rugby shirts and Top-Siders. Crowded, collegiate and post-collegiate.*	**Baltimore Country Club**. 4712 Club Rd., Roland Park. *Exclusive club in exclusive suburb. Sunday dinner.*
Cricket's. At the Quincy Market. *The Quincy Market is the spot for milling about and people-watching. Cricket's is a bar with a business-y crowd.*	**Hasty Pudding Club**. 12 Holyoke St., Cambridge. *This private Harvard club is older than the U.S. For private parties only.*	**Club Casablanca**. 40 Brattle St., Cambridge. *Known as "Casa B's." Only the upstairs is Prep. The center of the Prep universe, some say.*	**The Combat Zone**. Washington St., near Stuart. *Should be absolutely off-limits; male Preps go there to visit strip bars and ogle hookers.*
Wise Fool's Pub. 2270 N. Lincoln Ave. *For Preppies with the blues. Great blues artists. Hardcore jazz lovers.*	**Second City**. 1616 North Wells. *Famous improvisational comedy club. Go to late show around 1 a.m.*	**The 95th**. 95th Fl., Hancock Building. *Dressy. Go once to impress date and reaffirm socioeconomic status.*	**Pizzeria Uno**. 29 E. Ohio. *Before going to movies, Upwardly mobile people slumming.*
Red Fox. Chagrin River Rd., Gates Mills. *Bar, restaurant. Good service.*	**Gameskeeper's Tavern**. 87 West, Chagrin Falls. *Lively bar scene.*	**Rick's Café**. 86 North Main St., Chagrin Falls. *Big bar, live entertainment, good food.*	**Raintree**. 25 Pleasant Dr., Chagrin Falls. *The brunch place. Eggs Benedict.*
Cardinal Puff's. 4615 Greenville Ave. *Outdoor/indoor beer garden. Big SMU pickup spot.*	**Trader Vic's**. 5300 E. Mocking Bird La. *Skip dinner and drink instead. Located in Dallas Hilton Inn. Classic Prep watering hole.*	**Brookhollow Golf Club**. 8301 Harry Hines. *The place for deb parties, weddings, receptions. Chances are you'll attend one of them every Saturday.*	**Spanish Village**. 3839 Cedar Springs. *As New Yorkers eat Chinese food on Sundays, Texans get a weekly ration of Mexican food here.*

	Monday	Tuesday	Wednesday
EDGARTOWN	**The Colonial.** North Water St. *Big wicker couches that prevent great physical intimacy. Great noise that prevents great conversation.*	**The Colonial.**	**The Colonial.**
GROSSE POINTE	**Grosse Pointe Yacht Club.** 788 Lake Shore Rd. *Private. Drink your eyes out.*	**Sparky-Herbert's.** 15177 Kercheval Ave. *Bar/restaurant. Mid-30's crowd.*	**Sabre-Lancer.** 16543 E. Warren Ave. *Restaurant with good bar; smoked glass; paneling.*
HOUSTON	**Rosco's Cafe & Jazzbar.** 3230 Chimney Rock. *Live jazz, big-name performers. Backgammon tables.*	**Butera's.** 5019 Montrose. *Deli, very casual, with millions of different beers. The place to be seen, but closes early at 8 p.m.*	**St. Michel.** 2150 Richmond. *Jazz, very sophisticated atmosphere.*
KANSAS CITY	**Kansas City Country Club.** 62nd and Indian La., Shawnee Mission. *Mixed doubles, mixed drinks, mixed grill.*	**Kansas City Country Club.** *Swimming, bridge, tennis.*	**Entertain at home.** *Or get invited to a barbecue at a friend's house.*
LOS ANGELES	**Tom Bergin's Tavern.** 840 S. Fairfax Blvd. *Owned by Princeton alum. Irish coffees.*	**The Charthouse.** 1097 Glendon Ave. *In the heart of Westwood. Good steaks and lobsters, in the land of sprouts.*	**Joe Allen.** 8706 W. 3rd St. *Good drinks, hearty, sporty, rough wood kind of place.*
LOUISVILLE	**Troubador.** 3034 Hunsinger La. *Large disco, for Preps who can successfully execute a turn.*	**Captain's Quarters.** 6222 Guthrie Beach Rd. *Outdoor drinking by the riverbanks. Piano bar, food.*	**City Lights.** 117 West Main St. *Good dance music.*
MINNEAPOLIS/ ST. PAUL	**W.A. Frost & Company.** 374 Selby Ave., St. Paul. *St. Paul's bid for acceptance. Proto-Prep. Pickups.*	**Haberdashery.** 45 South 7th St., Mpls. *Formerly the home (for more than half a century) of a very Prep clothing store, Hubert W. White, original brass and wood fittings still here. Bar.*	**University Club.** 420 Summit Ave., St. Paul. *Traditional men's club, fallen onto hard times, now (discreetly) open to the public, for dinner, lunch, and room accommodations.*
NEW HAVEN	**Mory's Association.** 306 York St. *Known as Mory's, private club for Yalies. Whiffenpoofs perform every Monday night.*	**Old Heidelberg.** 1151 Chapel St. *Downstairs, dark, kind of ratty. German food and two large-screen TVs.*	**Fitzwilly's.** 338 Elm St. *Hanging plants and bentwood chairs. Big sandwiches and Bloodies in goblets. Overpriced.*

Thursday	Friday	Saturday	Sunday
The Colonial.	The Colonial.	The Colonial.	The Colonial.
Diamond Lil's. 18744 Mack Ave. *Oldest bar in town. Preppiest bar in town. Young clientele, pick-up action.*	Country Club of Detroit. 220 Country Club Dr. *Dinner with the other members.*	The Little Club. Lake St. Claire. *So private, it doesn't have a real address. No one even knows who's a member.*	Piper's Alley. 18696 Mack Ave. *Light supper: burgers, omelettes. Potted palms, ceiling fans.*
Kay's Lounge. 2324 Bissonnet. *Neighborhood bar with game room. Relaxed.*	The Hofbrau. 1803 Shepherd. *Texas roadhouse for steaks and heavy imbibation. Fraternity hangout.*	The Cadillac Bar. 1802 Shepherd. *Roast quail at this bar/restaurant. Famous for its Ramos Gin Fizzes.*	Cody's. 3400 Montrose. *Top floor (10th) with great view. Key spot. Good jazz, dress code.*
La Bonne Auberge. 610 Washington St. *Elegant French restaurant for requisite evening in town.*	River Club. 611 W. 8th St. *Mostly grownups, slightly nouveau.*	Kansas City Country Club. *Weekly dance. A must.*	Kansas City Country Club. *Tennis time. Its members obviously take advantage of the club's facilities.*
Tommy's Burgers. 2575 Beverly Blvd. *The food is suspect and so are the people. An L.A. tradition.*	The Baked Potato. 3787 Cahuenga Blvd., West. *Baked potatoes only, with all kinds of stuffing. Jazz too.*	The Polo Lounge. Beverly Hills Hotel, 9641 Sunset Blvd. *The place to be seen. Jet set hangout. Be prepared for corner table. A classic.*	The Nantucket Lighthouse. 22706 Pacific Coast Hwy., Malibu. *Go for name alone. Omelettes, blueberry muffins, champagne on the beach.*
Bauer's. 3612 Brownsboro Rd. *The #1 Prep headquarters in Louisville. Go any night after 9:30.*	Cunningham's. 500 S. 5th St. *Open 'til sunrise. Last resort when you want to meet another khaki dresser and the hour's late.*	Jim Porter's. 2345 Lexington Rd. *Old reliable, good any night late. Try to rent a space here during Kentucky Derby—if you leave, you might never get back in.*	Stay Home. *Or get invited to a friend's house for supper. Even if any restaurants did stay open on Sunday night, you wouldn't go.*
The Commodore. 79 Western Ave., St. Paul. *Restored hotel, bar, mecca of 1920's Prep revival. F. Scott himself used to frequent the place. Need we say more?*	Windfield Potters. 210 S.E. 2nd Ave., Mpls. *Cashing in on 1980's Prep revival, this is the place to go for drinks at the end of the workweek. Help is required to wear Weejuns, khakis, and Lacostes.*	Calhoun Beach Club. 2730 W. Lake St., Mpls. *Upwardly mobile lawyers, etc., play tennis, squash, and swim. Built in 1920's, formerly a Grand Hotel. Since no golf, members mostly 25-40.*	Woodhill Country Club. 200 Woodhill Rd., Wayzata. *Private. Old-line. Highest proportion of real Preppies in area. Suburban.*
George & Harry's. 381 Temple St. *"G&H" is the Prep mecca of New Haven. Small, somewhat unknown, waitresses wear orthopedic shoes.*	West of Eleven. 1104 Chapel St. *Pseudo New York restaurant. Connected to Mellon Art Center. Go after a performance at the Yale Rep. next door.*	Yorkside Pizza. 288 York St. *Overlit pizza place. Not best pizza, but most popular.*	Annie's Firehouse Soup Kitchen. 19 Edwards St. *Need a car to get here. Old firehouse. So organic, men won't go unless dragged by dates.*

	Monday	Tuesday	Wednesday
NEW ORLEANS	**4141 Club**. 4141 St., Charles Ave. *Backgammon, pool, adjoining restaurant.*	**Bart's Restaurant**. 7000 Lake Shore Dr. *Restaurant/bar for the 18-24 set. Right on the water.*	**Camelia Grill**. 626 S. Carrollton. *Open late, in the heart of the Prep district. Burgers and club sandwiches, freeze drinks.*
NEW YORK	**Swell's**. 1439 York Ave. *Banker, broker bacchanalian orgy. Sit according to alma mater. Horse and hunt decor. Unmarked storefront.*	**Hoexter's Market**. 1442 Third Ave. *Attractive and expensive restaurant, but bar is party to frequent pickups. After midnight people dance.*	**Sugar Mill**. 340 E. 79th St. *"The Mill". Pickup city. Couples almost never go together.*
PALM BEACH	**Peter Dinkle's**. 207 Royal Poinciana Way. *Sidewalk cafe, patio in back, crowded, especially during "high" season—Easter, Christmas. Horse-racing motif.*	**Alcazar Lounge**. Breakers Hotel, South County Rd. *Coat and tie required in this austere bar in the grand dame of American hotels, designed after Villa Medici.*	**264**. 264 South County Rd. *Bar/restaurant of the dark, polished wood genre. Everyone is a stockbroker, or lying. Home of the wrap skirt.*
PHILADELPHIA	**H.A. Winston & Co**. 15th & Locust St., S. Front St. *Prep McDonald's for burgers and fries.*	**Rusty Scupper**. 34 NewMarket St. *For the Preppy who won't eat anything but home cooking.*	**La Terrasse**. 3432 Sansom St. *Expensive food for high-class postgrads in law school or at Wharton.*
PROVIDENCE	**RISD Tap Room**. 235 Benefit St. *Art students who compensate for their hostility by being interesting to look at. Beer and wine.*	**Graduate Center Bar**. Charlesfield at Thayer St. *Brown bar, pitchers, wine, pinball, jukebox. Private.*	**Met Café**. 165 Friendship St. *Out of the way, slum bar, blues, beers, crowded, unsavory.*
SAN FRANCISCO	**The Oasis**. 241 El Camino Real, Menlo Park. *Old beer hall with great hamburgers and pinball machines.*	**Pacific Union Club**. 1000 California St. *Prehistoric Prep. Crusty old business types. Men only.*	**Perry's**. 1944 Union St. *Pickup bar where everyone claims to be an attorney.*
WASHINGTON	**Clyde's**. 3236 M St. N.W. *The definitive Prep bar. Maxwell's Plum with a big dose of young attorney.*	**Kramer Books Afterwords Cafe**. 1517 Connecticut Ave. N.W. *Watercress salad, quiche, Haagen Dazs, while reading books and magazines bought in adjoining bookstore.*	**F. Scott's**. 1236 36th St. N.W. *The Jazz Age re-created in 20th century Georgetown. Hardcore.*

Thursday	Friday	Saturday	Sunday
Spinnaker's. 1922 West End Park. *Disco right on the lakefront.*	**Metairie Country Club.** 580 Woodvine, Metairie. *Located in New Orleans' toniest suburb. Weekend din-din.*	**Valencia Club.** 1900 Valence St. *A private club for—get this—high school students. Members have to be proposed, and have to be 18 or younger. Resembles a frat.*	**New Orleans Yacht Club.** 403 North Roadway. *Sunny sailing day, lots of nautical drinking.*
Pedro's. 251 E. 85th St. *This is it. Looks and feels like college bar. Patrons speak unkindly of it, but they take it seriously.*	**The Ravelled Sleave.** 1387 Third Ave. *Although regulars profess to hate it, they always come back for more. Restaurant in back.*	**Mudd Club.** 77 White St. *"Hey, is this Soho?" Preppies go punk the one unpunk night of the week. Dancing to records and bands. Late.*	**J.G. Melon.** 1291 Third Ave. *Open every night until 4. Always crowded, bar and restaurant. Burgers, chili. Logo is pink and green.*
The Bath and Tennis Club. 1170 South Ocean Blvd. *Known as the "B and T," natch. Tea dances, place to sit by the pool if you're taking a long weekend. Private.*	**Taboo.** 221 Worth Ave. *Tiki-god paradise. Lamps look (and are) like plastic fruit. Older crowd at this bar/restaurant, coats and ties required.*	**Conchy Joe's.** 651 S. Flagler Dr., West Palm Beach. *The place to slum à la Jimmy Buffet island mentality. Steel band, imported beers, right on Lake Worth. Where Preps get down.*	**The Everglades Club.** Worth Ave. *The most old-guard of the old-guard, private clubs. Members under the age of 40 are nephews of other members. Very restricted.*
Saladalley, Entrees/On Trays, Hillary's. 4040 Locust St. *Philadelphia's answer to Prep heaven. From soup to nuts in three bistros in the same building.*	**Lily's.** 2nd and Lombard. *Meat market for newly employed Preps.*	**McGillin's Old Ale House.** 1310 Drury La. *One of Philly's few for rock 'n' roll dancing and casual food.*	**The Commissary.** 1710 Sansom St. *Self-service for the self-serving Prep looking for early morning merry. A must for brunch.*
Lupo's Heartbreak Hotel. 377 Westminster St. *Cavernous place, good name bands, dancing.*	**Rue de l'Espoir.** 99 Hope St. *French food, excellent bread. Quiche and profs.*	**L'Elizabeth.** 285 S. Main St. *Cramped bar, seating on couches. Expensive. To impress a date while ordering Brandy Alexander.*	**Silver Top Diner.** Route 6. *Open from midnight to noon. Truckdrivers and Preppies, the former, cool, the latter, acting cool; all ordering blueberry muffins. A ritual.*
Bohemian Club. 624 Taylor St. *Old-guard men's club where "bohemian" members allegedly support the arts. Summer camp is by Russian River.*	**Stanford Court Hotel.** 905 California St. *Beautiful old hotel with good bar, great restaurant. Advertises in New Yorker.*	**Henry Africa's.** 2260 Van Ness St. *Harley motorcycle in window. Bar specializing in singles.*	**The Alpine.** 42nd St., Palo Alto. *Cute bar with upstairs. Great views. Always crowded. Expensive drinks.*
The Tombs. 1226 36th St. N.W. *Very collegiate. Dark, downstairs, beer.*	**Day Lily Restaurant.** 2142 Pennsylvania Ave. N.W. *Chinese restaurant turned into UVA frat party on Fridays. Beer, pretzels, and Mount Vernon girls. Dead the rest of the week.*	**Déjà Vu.** 2119 M St. N.W. *Room after room of bar, restaurant, and dance floor. Boogie to oldies.*	**Burning Tree Club.** Burdet and River Rds., Bethesda, Md. *Get invited here for tennis and Bloodies.*

TOASTS, TENTS, AND THE *TIMES*

Getting Married

There comes a time in the young Prep's life when marriage is a logical event. It's not a matter of age, exactly. But one day the male Prep will wake up and notice that all his roommates are married and he can't find any single friends to take their places in his three-bedroom apartment. Or the female will realize that she cannot stand to be a bridesmaid one more time, and that she already *has* five pairs of sandals dyed to match five useless pastel-colored dresses. Marriage is the only alternative.

At this point, the Preps in question either get engaged to whomever they're seeing at the moment, or they find someone who looks promising at the next cocktail party and cultivate a relationship. Then they set their feet on the Nuptial Path, following a firmly established succession of events, each of which involves its own etiquette.

1. The Engagement Announcement. In the good old days, when most people still used the Social Register as a phone book, the *New York Times* wedding pages were a convenient way of assuring that everyone who mattered knew about the marriage of a Preppy scion. Now, since the space devoted by the *Times* to the announcements is meagre and the competition stiff, it is difficult to be sure that one's announcement will be included. The "importance" of the families of the bride and groom is the criterion for acceptance. Ancestors who signed the Declaration of Independence or invented the safety pin should be enough, but a stacked deck—a couple of senators, a railroad fortune, an ambassadorship—won't hurt. The *Times* staff checks each fact in the announcements that are submitted, so creativity isn't encouraged. If there's any doubt about whether or not the announcement will make it, it's best not even to try.

2. The Wedding Party. It is generally conceded that ten bridesmaids is overdoing it, but eight or nine are acceptable. The groom often has trouble digging up enough friends to

> **10 THINGS BRIDESMAIDS SHOULD NOT FORGET WHEN PACKING FOR AN OUT-OF-TOWN WEDDING**
>
> 1. Hot pink sandals for the rehearsal dinner
> 2. Pearls
> 3. Yellow and green Lanz nightgown (the summer version of the old flannel favorite)
> 4. Clairol Kindness electric curlers, to maintain that perfect pageboy
> 5. Diaphragm
> 6. Navy blue espadrilles
> 7. Maidenform bra
> 8. Five grosgrain hairbands, to match each outfit in the suitcase
> 9. Lip gloss (for the sultry made-up look)
> 10. Calling cards to slip to the ushers

satisfy some whim of the bride and—in trying to suit all nine of the bridesmaids—are becoming to none of them, the ushers look tremendously dashing in charcoal gray coats with striped pants, stiff collars, ascots, and pearl gray gloves. If the wedding is held in the evening (after 6:00 P.M., common in the South), the guests wear black tie (tuxedos and long dresses) while the ushers wear white tie (tails). In concession to the formality of the hour, the bridesmaids' dresses may be a bright or dark color, but the women still won't look as nice as the men.

4. Festivities. As the wedding date draws near, the schedule becomes crowded. During the final month or two, parents' friends, relatives, ushers, and bridesmaids all give parties. Showers present a great range of possibility: wine showers, bar showers, kitchen showers, tool showers, bed and bath showers—sometimes even showers to which guests bring an ornament for the new couple's future Christmas tree. There is also a series of cocktail parties, lunches, picnics, and dinner parties. The groom gets off fairly light—all he has to do is show up and be polite to the bride's family and friends. The bride, on the other hand, has to buy new clothes for practically every occasion and be sure that she doesn't break out or bite her fingernails. She also has to

match, and may have to recruit his entire bank training program. Juveniles carrying rose petals or rings are rarely seen. Occasionally, the groom's best man is his father, disgruntling the maid of honor, who has to walk down the aisle with him.

3. Clothing. Nowhere is wedding convention as strictly observed. If the wedding is at 4:00 or 4:30 (standard in the Northeast), the women wear identical pastel dresses and the men wear morning coats, also known as cutaways. While the women's dresses are chosen to

DISPLAYING THE LOOT

One of the chief advantages of getting married in front of four hundred people is that, if you play your cards right, you won't have to buy as much as a teaspoon for the next ten years. At a wedding that takes itself seriously, all those gifts should be laid out on tables covered with white damask where they can be admired, examined, or envied as the case may be.

1. Six soup mugs.
2. Limoges box.
3. Six Royal Worcester egg coddlers (return).
4. Tin tray with cardinal.
5. Ming Toi coffeepot (return).
6. Six Chinese export soup bowls and plates.
7. Lazy Susan.
8. Tulip pillow.
9. Formal china pattern—Limoges' *Lafayette*: dinner plates, service plates, bowl, coffee cups.
10. Crown Staffordshire's *Hunt Scene*: vegetable dish, bowl, coffee cup.
11. Crystal vase from Tiffany's (six

received, five returned).

12. Informal china pattern—*Botanic Garden*: canisters, dinner plates, covered casserole.

13. Green Dragon plate, Ming Toi plate, Real Old Willow plate, Flying Cloud plate: for decorative plate collection.

14. Six dessert plates with Audubon birds.

15. Six Royal Worcester dessert plates with fruit (return).

16. Silver salt and pepper shakers.

17. Small silver salt and pepper shakers.

18. Herend Rothschild Bird soup tureen.

19. Ginger-jar lamp with Provencal flower motif.

20. Royal Worcester's *Evesham*: covered casserole.

21. Staghorn handle steak knives.

22. Hunting prints.

23. Herend coffeepot.

24. Two Herend teapots (return one).

25. Herend chocolate pot.

26. Glasses with hand-painted polo players, two sets.

27. Five silver picture frames.

28. Butler's tray table with engraved plaque from the wedding party.

29. Rug with hunt scene.

30. Magazine rack.

31. Wastebasket with hunt scene.

10 WEDDING NO-NO'S

1. Performing relatives
2. Do-it-yourself ceremonies
3. Caviar
4. Name tags in the receiving line
5. Tuxedos that are any color but black
6. Enough food
7. Proofs of the formal photographs displayed at the reception
8. Fountains of champagne, or ice swans
9. A professional announcer at the reception
10. Disco

write thank-you notes for each party and each shower present, on the new writing paper she ordered from Dempsey and Carroll for the purpose.

5. The Wedding as Weekend. Prep wedding do not take twenty minutes, or even simply an afternoon. A real Prep wedding takes a whole weekend. On Friday night, the rehearsal is followed by the rehearsal dinner, given by the groom's parents. Dinner is interrupted by a series of toasts made by bride, groom, wedding party, and anyone else who has drunk enough champagne to think himself eloquent. The bridal lunch the next day gives the wedding party and out-of-town guests something to do before it's time to change for the wedding, and a chance to ingest some alcohol to palliate the hangover from the night before. Everyone wears dark glasses and drinks lots of Bloodies and picks at the chicken salad. The actual wedding—the least important part of the weekend—only takes a few minutes and many people miss it because they're still changing from lunch or decided to take a nap instead. The reception—the real center of the weekend—is followed by an informal dinner for the wedding party. There is usually another brunch the next day, affording ample opportunity for post-mortems.

6. The Reception in a Tent. Except in large cities, the Prep wedding reception takes place in a tent in the backyard of the bride's house. This is possible because all Prep houses have enough land not only to accommodate the tent, but to allow all four hundred guests to park their cars on the lawn. After the guests go through the receiving line they take the obligatory swing through the dining room to look at the accumulated presents on display, making sure that their own offerings are given a prominent place. They then move into the tent (either yellow-and-white or pink-and-white striped, decorated by the garden club with flowers from their own gardens). Fashion plates in high heels are punished for their vanity when they find that their heels sink deep into the grass at every step. Sensible Preps wear their Pappagallo flats and ancient little fur wraps over their chiffon dresses since it's often chilly. There is never enough food, always enough liquor.

7. Old-fashioned Music. Music at a Prep wedding is very traditional. The classic Preppy bands—Lester Lanin, Meyer Davis, Bill Harrington, Peter Duchin—produce bouncy but sedate tunes that everyone can dance to, even the bride who is seriously encumbered by her wedding dress (her mother's, cut down). The most typical song (played again and again through the afternoon; repertoires are not often innovative) is "Tie a Yellow Ribbon Round the Old Oak Tree." Lester Lanin bands hand out beanies at the end of each party.

8. The Wedding Announcement. Part of the wedding ritual takes place on Sunday morning when everyone flips immediately to the second half of the first section of the *Times*. What kind of coverage did the wedding get? How large was the Bachrach photo, how big was the headline, were all the bridesmaids listed? There is tremendous gratification in going into the office on Monday and having someone say "How was the wedding? I saw it in the paper."

A CAUTIONARY TALE

A young man who had been, in his day, an energetic advocate of light-hearted jokes played on his friends at *their* weddings—midnight phone calls, rice-strewn suitcases, getaway cars with empty gas tanks—greeted the occasion of his own nuptials with some trepidation.

Despite his expectations, all went well. No helpful soul offered reasons "why this couple should not be joined together." No water pistols appeared in the receiving line. No obscene telegrams were read, no cake was thrown, no goat appeared on the dance floor.

After an uneventful exit, the young man and his bride relaxed, reasoning that the likelihood of vengeful trickery had diminished. They reached their destination, and after a cursory inspection of the closets, got down to the business at hand.

The following morning, the groom called room service. "This is Chester Chester in room 417 and I'd like to order breakfast for two," he said. And a voice spoke up from under the bed. "Make that five."

HONOR'S CHOICE
Quiz #4

Lucky Honor. These two wonderful men are madly in love with her and want to marry her. She's ready to get married; but she has to decide who to choose: Carter or Taylor? Despite their similarly dazzling résumés, one is a less-than-promising prospect. Can you figure out which one, in Honor's eyes, is the more eligible Prep? For those to whom the choice is not obvious, the answer appears at the bottom of the page.

NAME:	CARTER DANFORTH 6′0″, 160 lbs., straight blond hair and blue eyes, ruddy complexion; looks like a lacrosse player from Maryland	TAYLOR NOBLE 6′5″, 170 lbs., wavy dark hair, blue eyes, horn-rims; a bit effete
BACK-GROUND:	Baltimore/Fisher's Island, Andover, Dartmouth	Philadelphia, Groton, Columbia, year at the Sorbonne, M.A. from Columbia Business
CAREER:	3 years at Morgan, recently moved to Brown Brothers Harriman	Account executive at BBDO on a toilet-paper account
CLUBS:	NYAC, Yale Club	University Club
OTHER:	Plays a lot of squash, has a nice baritone voice, reads *The Economist* in the bathroom, mixes a mean Bloody Mary, likes duck hunting	Divine dancer, very good at Scrabble, has a ballet subscription every year, lives alone in a wonderful apartment on West 76th Street
FAVORITE MOVIE:	*Heaven Can Wait*	*The Marriage of Maria Braun*
LAST BOOK READ:	*In Search of History* by Theodore H. White	*Justine* by Lawrence Durrell

THE CHOICE: Honor married Carter. His looks were actually a strike against him, since she is blonde and looks better with Taylor. But Taylor promised to be a bit difficult. Though he started with the right material (Philadelphia, Groton), who in his right mind would go to Columbia *twice*? And there's that year in France: that's all right for girls, but boys have better things to do with their time, and if you have to study abroad, Oxford is really much better. At least they speak English.

Carter's career is a real plus: investment banking is so *sound*! And Brown Brothers is full of such nice people. Everyone knows that advertising is risky, and besides, how embarrassing to work on a toilet-paper account.

Honor does harbor a secret yen to have the right to use the Ladies' Dining Room at the University Club, but she can always get Carter to join.

The basic problem with Taylor is that there's just no counting on him—imagine a ballet subscription? Movies in German? Living on the West Side?

Honor's parents are very pleased.

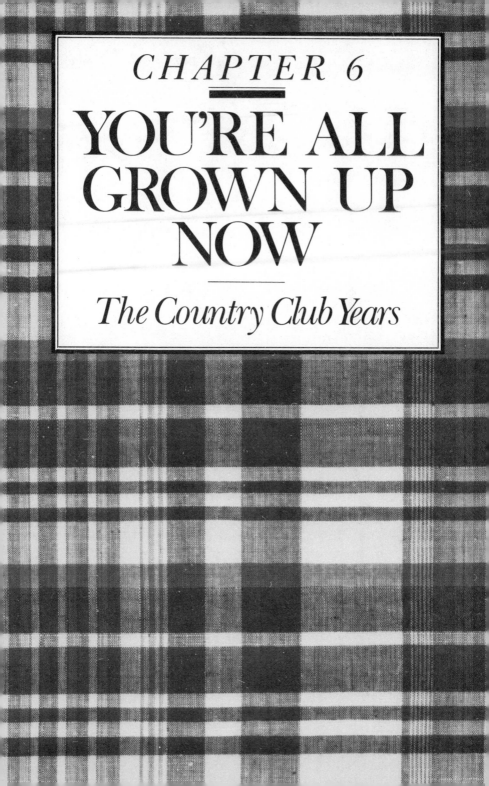

CHAPTER 6

YOU'RE ALL GROWN UP NOW

The Country Club Years

LIFE IN THE SLOW LANE

Although living in the city was thrilling, you always knew that a time would come when you'd leave. You'll miss it, there's no question—those winter dances for the benefit of Russian emigrés, drinking after squash at the athletic club, the convenience of just popping into Brooks for all your clothes.

But you're almost thirty now. It's time to settle down. So you'll sell the two-bedroom condominium and buy a house in the suburbs.

Preppies need certain amenities that other suburbanites don't require, and these necessities should be taken into account when choosing a suburb. Some features to look for when shopping for a new hometown:

a country club with eight tennis courts
a Ford/BMW dealership
decent train service
a good needlepoint shop
fertile soil for herb gardens
good private schools

What Preppies don't need are good public schools and a shopping mall.

Once you've chosen your spot and bought a house, life changes in subtle and unex-

THE CLUB CAR

At 7:29 on weekday mornings, a group of high-ranking executives walks through the grass and rubble at the head of the Bedford Hills train station in order to board the club car that is attached to the New York-bound train. These gentlemen pay rather hefty annual dues for the privilege of riding in a car separate from those used by common commuters. What they get for their pains are armchairs instead of banquettes, little tables, curtained windows.

Though each club car organization works slightly differently, the standard arrangement is that the association or club actually owns the car they ride in. The dues pay for its upkeep and a little something for the railroad company to tow it to Manhattan, as well as the salary of the man, should there be one, who serves tea, coffee, and ice water. On the Erie-Lackawanna car, this man now passes around subway tokens on a silver tray. Sic transit gloria mundi.

pected ways. The male of the species memorizes the train schedule and figures out where to stand on the platform so that the doors open in front of him. The female undergoes a sort of domestic metamorphosis, overseeing the renovation of the house, planning the garden, figuring out which butcher has the best price on lamb chops.

You'll need a station wagon—the little car you had in the city isn't big enough for hauling around flats of pansies (to border the front walk) and golf clubs at the same time.

And once you have the station wagon, you might as well have children.

And before you know it, you're bringing up little Preppies. The cycle has started again. You take them to your mother's house in Marion for the summer, where they learn to sail and to drive a Jeep. You start looking for boarding schools for the oldest. Will he go to your alma mater? Your youngest daughter wants a horse. The coat closet is littered with hockey sticks and tennis racquets. Your life is passing in front of your eyes.

A SAMPLING OF SUBURBS

New England

Avon, Conn.
Bar Harbor, Maine
Barrington, R.I.
Beverly Farms, Mass.
Centerville, Mass.
Chatham, Mass.
Chestnut Hill, Mass.
Concord, Mass.
Darien, Conn.
Dover, Mass.
Duxbury, Mass.
Fairfield, Conn.
Farmington, Conn.
Greenwich, Conn.
Hamilton, Mass.
Jamestown, R.I.
Kennebunkport, Maine
Lincoln, Mass.
Longmeadow, Mass.
Madison, Conn.
Manchester, Mass.
Marblehead, Mass.
Marion, Mass.
Narragansett, R.I.
New Canaan, Conn.
Newport, R.I.
Noroton, Conn.
Osterville, Mass.
Prides Crossing, Mass.

Rowayton, Conn.
South Dartmouth, Mass.
Southport, Conn.
Topsfield, Mass.
Truro, Mass.
Wellesley, Mass.
Weston, Conn.
Weston, Mass.
Woods Hole, Mass.

Middle Atlantic

Alexandria, Va.
Annapolis, Md.
Ardmore, Pa.
Bala-Cynwyd, Pa.
Baltimore, Md.
Basking Ridge, N.J.
Bedford Hills, N.Y.
Bernardsville, N.J.
Bryn Mawr, Pa.
Centerville, Del.
Chadds Ford, Pa.
Charlottesville, Va.
Chestnut Hill, Pa.
Chevy Chase, Md.
Cold Spring Harbor, N.Y.
Fair Haven, N.J.
Far Hills, N.J.
Garrison, N.Y.
Gladstone, N.J.
Gladwyne, Pa.

Guilford, Md.
Haverford, Pa.
Homeland, Md.
Katonah, N.Y.
Lancaster, Pa.
Lawrenceville, N.J.
Lloyd Harbor, N.Y.
Locust Valley, N.Y.
McLean, Va.
Middleburg, Va.
Oyster Bay, N.Y.
Peapack, N.J.
Princeton, N.J.
Purdys, N.Y.
Radnor, Pa.
Roland Park, Md.
Rosemont, Pa.
Rumson, N.J.
Rye, N.Y.
St. David's, Pa.
Sewickley, Pa.
Wilmington, Del.
Wynnewood, Del.

The South and The Rest

Aiken, S.C.
Alamo Heights, Tex.
Beaverton, Ore.
Bellevue, Wash.
Buck Head, Ga.
Chapel Hill, N.C.

Cherry Hills, Colo.
Clayton, Mo.
Edina, Minn.
Gates Mills, Ohio
Grosse Pointe, Mich.
Highland Park, Tex.
Hillsboro, Calif.
Hilton Head, S.C.
Indian Hills, Ky.
Kirkland, Wash.
La Jolla, Calif.
Ladue, Mo.
Lake Forest, Ill.
Lake Oswego, Ore.
Mercer Island, Wash.
Palm Beach, Fla.
Palm Springs, Calif.
Pasadena, Calif.
Pepper Pike, Ohio
River Oaks, Tex.
San Marino, Calif.
Shaker Heights, Ohio
Shawnee Mission, Kansas
University Park, Tex.
Upper Arlington, Ohio
Wayzata, Minn.
Winter Park, Fla.

IN PURSUIT OF PURSUITS

If there is one thing that the Preppy is dedicated to in adult life and career, it is leisure. There are many ways to pass all this free time, even beyond the usual golf games, bridge tournaments, and country club terrace-basking.

Activities for men are gardening, keeping the old Triumph in running order (which involves a nice, patronizing relationship with the garage mechanics), and finding good deals on bulk liquor.

For women, many towns still offer ladies' committees; it doesn't matter what they are for—anything called a ladies' committee is right. Women who are not employed will want to become involved in needlepoint, crewelwork, or making picture frames out of shells. Classes help to make these activities challenging. Kits help to make them easy. You may also want to be on the historical society and zoning board of your town, at least long enough to win permission to add that family room to your 1740 farmhouse.

Adults of truly strong character may go in for the most challenging avocations of all—the maintenance hobbies. These are: maintaining a gravel or shell driveway, maintaining a pool or tennis court (or both), maintaining a wooden sailboat, maintaining a horse, maintaining a waistline.

Remember this Prep watchword: Work hard, play hard, but if you can only do one, play hard.

THE PREFERRED HOBBIES

Bird watching
Boating
Collecting: antique cars; antique quilts; rare books; Chinese porcelain; weather vanes; pewter; boat models; Boehm; Steuben glass; Franklin Mint coins; Norman Rockwell plates and prints; Lilly Pulitzer prints; thimbles; tiny silver spoons (not what you think); Revere silver; birdcages
Gardening
Flower arranging
Fly casting
Fresh-water fishing
Furniture restoring
Shopping
Taxidermy

GREENER GRASS
The Country Club

Membership in a country club is one of the facts of Prep life in the suburbs. It perpetuates the Old Boy Network during leisure hours. It provides necessities such as tennis tournaments and golf caddies. It is a place to take house guests for lunch in the summer when you just can't be bothered. Though facilities vary from club to club, Preppies can count on most of the following.

The golf course. "The best natural-hazard golf course in Connecticut," they'll boast. That means that everyone loses four balls trying to get across the lagoon, and another three in the marsh. Though few members under age thirty seem to play, when they reach thirty-one, they'll know how.

The pool. Even if there's a beach nearby. The pool is full of eleven-year-olds playing "Marco Polo" until they're blue around the lips. "Adult swim" provides matrons a chance to put on their petal bathing caps and perform five sedate laps of breaststroke (keeping their heads out of the water at all times). Once every summer, teenagers are caught skinny-dipping after dark, causing a scandal.

The beach. If there is one, it's the center of action. Mummies sit in beach chairs in long rows facing the water, do needlepoint and discuss their children. Beach boys put up umbrellas and flex their muscles for the adolescent girls. Hardy swimmers (usually in their forties) breaststroke out to the raft in high waves. Low tide reveals beer cans and dead flounder on the sand.

The tennis courts. At least eight of them. The tennis pro (a good-looking blond from a nearby club) gives private lessons to matrons and runs junior tennis clinics. Competition is the major focus here, and tournaments (round robin, member-guest, father-son, Memorial Day, Labor Day) take place almost weekly. The first court (closest to the pro shop and the pavilion) is the exclusive turf of brash youngsters with wicked serves, or their fathers who can still beat them.

The grill. No wet bathing suits, please. The menu is the same everywhere; club sandwiches, hamburgers, lemonade. Some clubs boast a specialty, like peanut butter and bacon. Though you can bring your lunch to the club in a cooler, it's much more fun to order—and sign for it.

The clubhouse. In some cases, separate from the beach house, and more elaborate—the setting for dances and wedding receptions. Most clubs have a formal dining room (the food is generally worse than the grill food) and, naturally, a bar. Clubhouses range in atmosphere from the posh (little pots of geraniums and whiskey sours in indi-vidual shakers) to the rustic (green wicker rockers and mildew).

The locker room. Where the golf shoes are kept and all the best gossip is heard. Women's locker rooms often boast vanity tables with combs and face powder in an improbable shade, and a supply of hair nets. Men's locker rooms provide no privacy; the shower and changing rooms are always communal just like Prep school.

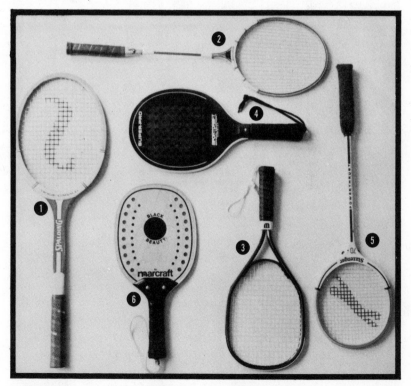

1. **Tennis.** The essential country club sport.
2. **Badminton.** "It's a fast game," say its players. Fast, but sissy.
3. **Racquetball.** Fast, sweaty, and a little bit proletarian.

4. **Platform tennis.** (also known as paddle tennis) played by doubles in Darien.
5. **Squash racquets.** The game every Preppy can play.
6. **Paddleball.** If Preppies play, they don't admit it.

THE COUNTRY CLUB YEARS. After forty. They've made their fortune and have become relaxed, confident and fun-loving once again. This happy couple is enjoying an evening at the country club; they have already decided to sell the company and enjoy the good life while they're still chipper. And what could be more enjoyable than a brisk round of golf followed by drinks on the terrace? Or a surer emblem of the good life than these sprightly resort clothes?

Brylcreemed hair, going gray at the temples no sideburns

bags under eyes from too much drinking

deep tan

yellow Lacoste, collar finally worn folded down

tennis forearm

gingham belt, leather trim

pockets empty except for key ring with keys to Mercedes sedan, house, burglar alarm

gold watch, kept 5 minutes fast; striped grosgrain watchband

white button-front boxer shorts

green poplin pants with cute yellow tennis racquets

cuffs

no socks

slip-on tassel loafers, polished every night

*flag always flying
at the country club*

PREP PERSONA
No. 5

*wash and wear hairstyle,
ash blonde hair going gray*

*frosted coral
lipstick (dates
from 1971)*

*white plastic bead necklace
white bracelet and earrings to match*

freckles on chest from too much sun

*hot pink scoop neck T-shirt with
white piping*

*his navy blue blazer over shoulders,
in the pockets: his half-frame reading glasses
in needlepoint case made by daughter
(his wife will use them to read the menu);
two Cross pens; Brooks Brothers wallet with
credit cards, monthly commuter ticket, no cash*

*wedding ring,
engagement ring,
diamond
and sapphire
guard ring*

*tennis
figure*

*patchwork
wraparound
long skirt*

*white thong
Bernardo sandals*

GO-TO-HELL-PANTS

In casual wear it is considered very spirited, very fun-loving to wear one offbeat, loud item—usually the pants. Only one item of clothing may be this way, however. The total outfit must be traditional—the usual uniform—with the one exception. Tom Wolfe refers to pants in "go-to-hell" colors; that's okay, but the pants must never be in a go-to-hell cut—that remains strictly classic. The favored color is lime green, but go-to-hell pants come in other similar shocking colors. They may also have embroidered figures on them, but only appropriate figures (See "The Duck Motif"), or a wild print—but only an approved wild print. Being fun-loving should never be confused with being nonconformist. Occasionally a go-to-hell blazer may be worn with plain pants. There is not a go-to-hell shirt.

THE OLD BOY NETWORK
How It Works

HENDERSON CRAM lives in GREENWICH, Conn., and summers on NANTUCKET. He is on the ART MUSEUM BOARD OF TRUSTEES and the ORPHAN'S HOME BOARD OF DIRECTORS. He went to ST. GROTTLESEX SCHOOL and to college at OLD IVY, and he is a member of the RACQUET CLUB and the WINDY BRAE COUNTRY CLUB.

CRAM's daughter MARY BUNDY CRAM (known as BUNDY) wants very much to come out at the DEBUTANTE COTILLION. So CRAM calls his friend, MORGAN HACK, whom he knows from ST. GROTTLESEX, OLD IVY, the ART MUSEUM BOARD OF TRUSTEES, and NANTUCKET. HACK's ex-wife, BITSY HACK HICKS, was the roommate (at MISS HAVISHAM'S SCHOOL) of MITTENS CRUMB, who is the director of the DEBUTANTE COTILLION. CRAM, through HACK, through HICKS, through CRUMB arranges to have Bundy put on the deb list.

CRAM's son, HENDERSON CRAM III, known as TRIP, wants to go to ST. GROTTLESEX SCHOOL. (Actually, CRAM wants TRIP to go to ST. GROTTLESEX. TRIP wants to work on an oil rig.) So when CRAM has his weekly squash game at the RACQUET CLUB with his old ST. GROTTLESEX friend and GREENWICH neighbor, TALCOTT FUNK, he mentions this. FUNK, on the ST. GROTTLESEX BOARD OF TRUSTEES, writes the school a letter of recommendation on behalf of TRIP, who is promptly admitted.

CRAM himself very much wishes to join the YACHT CLUB. He takes another GREENWICH neighbor, MADISON MUDD, to lunch, and steers the conversation toward sailing. MUDD knows CRAM to be a worthy citizen since they both serve on the ORPHAN'S HOME BOARD OF DIRECTORS, and he knows that CRAM is a member in good standing of two clubs to which he, MUDD, also belongs— the RACQUET CLUB and WINDY BRAE COUNTRY CLUB. He suggests to CRAM that since CRAM is such an avid sailor, he will mention CRAM's name at the next meeting of the YACHT CLUB MEMBERSHIP COMMITTEE.

CRAM is the chief executive officer of the NATIONAL HOLDING CORPORATION, which wants very much to absorb both CONSOLIDATED INDUSTRIES, INC., and UNITED PRODUCTS CORPORATION. He arranges a meeting with the presidents of those companies, WINTHROP PUCE and SCHUYLER TWITT, respectively. (WINTHROP PUCE is the brother of HAMILTON PUCE from NANTUCKET, the ART MUSEUM BOARD OF TRUSTEES, and the RACQUET CLUB; CRAM knows TWITT from GREENWICH, the ORPHAN'S HOME BOARD OF DIRECTORS, and WINDY BRAE COUNTRY CLUB). CRAM hopes that the two men will merge their companies, making them an ideal package for takeover by NATIONAL HOLDING CORPORA-TION. But the plan fails due to reluctance on the part of PUCE and TWITT—they don't know each other.

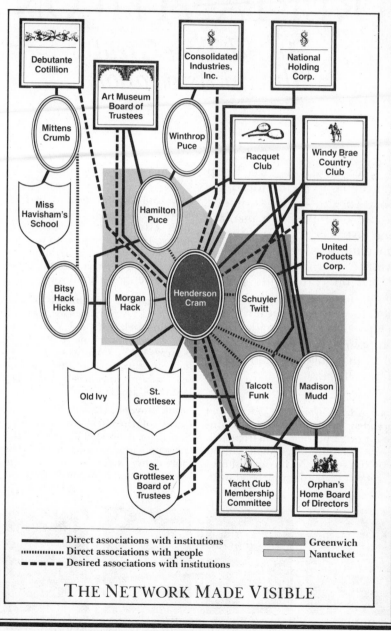

THE NETWORK MADE VISIBLE

THE PREP PANTHEON

An All-Time Great Alumni Association

Elevation to the Prep Pantheon is an honor open only to those Great Preps whose example both inspires and instructs. As the prototypical alumni association and ultimate reunion, the Prep Pantheon transcends school affiliation and year of graduation to gather together those people who have made their Preppiness not merely a way of life, but an illumination of life. The roll call:

John Adams. *Harvard, 1755.* Second president of the United States. Ancestor of 23 percent of metropolitan Boston's Preppy population. On his first visit to France, he established a Preppy tradition by rudely addressing everyone in English, including Louis XVI.

Cleveland Amory, *Milton Academy '35. Harvard '39.* Editor, *Celebrity Register.* The self-appointed *arbiter Preppianum.* His *Proper Bostonians* defined Prep for the postwar generation. Actually he gets in because of the priceless whiskey growl of his voice.

Louis Stanton Auchincloss. *Groton '35. Yale U. '39. Virginia Law.* Partner, Hawkins Delafield and Wood. Author, *Rector of Justin,* more. Regularly portrays WASP financiers who cry in their martinis because they can't be sea captains like great grand-dad Jedidiah. Life is tough.

Frank Boyden. *Amherst '02.* Headmaster of Deerfield for more than fifty years, converted it from a dying day school into a citadel of Prep. His philosophy: "There's nothing in the world like good hard work." Most un-

Cole Porter

Franklin D. Roosevelt

George Bush

George Plimpton

Prep. But could he raise funds!

William F. Buckley, Jr. *St. Thomas More and St. John's, Beaumont (England), and Millbrook, Yale '50.* Author, critic, publisher, television personality. Earned an immediate place in Prep Pantheon for his first book, *God and Man at Yale.* Would have made it anyway for his patrician demeanor, number 2 pencil, and amazing curling tongue.

McGeorge Bundy. *Groton '36. Yale '40.* Prep as paragon. Top grades at Groton and Yale. Personally solved the Dominican crisis. Quoted Heraclitus in the original. *And* you could put his last name before his first and it would still sound top drawer. Disgusting.

George Herbert Walker Bush. *Andover '42, Yale '49.* Businessman, congressman, U.S. envoy to Peking, U.S. ambassador to the United Nations, candidate for vice-president of the U.S. Qualified for Prep Pantheon because of impeccable breeding and manners. Described by Ronald Reagan as "a Preppy, a Yalie, a sissy."

Dick Cavett. *Yale '58.* Actor, author, television talk show host, friend of Woody Allen, and everyone else. Can talk about origins of the bicameral mind, choreography, France, anything. Often wears sneakers and slouch hat—and invites Yale professors on.

Archibald Cox. *Harvard '34. Harvard Law '37.* As Watergate special prosecutor, inspired the nation with the awesome totemic power of skinny bow ties. The rumor: whoever took his Harvard Law School course flunked. Crusty old bastard.

F. Scott Fitzgerald. *Princeton '17.* Chronicled the Jazz Age. Wrote *The Great Gatsby.* Blew the Prep cover on hopes and disillusion. Said it all.

Isabella Stewart Gardner. The "Queen of Back Bay" lived in the Fens (unfashionable), hung out with Jewish art connoisseurs (unconscionable) and visited Italy far too often (unhealthy). Obeyed a not-so-secret rule of Prep: break all the rules—just look good doing it. They'll eat it up.

Edward S. Harkness. *Yale 1897.* Not remembered as the director of the Southern Pacific Railroad. Donated nearly $30 million to construct the Harvard houses and Yale colleges, thus ensuring that Preps always had oak-paneled common rooms for getting wrecked after The Game.

Katharine Hepburn. *Bryn Mawr '38.* Actress, legend in her own time. Took the sockless look to the MGM sound stage. Possesses flawless Prep accent and full woodsy wardrobe.

Oliver Wendell Holmes Jr. *Harvard 1861, Harvard Law 1866.* Boston Brahmin. Did not achieve divine status until the age of sixty, when he became a Supreme Court justice, and sported a white mustache that looked swell in portraits. Dozed constantly on the bench, waking up just in time to help deliver landmark decisions.

Noor Al Hussein, *ci-devant* **Lisa "Buck" Halaby.** *Princeton '74.* Wife of

F. Scott Fitzgerald

Clare Boothe Luce

Isabella Stewart Gardner

Noor Al Hussein

King Hussein of Jordan. Prep gone native. Described ecstatically by *Time* as "blonde, blue-eyed, and lissome," the Light of Hussein almost misses the Pantheon because she married a man whose blazers fit perfectly.

Grace Kelly. *Stevens School. American Academy of Dramatic Arts.* Advocacy of breast-feeding has racked up points against Grace, but her role in *High Society* is recorded on celluloid and that will never fade. As the avatar of blonde arctic Prep women, she rivals Dina Merrill.

Caroline Kennedy. *Concord Academy '75. Harvard '80.* On technical points Preppier than Mummy. During four years at Harvard Square, an unnatural fiber never went near her body (except for the shell of her L. L. Bean down vest). Her lacrosse game was ruthless, her brunch technique dazzling (smoked heavily, sat with the descendants of three other presidents).

Anne Morrow Lindbergh. *Miss Chapin's '24. Smith '28.* The first female glider pilot. Daddy a Senator, Mummy president of Smith, husband a hero. The *New York Times* described her first novels as "small works of art." *Small* is the operative word; greatness is an indulgence a good Prep does not permit herself (but she has a house in the country).

John Vliet Lindsay. *St. Paul's '40. Yale '44.* Former Mayor of New York City, master of political fence-straddling (cf. George Bush). Imparted to the Big Apple the well-known Preppy habit of spending somebody else's money. Wore khakis on walking tour of Harlem.

Alice Roosevelt Longworth. Daughter of T. R. "The other Washington Monument." Wore her wedding pearls until the day she died, told Senator Joseph McCarthy not to call her Alice, and never said anything that couldn't be quoted.

Clare Boothe Luce. *St. Mary's.* Editor, *Vogue, Vanity Fair.* Wed to Time-Life.

Elegant, conservative, eyes courtesy of U.S. Steel. Her film temple to Prep: writing the screenplay for *Come to the Stable*, a 1949 story about French nuns enduring hardship in suburban Connecticut.

Charles Follen McKim. *Harvard 1867, Ecole des Beaux Arts 1870.* **William Rutherford Mead.** *Amherst 1867.* **Stanford White.** *A.M. NYU 1875.* Literally the foundations of New York Prep. The architectural firm of McKim, Mead and White designed the Century Association, the Harvard Club, the Metropolitan Club, and the University Club—thus ensuring continual shelter and soggy Cheddar cheese and crackers for the richest WASP drones of the city.

Barbara ("Babe" or "Babs") Cushing Mortimer Paley. *Winsor School, Westover.* Came out, Boston 1934. 13 times #1 on the best-dressed list. Her *Times* obit says it all: "For years she was the inspiration for the mannequins that lined the windows of Lord and Taylor's."

George A. Plimpton. *Exeter '44, Harvard '48.* Author, publisher, professional amateur. Edits the *Paris Review.* Wrote *Out of My League*, and other books. Admitted to Pantheon not only for his thoughtful and witty career in letters but also for his abilities as a diverting host to other Preps.

Cole Porter. *Worcester Academy, Yale '13.* Wrote most popular music worth listening to, including the Yale fight song "Bulldog, Bulldog" for which he received instant nomination to the Pantheon.

Franklin Delano Roosevelt. *Groton 1900, Harvard '04.* Before his years in office as president of the U.S. only birthright Preps knew about cigarette holders, fireside chats, little dogs, and reckless offspring.

Elliot Richardson. *Harvard '41, Harvard Law '47.* Held numerous Cabinet posts under Nixon and Ford. The ideal representative of a dying subspecies of Prep—the Unsmiling Public Servant—Elliot has never quite gotten what he wanted (the vice presidency, a complete term as U.S. attorney general). Since 1977 he's been discussing the ownership of manganese nodules at the U.N. Law of the Sea Conference. For that he deserves the Pantheon (he would not appreciate the gesture).

Sargent Shriver. *Canterbury School, Yale '38. Yale Law '41.* Founder of Peace Corps. Husband of Eunice. Intimately linked with the legend of you-know-who. The classic (albeit apocryphal) Shriver story: at a 1972 campaign stop in West Virginia, Shriver, McGovern's running mate, tells a tavernful of miners, "You guys are great! Bartender, beers for the house—and a Corvoisier for me!"

Adlai Ewing Stevenson. *Choate '17, Princeton '21.* Governor of Illinois, later leading patrician liberal Democrat and unsuccessful presidential candidate. Middle-aged women in New Canaan still cherish his campaign buttons—and weep over them after the third Manhattan.

Garretson Beekman Trudeau. *St. Paul's '66, Yale '70.* Creator of *Doonesbury* (from "doone," St. Paul's slang for "out to lunch," and Charles Pillsbury, Trudeau's Prep-school roommate). The mouthpiece of the Prep *zeitgeist* in the Age of Rage: "At college my three main interests were—in descending order of importance—a steady supply of recreational drugs, a 2-S draft deferment, and overthrowing the Nixon Administration."

Gloria Vanderbilt. A tribute to the granitelike endurance of blue blood, despite Gloria's best effort to prove otherwise. The jeans, that unpleasantness at River House, the elopement at age 17—they are all for naught. She's a Vanderbilt—and her funny hairdo would still pass muster at Miss Porter's. Nice try, Gloria.

FOR ALUMNI ONLY

It is the duty of the alumni association to see to it that graduation is merely a landmark, not the end of the Preppy's relationship with his education. College alumni associations try to keep a permanent room in a hotel or have a building all their own—in New York City for the most part. The leading examples of the latter are Harvard, Yale, and Princeton (often considered the Howard Johnson's of clubs by virtue of its decor).

For the graduate who is unable to make it to the big city, Prep school and college alumni organizations publish monthly bulletins—nicely packaged periodicals with announcements of alumni get-togethers, marriages, deaths, and special interest articles (Backgammon—That Simple Game). Placed on the last page of the bulletin—as if in afterthought—is the contribution form and envelope. And generally, in the competition for the donation dollar, the Prep school wins out over the college. The former is, after all, a little smaller, a little further back in the lustrous past, a little closer to the Prep heart.

OFF THE WAGON
The Tailgate Picnic

A few hours before the football game begins, station wagons arrive at a grassy field near the stadium. The Prep cars go to one area and park, their tailgates facing each other in rows or a loose circle. Picnics with Bloodies are arranged on the open tailgates. After a couple of Bloodies, the men develop bone-crushing handshakes, which they exchange. There is much backslapping and the talk is very, very hearty. Later, the men take their pipes and sit in the stadium bleachers with their wives. They cover their legs with stadium blankets and, when the game begins, fall asleep.

1. Dog with college muffler about to steal food.
2. Underwood deviled ham.
3. Scotch eggs in imported-cookie tin.
4. Ry-Krisp crackers.
5. Stoned Wheat Thins, slightly stale.
6. Cheese platter: Jarlsberg, Brie, Edam, Cheddar, Bonbel.
7. Loaf of Italian bread.
8. Whole stuffed turkey.
9. Picnic basket from Abercrombie & Fitch.
10. Extra Bloody makings bought on the way to the stadium.
11. Quiche Lorraine purchased at gourmet deli.
12. Bloody mix in Tropicana orange juice jar.
13. Orange juice for screwdrivers.
14. Pepperidge Farm cookies: Mint Milano and Nassau.
15. Country club sticker.
16. Chest of beer for son's friends.
17. Ham and Swiss cheese sandwiches without crusts.
18. Chocolate cake with walnuts.
19. White wine for the women.
20. Mr. & Mrs. T's Bloody Mary mix.
21. Liquor.
22. Scotch cooler.
23. Liquor.
24. Tartan blanket spread over lowered tailgate obscuring other college and secondary-school decals.
25. Thermos of whiskey sours.
26. Thermos of Pimm's Cup.
27. Owner's monogram in nautical flag tiles.
28. College decal.
29. Hip flasks waiting to be filled with liquor for actual game.
30. Pecan pie from Great-grandmother's can't-miss recipe.

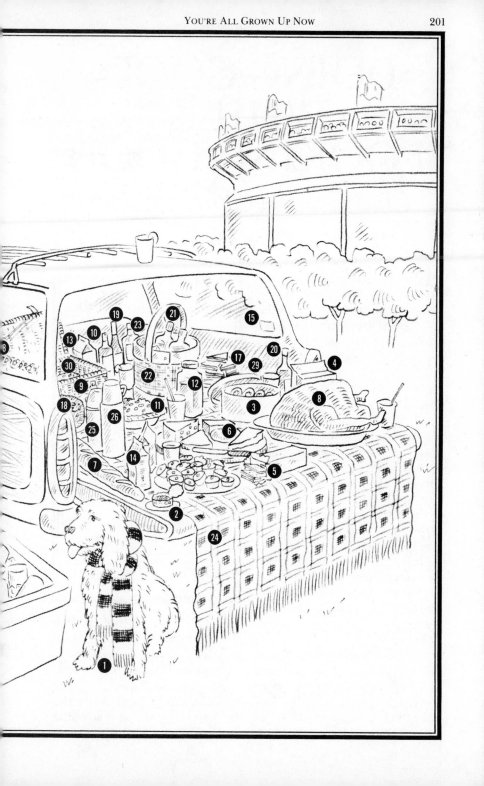

DOING GOOD WHILE LOOKING GOOD

Charities and Charity Events

There are, naturally, many forms of volunteer work. Keeping the files at the blood bank and restoring the herb garden at the historical society are prime Prep activities. So are running the Christmas pageant at the church and manning the information desk at the art museum. Preps are also fond of shoring up dilapidated structures, and coming to the aid of endangered species, especially if they are cute and furry.

But what Preppies do best is raise money, and the easiest way to do that is to provide entertainment (tax-deductible, of course) for their friends. Preps are so fond of giving parties—it makes perfect sense to get Brownie points for doing it.

Dances. The perennial favorite. A spectacular setting such as an armory is perfect. Wives wear that divine brocade they bought six years ago and force their husbands to put on black

---

THE FAVORED CAUSES

For Preps, some of the most important local and national causes:

Boy's club
YMCA
Day care center
Zoo
Art museum
Theater group
Preservation society
Botanical society
Red Cross
Save the Children
Project Hope
Planned Parenthood
Outward Bound
United Fund
American Cancer Society
ASPCA

---

tie. The dancing fervor that distinguishes Preppies in their youth has faded—now, they do little more than a stiff fox trot.

Theme Fairs. Medieval, Renaissance, Old English are the favorites. Booths with strolling troubadours, and ninth graders dressed up in period costumes are featured. Since scholarship is not a fundamental of Prep life, historical accuracy is wanting.

Bazaars. Especially at Christmas. Held either at the church or at the school. The ladies in charge spend six months in advance making gingham tea cozies and rounding up slim but matronly models for the fashion show.

Auctions. Wives get their husbands' companies to donate goods. If the auction is held in the school auditorium, everyone wears black tie and pretends it's Sotheby's in Monte Carlo.

Antique shows. Dealers from the surrounding area display their wares in the gym, the parish hall, or the ballroom at the hunt club. A patron's cocktail party before the opening day adds the required festive air.

Show houses. Enterprising ladies find an empty house, then persuade local decorators to "do" a room each. Everyone turns up to see how a decorator would handle the fireplace. They go home satisfied that theirs looks much nicer.

House tours. Committee leaders bully people who owe them favors into letting the hordes through their homes. If your house is on a tour, you have to bolt down everything movable. If you go on the tour, you do *not* look in the closets.

THE JUNIOR LEAGUE

The Junior League is one of the finest institutions in the Prep world. Made up of women who are actively interested in charity work, it is a national organization divided into local chapters. A typical member is married, thirty-five years old, intelligent, well educated, fond of Lilly shifts and low heels. She is also very serious about the League.

The League means business—prospective members have to be proposed by several women and letters must be written, vouching for their good character. Then for several months candidates are provisional members, undergoing official League training. Finally, as full members, they are required to devote at least two hours a week to volunteer work—tutoring, day care, staffing a rape hotline—through the Junior League.

Young women moving to strange cities such as Huntsville, Ala. might join the League as much to meet the right people as to do good works. Nonetheless, work they will as their mothers did before them, giving the Junior League the continuity and strength of a true Preppy bastion.

PREPMOBILES

What's the point of going to the Right Places if you don't travel in the right style? Drive off the ferry on Nantucket in a Firebird Trans-Am and you're really nowhere at all.

The car is as much a key part of Prep paraphernalia as a club tie or the ubiquitous duck. If, that is, it's the Right Car—the Proper Make, in an Accepted Color, Appropriately Adorned.

MAKES

Land Rover, Toyota Land Cruiser, Jeep (but no flashy paint job, please), International Harvester, Jeep Wagoneer. This type of vehicle is essential, according to the rationale that, of course, you live in a place where the roads are private and unpaved or covered with mud. Judging by the distribution of these machines, Manhattan and Greenwich, Conn., are two such places.

Woody wagon—especially Ford Country Squire. This is the quintessential family car. It has room for both parents, the four beautiful children and, in the back separated by a wire barrier, the three beautiful dogs. These wagons tend to migrate several times a year, each time in different plumage. In late spring, they are full of beach things and can be spotted on ferries off Fisher's Island, the Vineyard, etc. In late summer, they are on the ferry, going back to the mainland, filled with the same gear except now all this equipment has been bleached by the sun and salt and there is sand *everywhere*. In the fall, the wagon is full of trunks, stereos, and tennis racquets on the way to the schools identified by the decals in the rear window. And in the winter, the car is heading north, topped with a ski rack.

Volkswagen. Originally a simple matter of reverse snobbery—now made even better by their having become expensive.

BMW. An extension of the reverse-snob idea. Here is an expensive toy whose compact-car appearance is supposed to say,

THE PROPER MAKES

Jeep Wagoneer   *Volkswagen Rabbit*   *BMW*

"not showy, just sensible." Of course, since anyone worth his or her salt knows that this is a costly, high-performance car, it achieves a very desirable encoded flashiness.

Volvo, Peugeot, Mercedes-Benz. More of the same. Everyone is supposed to recognize right off that you've dropped a wad of bills on the car, and at the same time they're expected to see that you're a person of understated taste. You have bought the car, presumably, not as a status symbol but simply because you *care* about good machinery. That a basic Toyota performs most of the functions of these cars is never mentioned.

Any English car. It's English, and that's good enough.

COLORS

Green. Racing green is right; seafoam green is a *no*.

Red. Fire-engine or maroon are fine.

Blue. Navy blue is a yes; powder blue a don't.

Metallic. Silver works, but bronze doesn't.

White, tan, or yellow. No.

ADORNMENT

Hood. Horse, dog, or duck hood ornament is showy but acceptable.

Side front doors. Broad, red stripe running just below windows. The name of your house (e.g., Foxbelly Farm), professionally lettered. Monogram in nautical flag tiles.

Rear window. Nantucket flag decal. Two or more college or Prep school decals. Audubon Society decal. Museum or public TV decal. Ducks Unlimited decal. Beach parking permit—especially one available to residents of beach town only.

Roof. Ski rack. Year round.

Rear bumper. "I'd Rather Be Sailing" sticker. "I'd Rather Be Skiing" sticker. Over-sand vehicle permit.

Body. Salt stains from seawater. Scratch marks from excited dogs.

Rear package shelf. Throw pillows for long drive to summer place. Tennis and squash racquets are not kept here—the sun is too punishing. But they should be in the car at all times, because you never know.

Glove compartment. Maps of New England. Ray-Ban sunglasses.

Hanging from rearview mirror. Nothing. Ever.

Volvo   Peugeot   Mercedes-Benz

SUMMER IS A VERB

To summer (in plain language, to *spend the summer*) someplace other than where you live and work the rest of the year is key, and to summer in the *right sort of place* is crucial.

Where are these places? Primarily, at the beach. Or in the mountains. Beside a lake or river. The highest concentration of summer enclaves is along the Atlantic coastline from Maine through Connecticut, on the mainland and on the islands. Also in the Green Mountains of Vermont, the White Mountains of New Hampshire, the Berkshires in Massachusetts, the Adirondacks in New York. Resorts appear again on the coast of New Jersey, and in Virginia and the Carolinas. (Once you get too far south, however, you find yourself in winter resorts.) Prep resorts appear by the Great Lakes, in the Thousand Islands in the St. Lawrence River, and even in Canada. As far as the Prep is concerned, there are no summer places on the West Coast because there it is *always* summer. At least compared to New England.

The summer is the high point of the Prep year, the time when Prep blossoms into fullest flower, the point of reference for everything else in life. You choose your clothing, car, friends, pets, on the basis of where and how you summer. The Jeep because you summer on rough terrain. The sailboat motif because you sail during the summer. Your spouse because you grew up summering together on the same beach.

Your winter house is decorated to remind you of where you summer (charts, memorabilia). You wear Nantucket Reds, perhaps, to a cocktail party in Manhattan. All year you think about the summer, when all things Prep come together under the sun.

Those members of the family who work come out to the summer place on weekends. The rest of the family is there from Memorial Day to Labor Day. There are activities to keep the family busy—shopping, eating lobster, swimming, sailing, planning parties, tanning, attending parties, shopping some more—in general, expending the most possible vigor in pursuit of relaxation.

Memories of the summer are of racing down from the city to make the ferry in time, of suddenly chilly nights when you walk home in a fog so thick you could get lost in your own driveway, of the big blowout that last night on the beach when everyone goes skinny-dipping.

You remember strenuous regattas, and long, lazy evenings drinking Mount Gay rum and tonic (with lime) on the porch. This last summer is always the best summer that ever was, or ever could be.

THE ISLANDS

The highest concentration of Prep summer homes seems to be on islands. Islands, after all, often seem apart from time—little worlds where traditions die slowly and where outsiders rarely drop by casually. And islands are special places, too—ideal for people who see themselves as special.

Mt. Desert Island, Maine
(Bar Harbor is here.)
Vinalhaven Island, Maine
Monhegan Island, Maine
Nantucket Island, Mass.
Martha's Vineyard, Mass.
Cuttyhunk Island, Mass.
Great Island, Mass.
Block Island, Rhode Island
Jamestown Island, R.I.
Fisher's Island, N.Y.
Gardiner's Island, N.Y.
Shelter Island, N.Y.
Hatteras Island, N.C.
Isle of Palms, S.C.
Hilton Head Island, S.C.
Sea Island, Ga.
Saint Simon's Island, Ga.
Key West, Fla.
Sanibel Island, Fla.
Captiva Island, Fla.
Mackinac Island, Mich.

THE RIGHT TACK
Sailing

Of all sports, sailing is perhaps the most ideally suited to the standards of the Prep culture. It offers fresh air, physical and intellectual challenge, and the thrill of being financially frivolous—in fact, sailing is often described as standing in a cold shower tearing up $100 bills. Preppies enjoy the novel experience of cultivating what are commonly considered blue-collar skills: mechanics, engineering, and repetitive labor. What makes a sailor different from an auto mechanic, besides not getting paid, is that it is virtually impossible for him to get dirty. Sweat is scoured off by clean salt air and water and sailing all day can beat Clairol at turning brown hair blond.

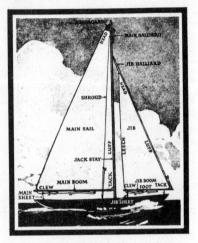

The boat. Face it, you've got to get your own. An all-wood craft is preferable, but Fiberglas, after a twenty-five-year race-winning trial period, is acceptable. Wood decks are highly recommended; wood-finished interiors absolutely essential. Electronic navigational gear—digital, of course—should be copious. Anything less than thirty-five feet will be considered a sign of a depleted family till, unless it is an accessory to a larger yacht. Interior decoration by wife, but should retain masculine flavor.

The outfit. Faded brick-red pants, shirt with boat name sewn on where the crocodile usually is, Top-Sider moccasins. It is permissible to replace red pants with khakis and moccasins with blue canvas sneakers. Your choice of yellow, orange or chewing-gum green foul weather gear.

The yacht club. Possibly more important than the rig itself. They may vary in character but all serve the function of tribal bonding. Clubs are extremely selective not only of their own members, but of which other clubs may be allowed guest privileges. Activities within the clubs center around, in order of importance, sailing, drinking, and the dinner dance. Events such as the weekly races and regattas are significant only to the fringe of racing fanatics who undermine the tightly woven social fabric by consorting with nonclub members.

The cruise. The most prominent of all yacht club functions. The yacht owner and his wife invite two other couples to join them as the flotilla sails from harbor to harbor. The owner's kids do not attend because they have to stay on the mainland and take tennis, swimming, and sailing lessons. It is at the arrival of each night's anchorage that the cruise manifests its true purpose: an ocean-going debauch. Several boats raft together at anchor making for a night the private little islands that are every Preppy's dream world. Sailors know people in every port and invite them for drinks on board and then everyone goes ashore for dinner, during which the women will discuss the problems of humidity on a boat and the men will talk about their newest gear and compare bad-boatyard stories.

A dinner dance always culminates the cruise. The Lilly dresses and jackets make a floral bouquet under the yellow-and-white tent. After the lobster or beef stroganoff, everyone dances for hours to accordion arrangements of Cole Porter.

Races. On those occasions when you actually want to race your boat, the correct crew should be composed of the owner, two large rugby players, and three or more college varsity sailors (preferably from Harvard, Yale, USC, Tufts, or Tulane) to do most of the driving. Racing can be fun, but don't overdo it or you'll estrange yourself from intimidated fellow club members.

RACES AND PLACES TO BE SEEN

Bermuda Race
New York Yacht Club Cruise
Block Island Race Week
Edgartown Regatta

Beyond the necessary, but good to mention over Bloodies:
Southern Ocean Racing Circuit
Transpac
Sydney-Hobart
Halifax
Admiral's Cup
Onion Patch

The Ultimate, Incomparable, and Awe-Inspiring Feat:
To sail in the America's Cup, even the trials. This is probably good enough to get you both the job and the girl of your pink-and-green dreams.

THE RIGHT CLUBS

ON THE GOLD COAST:

NEW YORK YACHT CLUB. As good as the Social Register.
LARCHMONT. Membership list is like a Hall of Fame.
NOROTON. Packed with talent, but no booze.
PINE ORCHARD. Takes three references for night anchoring.
NANTUCKET. Must be able to play tennis to join.
EDGARTOWN. Happens to be on the water.
PEQUOT. Most members just watch from the porch.

NOT ON THE GOLD COAST:

SOUTHERN. A fortress of the New Orleans elite.
ST. FRANCIS. Republican conclave under the Golden Gate.
NEWPORT HARBOR. Invaded by California surfers turned sailors.
SAN DIEGO. Another outlet for a city of sports maniacs.

CLOSET PREPS
Quiz #5

The following is a list of twenty persons you would perhaps not expect to have graduated from Prep school. Not because you don't think they're wonderful, but because they have somehow sublimated their Preppiness—in the glitter of show biz, for the most part. If you can match the celebrity with his or her school, fine, if not answers are supplied at the bottom of the page.

The Graduates

1. John Carradine
2. Natalie Cole
3. Bruce Dern
4. Lawrence Ferlinghetti
5. Gil Scott-Heron
6. Abbie Hoffman
7. Jack Kerouac
8. Tommy Lee Jones
9. Jack Lemmon
10. June Lockhart
11. Johnny Mercer
12. Vincent Price
13. Renée Richards
14. Cesar Romero
15. Randolph Scott
16. Grace Slick
17. James Stewart
18. Shirley Temple
19. Sigourney Weaver
20. Jesse Colin Young

The Schools

a. *Andover*
b. *Castilleja*
c. *Choate*
d. *Collegiate*
e. *Ethel Walker*
f. *Episcopal Academy*
g. *Fieldston*
h. *Horace Mann*
i. *Mercersburg*
j. *Northfield Mt. Hermon*
k. *St. Louis Country Day*
l. *St. Mark's School of Texas*
m. *Westlake*
n. *Woodberry Forest*
o. *Worcester Academy*

Answers:
1f; 2j; 3c; 4j; 5g; 6o; 7h; 8l; 9a;
10m; 11n; 12k; 13h; 14d; 15n;
16b; 17i; 18m; 19e; 20a.

CHAPTER 7

PREP
SPOKEN
HERE

DERIVATION OF THE WORD

Erich Segal (Midwood High School '54—Brooklyn) definitely does not consider himself a Preppy, but he is the person responsible for introducing the word into common usage. "Just what is a Preppy?" he asked himself. "He's a guy who dresses perfectly without trying to. He appears to do everything well with ease." Just like Oliver Barrett, IV, the protagonist of his best-selling 1970 novel, *Love Story*.

> "Do you have *The Waning of the Middle Ages*?"
> She shot a glance up at me.
> "Do you have your own library?" she asked.

> "Listen, Harvard is allowed to use the Radcliffe library."
> "I'm not talking legality, Preppie, I'm talking ethics. You guys have five million books. We have a few lousy thousand."

Segal's signature work was translated into thirty-three languages, that is except for the word "Preppy," which defied translation, its concept so quintessentially American. But since Segal is also a classics scholar, *The Official Preppy Handbook* asked him to provide us with the etymology of the word. "It's a derivative of the word 'preposterous'." Of course.

ACCENT ON ACCENTS

Preppies love to talk. So, as well as having their own style of dress, their own schools, their own sports, they have their own way of speaking. Different parts of the country feature different accents, but within most regions there is a distinctive Preppy sound. A Northerner may not be able to distinguish between Prep and non-Prep versions of a Southern drawl, but a blindfolded Virginian would have no trouble pointing out the individual who intends to go foxhunting in the group.

BOSTON BRAHMIN

It's not what people think. It's not the broad "a" of the cliché, "I pahked my cah ..." It's not the Kennedy accent, which belongs to their family alone. Rather, it is a mixture of 70 percent British and 30 percent Maine, and it oozes aristocracy. What sounds to the untrained ear like a broad "a" is really the dropping of the following "r"—a habit more English than East Boston. The Boston Brahmin accent cannot be learned; it can only be inherited.

NEW ENGLAND NASAL NIP

The sign of winters spent on isolated campuses, this accent is largely a matter of diction. Involves strategic pauses during which a low-pitched gravelly "ahhhh ..." is heard. This suggests a bumbling fool. Yet it is clear that the speaker could slay any opponent in verbal volleyball. It is

part of an effort to sound offhand— to seem to be groping for words. But the speaker only gropes for easy words. Use of SAT words is as casual as breathing. Example: "Ahhhhh ... but surely you don't mean to .... ahhh .... suggest that .... ahhh ... his behavior in any way adumbrates malversation .... because, ahhhh ... after all ... none of us is prepared to ... ahh ... to ahhh .... agree with you on that." For further instruction, listen to William F. Buckley, Jr.

LOCUST VALLEY LOCKJAW

A common self-imposed affliction among those with inherited wealth, becoming more severe as the money is squandered away. This social disease is characterized by a chronic clenching of the molars while speaking, the use of the anterior nasal passages instead of the more usual mouth for resonance, the upward tilt of the chin (and consequently nose), and the languid look of bored superiority when one is compelled to engage in conversation with a social gnat. Numerous case studies indicate that the severity of L. V. Lockjaw is directly correlated to the length of one's driveway. Can be found wherever Polk's Social Directory issues a summer edition.

MANHATTAN NEUTRAL EXPRESS

Characterized by a complete absence of any dialectal distinction. The conscientious teachers at St. Bernard's, Horace Mann, and Riverdale have so thoroughly grilled their charges for saying "twenny" instead of "twen-tee," that native New York Preppies, in learning to enunciate, have lost all of their Yiddish, Italian, and Irish influ-

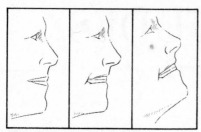

Three Steps to Perfect Lockjaw. *1.* At rest. *2.* Jaw begins forward thrusting movement. *3.* With front teeth firmly clenched, sound is forced through nasal passages for a resonant—not harsh—nasal tone. *Draw out all accented vowels as long as possible.* Reeeeally.

ences. They also have difficulty imitating the leisurely Locust Valley Lockjaw because they're too used to the 50 wpm rat-tat-tat speed of arguments with cabdrivers over the fastest route to the New York Athletic Club.

MADEIRA-FOXCROFT STRATFORD-ON-POTOMAC PATTER

Perhaps it's the influence of the daughters of foreign dignitaries living in nearby Washington, but these lasses speak with a sort of quasi-British-uppercrust tone, ending their sentences with a questioning lilt, "We just had a smashing time at field hockey today." "Oh, really?" They believe this intonation will help them pass for British when they spend their junior year in college abroad.

VIRGINIA REDNECK BOY DRAWL

Southern Prep courts hillbilly twang in the halls of Woodberry Forest, EHS, and VES as sons of southern gentlemen drag out their vowels and boomerang them back in distorted form like mountain moonshiners. The monosyllabic affirmative "yeah" becomes the sesquipedalian "yeeee-aaaayyyy-uuuuhhhh." Such phonetic slaughter will prepare them for fraternizing with the real McCoys at UVA, UNC, and Georgia.

GROSSE POINT MONOTONE

Lips are never to be moved while speaking; mouths are opened only for whiskey sours and steaks at The Little Club. This unrelieved droning perfectly conveys the Prep attitudes of boredom and cynicism, allowing emotion only with a slightly curious, "Oh?" Rumor has it Peggy Lee recorded "Is That All There Is?" in Grosse Point.

CHICAGO-COLORADO HYBRID

The ubiquitous Chicago "a"—used whether it's welcome or not, as in "Cha-ca-ga," "Jahn" and "alaphant"—cohabits with the Colorado laid-back slur ("You . . . wanna . . . go . . . skiin'?") among the Latin, Francis Parker, and University of Chicago Lab School set who hit the slopes in Aspen by day and fly back home to grab a pizza at Uno's at night. Since the Windy City Preppies commingle with the Boulder Bohemians, the latter absorb the former's linguistic quirks, thereby making it impossible to tell who's coming or going.

HOCKADAY (AND HIGHLAND PARK) HEIGHTENED HARMONY

The "pretty-sweet" Preppy girls at these schools (note: technically, Highland Park is registered as a public school, but since most of its students are members of country clubs, it has a private school's Prep quotient) take the Texan twang and sugar-coat it by stretching certain words to extreme lengths. This practice is customarily employed for compliments—"This Cadillac is gggrrreeeaaattt," "This party was so much ffffuuunnn," "This is the best quiche I've ever hhhhaaaddd,"—but can also serve as an insult in disguise: "Oh, you aaallll-wwwaaaayyyssss look so cute in that sweater." (In other words, "Why don't you wear something else once in a while?")

ATTITUDES
A Usage Guide

Entrance into Mondo Preppo is guaranteed by a common sensibility. The attitudes of this sensibility are expressed in a particular tone of voice, using practiced inflections and special terminology. They tell the listener where you were raised, where you went to school, and when you graduated. Call it semiotics, or call it silly, but don't call it snobbery. Preps aren't snobs. They're neat.

Ennui. It's the most consummately Prep of all attitudes. Don't worry that this is contrary to genetic effortlessness; effortlessness is hereditary, but ennui is learned. Hailing from the "Oh-it's-such-a-bother" school of thought, ennui comes from retaining your natural impulses that once regarded an idea as promising, to thinking it's tiresome. You won't get excited; you are too tired from dancing until four this morning.

Cynicism. An extension of ennui maintaining that not only are you bored, you are in a state of disbelief as well. And you cannot be convinced otherwise. Cynical speech is characterized by a lengthen-

ing of vowel sounds in the syllable that is normally accented, i.e. "Woooonderful." Derivation of this attitude can be traced to the manufacture of the first synthetic fabrics. "That sweater's prooooobably acryyyyylic." Cynicism is more than a pose; it's also a handy time saver. By deflating your companion's enthusiasm, you can cut conversations in half.

Sarcasm. Again, as with the two dispositions cited above, sarcasm connotes a weary lack of interest. A well-aimed, "Oh, really?" will indicate to the speaker that you *actually* have better things to do. Sarcasm masquerades as the Preppy's sense of humor. If a colleague is wearing a short-sleeved shirt with the Table of Elements depicted on the back, it would be absolutely appropriate to comment, *"Nice* shirt." Similarly with an ungainly main squeeze: *"Nice* girlfriend." That takes care of *that*.

Joie de vivre. Preppies are social creatures. Sitting alone in a darkened room with a bottle of Dewar's would never occur to a Preppy. A bottle of scotch means it's time for a party. Intimate to a Preppy

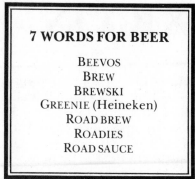

7 WORDS FOR BEER

BEEVOS
BREW
BREWSKI
GREENIE (Heineken)
ROAD BREW
ROADIES
ROAD SAUCE

means thirty close friends. This joie de vivre has linguistic manifestations. It presupposes the existence of the word "Let's" before such words and expressions as, "go Borneo," "tie one on," and "dance." This attitude is unfamiliar with the concepts of lonely and melancholy. It doesn't know the word "no." It condones excess.

Esprit de corps. While pooh-poohing the description, "elite," Preppies do assay a certain amount of exclusivity. Hence, without ever planning it, they've developed their own parlance, designed to be understood by other Preppies. The phenomenon of constantly coining new phrases is nowhere so prevalent as among Preppies. The joy of hearing your expression on the lips of a stranger is unmatched, and determines that the stranger is actually another member of the club. Only a Preppy knows what "Tapioca," "Scoots," and "G and T action" mean, and whether the communication occurs among celebrants at a post-Princeton-Dartmouth game party, or not until the big move to the big city, or mysteriously, in one's sleep, it works.

Enthusiasm. The charmed life of the Preppy leads to a disproportionate use of superlatives, expressing a seeming limitless enthusiasm. For girls, especially, "cute" is the supreme accolade. Anything can be cute: a boat, a boy, a set of directions to Westport, a campus, a politician (George Bush). Boys show a marked preference for "great" as in, "Hey, you've really got a great car/boat/mother/needlepoint belt/beer-can display!" The trick with enthusiasm is that it should be undifferentiated. If one thing is great or cute or both, then everything else is, too. Preppies are generous with praise.

Worldliness. The Prep has traveled extensively in at least two continents by the time he or she hits puberty. The first Audi was trashed on the Vineyard at age fifteen. Life holds little mystery; Preps like to think that they've seen it all and in five different languages. This means their own language is freely sprinkled with foreign phrases—never entire sentences—in casual chatter. Even with the filling station attendant. They don't care if they aren't making themselves understood. That's the other person's problem.

THE LEXICON

Air hose *n*. New loafers worn without socks.

a little tongue sushi *n*. French kissing.

at school *adv. phrase*. Prep code for *in prep school*. "Where were you at school?" always means, "Where did you prep?"

Attitude Adjustment *n*. 1980's version of Happy Hour.

awesome *adj*. Terrific, great. "The saxophone player is awesome."

Bagging z's *predicate phrase*. Taking a nap.

best *adj*. Most Prep.

big fella *n*. Affectionate name used by men with and to each other. Not condescending.

Big Green *n*. Dartmouth College.

big guy *n*. Same as "Big Fella."

Big Red *n*. Cornell University.

bit *adj*. Disappointed by unexpected bad luck. "I bet he was bit when he found out he was cut from the lacrosse team."

Bloody *n*. Bloody Mary.

blow away *v*. To impress, overwhelm. Also, *blow me away*: "I'm impressed."

blow-out *n*. A big party. Usually includes live band and black tie attire. Celebrants always drink more than they should but term confers permission to do it to the max.

blown out *adj*. Wasted, tired, hung over.

bones *n*. Marijuana cigarettes, joints, "j's." (Also: nickname for Yale's secret society, Skull and Bones.)

booted *v*. Expelled from school. (Also: vomited.)

brothel stompers *n*. suede shoes.

Bruno *n*. Brown University.

Carl Comedian *n*. Sobriquet for an unsuccessful joke teller.

chew face *v*. Make out, kiss.

classic *n*. Person, object, or social gathering that's different or strange.

completely cute *adv. phrase*. Handsome; used by women to describe men. Same as 1950's "dreamy."

cool *adj*. Why you still smoke cigarettes. What jazz is. Something you like that's too hip or naughty to be cute.

_____ city *n*. The condition of something being rife, as in "tweed city," (second floor bar, Yale Club) or "nerd city" (the Engineering Department).

Crimson *n*. Harvard University.

cute *adj*. Most supreme Prep accolade. Favored by girls.

cutest *adj*. Most Prep.

Daddy *n*. Whether you're talking to him or about him. Often, but not always, still married to Mummy.

darling *adj*. Synonymous with cute. Applies especially to clothes and animals. A favorite of saleswomen.

dead attractive *adj*. Same as completely cute.

divine *adj*. How an older woman looks when you mean to be complimentary.

Dobbs *n*. The Masters School, Dobbs Ferry, N.Y.

dork *n*. A clumsy person who does not know Prep sayings and attitudes.

dorky *adj*. That which is characterized by clumsiness or ignorance of, for instance, how to mix a Bloody.

drop trou *v*. (*Trou* rhymes with *cow*.) Let down one's pants. What Preppy guys do to break the ice at parties. A real hoot, especially when they wear "wild" boxers.

drugs *n*. Marijuana. Makes speaker sound cavalier, dangerous, criminal, wild.

Eat my shorts *v*. Drop dead, go jump in the lake.

Eli *n*. Yale University.

excellent *adj*. A good idea. Said in reference to trivial plans, e.g., "I'll make some coffee." "Excellent."

Fag tag *n*. The loop on top of the back pleat on button-down shirts. Also, ripcord.

Farmington *n*. Miss Porter's School, Farmington, Conn.

fire up *v*. Engage in sexual relations, as in "I'm going to fire her up."

flamer *n*. He who commits a *faux pas* or obvious error. Also, the *faux pas* itself.

fruit loop *n*. Same as fag tag.

Game *adj*. Admiring term by which a girl is described by boys as being a good sport, ready for anything. Fun.

get Chinese *v*. Get really stoned.

getting low *v. phrase*. Getting high.

go for it *predicate phrase*. Let's get carried away and act stupid. May also be used as an adjective, as in "Ted Turner—what a go-for-it attitude that guy has."

good-attitude student *n*. A jerk. One who is favored by the school administration, but not by peers.

good old boy *n.* Prep school alumnus.

greatest *adj., adv.* Most Prep.

gross *adj.* Disgusting. As in food or rude behavior. Also, "gross me out."

Heavy _____ **action** *n.* Whatever one does a lot. "Heavy tanning action."

• **hide the salam** *v.* Salam is short for salami. Sexual intercourse. Used with "to play," as in, "Then we played hide the salam."

hoot *n.* That which is amusing. Woody Allen is a hoot.

hop on a babe *v.* To pounce on a woman; have sex with a female. (Male initiated, of course.)

horizontal rumble *n., v.* Same as firing up. Doing it. Sexual relations.

how arch *adv. phrase.* Inappropriate. Wrong, as in dark blue slacks with light green socks.

howl *n., v.* A cry of derision. To make fun of.

Icky *adj.* Not quite gross enough for "gross." Used only by girls. Also, "ickypoo."

in a big way *adv. phrase.* An intensifier. As in, "I got crocked in a big way."

intense *adj.* Anything *really* fun. Such as college.

in your eye *phrase.* "You're mistaken, know-it-all." Directed toward someone who insists that Cole Porter went to Harvard.

irony *n.* The preferred observation. Mentioning irony indicates a fine mind and insightful intellect. Best when discussing Cinema and Literature.

Jacked out *adj. phrase.* Angry, pissed off.

Key *adj.* Crucial, especially to being Prep. As in key colors (pink and green), or used alone: "Webbed belts are key."

Lame *adj.* Weak, pathetic. Used to describe all jokes.

light up a few *v.* Smoke. Indicates largesse, as in, "Let's light up a few bones/rettes."

love *v., n.* What a girl feels about ice cream, add-a-beads, sailing, and needlepoint.

lunch *v.* Meet for midday meal. "Shall we lunch tomorrow?"

Major *adv., adj.* Signifying large quantities or anything being done in a big way, as in "major slalom action."

Mummy *n.* She's Mummy if you're talking to her or about her. Never too old to use term. *Never* "my mother" or "Ma."

must *n.* Something you *have* to have; a movie you cannot miss. "It's a must."

Neat *adj.* Something cute, but not as cute as cute. Neat is sweet.

need a foghorn *adv. phrase.* To be confused or unaware.

nice *adj., adv.* Not nice. Awful. Sarcastic.

Old **Nassau** *n.* Princeton University.

on fire *adv..* When you've made a social gaffe, you're on fire.

on the rag *adv.* Testy, snappy. Originally from girls' schools, but now coed.

outrageous *adj., adv.* Lively, funny, or just somehow memorable. "The traffic outside the stadium after the game was outrageous."

outstanding *adv., adj.* Synonymous with excellent but delivers bigger wallop. (Pronounced with drawn out second syllable.)

out to lunch *adv. phrase.* Confused or unaware.

Panic *n.* Something or someone hysterically funny.

parallel parking *n.* Sexual intercourse.

12 FOREIGN PHRASES

A domani (Italian) Much better than offensive *ciao.*

Al fresco (Italian) Out-of-doors, where you picnic.

Assez bizarre (French) Applies to Fellini and Bergman films, when you're trying to score.

Dinero (Spanish) Dollars, money. "I'm running out of dinero." Very cute.

Je ne sais quoi (French) "I don't know what," as in, "This wine possesses a certain *je ne sais quoi.*"

Nouveau (French) Literally, "new," short for "nouveau riche." Read: vulgar and showy.

Par chance (French) "By chance." Used only by debutantes.

Partir (French) "To leave." "Are you about to *partir?*" Grammatically incorrect, of course, but it shows that the speaker has a charming, wry sense of humor.

Perrier What you drink when you're hung over. With a lime wedge.

Peut être (French) "Maybe." Easy to insert into any sentence.

Schnell (German) "Fast." "*Schnell*, get into the car."

Très declassé (French) For inappropriate behavior, or dreadful restaurant.

poo *n.* Champagne. Humorous. When people think they're hilarious by referring to the bubbly as "shampoo."

psyched *adv.* Psychologically predisposed, enthusiastic, brainwashed, ready.

Rally *v.* To go Borneo. Do it to the max. Go for it big guy.

rat *n.* New student at Prep school.

really *adv.* Universal term of agreement and emphasis. Can be used as a complete sentence.

reel in the biscuit *v.* Lure a girl to bed.

reel it in *v.* Congratulatory advice awarded to prankster permitting him to exult in his triumph in having "hooked" (deceived) a "fish" (dupe).

rettes *n.* Cigarettes. The cool jargon, as opposed to "butts."

riding the porcelain Honda *v.* The runs. Montezuma's revenge.

rude *adj., adv.* In bad taste; without class, gauche, bad. When impolite is meant, the word impolite is used.

St. Grotlesex *n.* St. Mark's, Groton, Middlesex, St. Paul's. Refers to this group.

scoots *n.* Dollars.

scream *n.* Ice cream. Usually Haagen Dazs.

she doesn't have both oars in the water *adj phrase.* Spacy girl. Can apply to boys too.

____ski *suffix.* Appended to any word, "ski" will enhance the humor quotient. Prepski.

shoe *adj.* Top-drawer. Very acceptable.

skied *adv.* Psyched. I'm ready for the challenge. Pronounced sky-ed.

smash mouth *v.* To kiss.

someone blew out his/her pilot light *adv. phrase.* An individual who is spacy.

spaced *adv.* Head in the clouds.

stitch *n.* Someone or something funny.

stitch and a half *n.* Even funnier.

stitches *n.* The state you're in when you find something funny.

stop moing me *v.* Don't touch me. When boys inadvertently touch each other in elementary and secondary school; homophobic. (Also, mo, moing out, heavy mo action.)

sucked *adj.* Disappointing. Used mostly in the past tense, e.g., "The seminar/the concert/the South of France sucked."

suck face *v.* Same as chew face. Get to first base.

8 EXIT LINES

"Let's cruise." (en route one may decide to "swing by Wellesley or Pedro's")
"Let's bolt."
"We're golden."
"We're history."
"We're out of here."
"Let's get the hell out of Dodge."
"Let's split this scene, man." (*satirical*)
"Let's act like a preacher and get the hell out of here." (*humorous*)

super *adj.* Good. As opposed to "cute," it refers to an experience, not a thing. "We had a super time at the club."

swap spit *v.* To French kiss.

Talent *n.* Boyfriend or girlfriend. Newer version of "my better half."

tapioca *adj.* Flat broke, "tapped." Also, Tap City.

to die *adj.* Wonderful, fantastic. As in, "the party was to die," or, "He was to die cute."

too much *adj.* Amusing, fun-loving. Used to modify someone who's passed out at a party.

tossed *v.* Kicked out of school. (also, vomited.)

to the max *adv. phrase.* All the way. In drinking, consume a whole keg. In sex, go to home plate. In parties, dance and drink and throw up.

trash *v.* To goof, make fun. "We trashed Swell's" means "We wore polyester and made fun of everyone at Swell's."

tremendous *adj.* More key than "excellent," if possible.

tuna *n.* Either steady girlfriend or recent acquisition. "Catching tuna in Bermuda." (Also: marijuana.)

Unreal *adj.* Pleasant, enjoyable; used to describe concerts, movies, parties, cars.

Walk on *v.* Get lost. Usually aimed at someone who has suffered extreme embarrassment on the playing field or on a date and should know better than to show his face.

white bread *adj.* WASP-y, bland. Suggests Velveeta, Kleenex Boutique tissues, Tricia Nixon Cox.

wild *adj.* Dirty, dangerous, or inclined toward wearing a lot of black. Wild is the time you had when you went slumming. If you are considered "wild" you generate awe.

worst *adj.* Least Prep. By extension, most boring.

Za *n.* Pizza.

zoned *adj.* Blitzed, exhausted, burned out.

THE ABBREVIATED VERSION

Preppies would rather take it easy. They'd prefer not to expend energy speaking. For the sake of basking in their own ingenuity as well as camaraderie, they've developed a codified set of abbreviations which cut conversation time to a minimum while insuring that non-Preps will have no idea what or whom is being discussed.

A.T.D. *Absolutely to Die.* Too much cuteness/nerve/rudeness.

B² *Brooks Brothers.* The key store. Universal abbreviation.

B.M.O.C., *Big Man on Campus.* Mr. Prep. A future husband.

C.B.C. *Couldn't Be Cuter.* A favorite of girls.

D.P. *Dom Perignon.* Said by college kids, even though they can rarely afford it.

E.C.T. *Estimated Cloud Time.* Go inside and get a drink.

F.T.P. *Falling To Pieces.* Useful when you're hinting for a vacation.

G&T *Gin and Tonic.* What you drink at the club before, during, and after a tennis game.

H² *Hot and Heavy.* An intense romantic relationship.

H.T.H. *Home Town Honey.* That person on whom you cheat while you're away at school or college.

I.B.M. *Instant Big Mouth.* Martini—usually used in the plural.

K.P.O.C. *Key Prep on Campus.* The ultimate B.M.O.C. Wears the most frayed shirts, patched down vests.

N.O.C.D. *Not Our Class, Dear.* He's not for you, believe me. **N.O.K.D.** *(Not Our Kind, Dear)* is also heard.

N.T.B. *No Talent Bum.* He's only interested in your bank account. Used by women after they've learned the hard way.

O.O.C. *Out of Control.* Preceded by any pronoun. Screamed while reeling from too much drink.

O.T.W. *Off the Wall.* Mildly crazy, charmingly insane, as in wearing evening dress with Newmarket boots.

P.D.A. *Public Display of Affection.* Kissing, necking, sexual relations done outside of one's dorm room or frat room.

P.T.H. *Peak Tanning Hours.* The hours between 10 A.M. and 2 P.M. when classes are empty in the spring.

R&I *Radical and Intense.* Heavy. Great. Defies emphasis.

S.A. *Sex Appeal.* What Montgomery Clift had that Mummy liked.

S.O.T. *Same Old Thing.* Boring Saturday night. Can be applied to an individual also.

T.B.A. *To Be Avoided.* Person, movie, parent, activity.

T.D.C. *Total Design Concept.* A house or wardrobe that is thoroughly coordinated. Often used sarcastically.

T&T. *Tanqueray and Tonic.* Yummy, but a little nouveau.

T.T.F.W. *Too Tacky For Words.* Applied to vans with painted sunsets.

U.R.L. *Un-Requited Love.* Bittersweet when you are afflicted, annoying when it's someone else.

V&T. *Vodka and Tonic.* Gets you smashed fast.